CAMBRIDGE STUDIES IN CRIMINOLOGY VOLUME XX
*Editor:* Leon Radzinowicz

# BORSTAL RE-ASSESSED

THE HEINEMANN LIBRARY OF CRIMINOLOGY
AND PENAL REFORM

By the same author:

*Sentencing in Magistrates' Courts*

*Publisher's Note:* This series is continuous with the Cambridge Studies in Criminology, Volumes I to XIX, published by Macmillan & Co. London.

# BORSTAL RE-ASSESSED

*by*

## Roger Hood

*Lecturer in Social Administration*
*University of Durham*

HEINEMANN
LONDON

Heinemann Educational Books Ltd

LONDON   MELBOURNE   TORONTO

SINGAPORE   CAPE TOWN

HONG KONG   AUCKLAND

IBADAN

Published by
Heinemann Educational Books Ltd
48 Charles Street, London W.1
Printed in Great Britain by
Morrison & Gibb Ltd, London and Edinburgh

# CONTENTS

# Author's Preface

THIS study is concerned with the English borstal system for boys. It does not attempt to deal with the rather different situations in Scotland and other countries. It is also not concerned with the separate issue of borstal training for girls.

Throughout the book borstal is spelt with a small 'b', in line with current practice, except where referring to the particular institution at Borstal or where it appears in quotations from a period when it was customary to use the capital letter. In the footnotes, the Annual Reports of the Prison Commissioners are referred to as *P.C. Report*, Annual Reports of the Central After-Care Association is *C.A.C.A. Report*. To avoid confusion the term Prison Commission is used throughout, even though since 1963 it has become the Prison Department of the Home Office.

I am particularly grateful for advice and criticisms to John P. Martin, F. H. McClintock and Nigel Walker. I would also like to thank Mr Frank Foster, Director of Borstal After-Care for his readiness to make available to me the Minutes and other papers of the Borstal Association and giving me permission to quote from them.

Finally, I thank Professor Leon Radzinowicz who guided my work at all stages and encouraged me to persevere with it.

R.H.

*July* 1965

# Foreword

## by

## LEON RADZINOWICZ

THE borstal system has been one of the most significant contributions made by this country to the penological theory and practice of the twentieth century. Now, however, it is going through a crisis. Under recent legislation the demands upon it, in range and scale, are becoming greater than ever. At the same time its effectiveness is subject to question. Before the war the success rate, in terms of those not reconvicted within two years of release, was as high as 70 per cent. Now, at 36 per cent, it has almost been halved.

Several reasons have been suggested for this. It can be argued that the extended use of other measures has left borstal to handle a hard core of the most difficult young men. Also that their subsequent behaviour must be seen in the general perspective of juvenile and young adult crime, which has more than doubled even in the past ten years. But whatever the causes, the fact remains that the fall in success is a symptom of failure to deal with modern conditions, and it may be that the borstal system, under the onset of middle age, has lost some of its zest and originality in tackling new problems.

It is this that makes Dr Hood's re-assessment, with its wide historical sweep in relation to changes in the social scene and in the attitudes of courts, so opportune and potentially so valuable. It confirms his claim to be one of the ablest of the new generation of young criminologists.

It also shows how necessary, to any advance in the understanding of our penal system, is this kind of study in depth as compared with the more superficial visiting and questioning on which we still seem to rely too much.

This volume marks the opening of a new series published on behalf of the Cambridge Institute of Criminology by Heinemann. We look forward to a long and happy collaboration with them.

L.R.

*Cambridge, July* 1965

# The Problem

DURING the 1930's borstal stood at the height of its reputation. The austere, discipline-orientated regime developed by its founder, Sir Evelyn Ruggles-Brise, had been replaced by the new educationally based ideas of Alexander Paterson. Paterson abolished the staff's prison uniform, strengthened its educative role, imported men from public schools and universities as housemasters, established open institutions and fired them with a missionary zeal. He believed, and persuaded others to believe, that the 'British lad' had good in him that had simply been thwarted by a bad environment—and that this good side of his nature could be brought out by methods in some ways similar to those used at the great public schools. Borstals were often likened to public schools and boys were sent there 'for their own good'. Paterson aimed to dissociate borstals completely from their prison roots and to make them entirely educative. He communicated his enthusiasm and hopes to the judiciary—borstal was seen as a panacea for adolescent crime where boys would be taught a trade, educated and taught to develop their sense of responsibility. The statistics of results produced by the Borstal Association (which organized after-care) were very encouraging. Two years after their release in 1936, 70 per cent had not again been convicted, and of those convicted only 12 per cent came before the courts more than once. By 1939 borstal was seen as an enormous success. With improvements and expansion along the lines Paterson had developed, it was hoped to nip in the bud the vast majority of potential persistent criminals. The Prison Commissioners confidently looked to the time when they could close many of their prisons.

In strong contrast, the sixties, far from being a period of optimistic plans for the future, is a time ripe for the reappraisal

of both the role of borstal in the penal system and its methods
of training. The results are no longer encouraging. In fact, they
are a startling contrast to those achieved in the thirties. Two
years after boys had been released in 1960, only 36 per cent had
not been reconvicted and of those convicted as many as 39 per
cent appeared before courts more than once. Boys have
certainly been more difficult to train in post-war years. After
the war the number of escapes rose phenomenally, and have
remained far above the pre-war level. The Prison Commissioners were forced to conclude that instead of expanding the
number of open institutions they needed more secure establishments. The hope that borstal could develop along 'open-lines'
was shattered. As a logical corollary to the new emphasis on
closed institutions and the growing liberalizing of the special
prisons for young offenders the two systems of borstal and
imprisonment were joined together as 'custodial training' by
the Criminal Justice Act 1961. Parallel to this renewed emphasis
on discipline, much of the enthusiasm formerly lavished on
borstal has been transferred to the short-term detention
centres.

There have been some notable advances in training methods
since the war, particularly the introduction of group counselling. But the major problem has been that of re-examining
objectively the principles of the thirties in the context of the
intervening social change. In face of increasing difficulties in
training young offenders it is necessary to examine the appropriateness of current methods to the problems of today's
delinquents. Such an appraisal will prove a major task for the
Royal Commission on the penal system.

It is not the purpose of this study to describe the daily
regimes and atmosphere of the contemporary borstal system.
The intention is to provide an historical and critical perspective
on how the system has grown, developed and changed. When
new proposals for the 'remedy' of delinquency are considered
it should prove instructive to look back on the most famous,
and most hopeful, penal experiment of this century and enquire
how and why it lost both prestige and promise.

*1965*

ROGER HOOD

# I

# Borstal Begins

*The Gladstone Committee*

Before the borstal scheme was established as an experiment in 1900[1] there had been no special form of prison treatment for young offenders between the ages of 16 and 21. In fact, anyone over 16 was committed to prison and treated there in the same way as if he were an adult. In its assertion that this age-group was worthy of special treatment, the Gladstone Committee of 1895 made a revolutionary break with English penal traditions. Its two main recommendations for treatment were:

(*a*) The age of admission to reformatories should be raised from 16 to 18, and of detention to 21 . . . We assume that before the age was raised the satisfactory conditions of the schools would be ascertained . . . (and) the proposal would have to be looked at from the point of view of the reformatory managers.

(*b*) We are of the opinion that the experiment of establishing a penal reformatory under Government management should be tried. It should be begun on a moderate scale, but on a design which would allow of large expansion if the results were proved to be satisfactory. The Court would have the power to commit to these establishments offenders under the age of 23, for periods of not less than one year and up to three years, with a system of licences graduated according to sentence, which should be freely exercised.[2]

Furthermore, the Committee went on to outline the sort of reformatory it had in mind:

The penal reformatory should be a half-way house between the prison and the reformatory. It should be situated in the

---

[1] It was actually started at Bedford Prison and not moved to Borstal (Rochester) Prison until the following year.

[2] *Report from the Departmental Committee on Prisons* (C. 7702, 1895), para. 84, p. 30

BORSTAL RE-ASSESSED

country with ample space for agricultural and land reclamation work. It should have penal and coercive sides which could be applied according to merits of particular cases. But it should be amply provided with a staff capable of giving sound education, training inmates in various kinds of industrial work, and qualified generally to exercise the best and healthiest kind of moral influence.[1]

Despite the fact that previous enquiries 'almost altogether overlooked this all important matter'[2] the Committee was 'unable to elicit from any witnesses a serious objection to the scheme'.[3] There appeared to be sufficient evidence for a drastic change in penal methods.

The Committee said that it was 'certain that the ages when the majority of habitual criminals are made lies between 16 and 21'. Its evidence mainly rested on a study made by G. P. Merrick, the Chaplain of Holloway and Newgate, of about 2,000 prisoners with whom he dealt in 1893. His method of study was largely to note the ages of offenders imprisoned for several serious offences. In conclusion he stated that 'it will be observed that there are more burglars at the age of 18 than at any other age, and that from that age the numbers decline very rapidly'. In looking at the age of thieves he also wrote, 'it will be observed here also what a fatal age 18 is for wrong-doing.'[4] Merrick's figures gave no indication of how many of these boys were likely to get into trouble again, nor did they show whether habitual criminals had in fact been imprisoned

[1] ibid., para. 84b
[2] ibid., para. 29
[3] ibid., para. 84b
[4] ibid., para. 29, and Appendix 17 of the *P. C. Report*, 1894–95, pp. 80–81. An example of the sort of evidence Merrick produced is as follows: 'Of ordinary thieves, the youngest in 1,023 cases was 10 years of age, while the oldest was 72.

10 years of age produced 1 offender
13 years of age produced 1 offender
14 years of age produced 3 offenders
15 years of age produced 14 offenders
16 years of age produced 16 offenders
17 years of age produced 32 offenders
18 years of age produced 55 offenders
19 years of age produced 49 offenders
20 years of age produced 46 offenders.'

when under the age of 21.[1] The fact that this age group provided the highest number of prisoners was taken as reason
enough for believing that it would contain the vast majority of
future habitual criminals. This was also the opinion of others
who gave evidence.[2] It had been noted that after 30 a 'very
distinct decrease in the number of prisoners proportionate to
the population of the same age sets in'.[3] The Committee
believed that a natural tendency to the abandonment of crime
could be speeded up and strengthened by taking special pains
with the prisoners at the age when they were most numerous.
But in any case, there were no available figures whereby the
Committee could have checked Merrick's assertion: methods
available to the police for recording and checking previous
offences were still unsophisticated. Yet it was the *impression* of
prison governors that once a young person had served a short
sentence, the dread of prison would vanish, he would be
corrupted and undoubtedly return for a life-time's succession
of short sentences. Undoubtedly there were some for whom this
must have been true: but for how many the Committee was
not to know. It was enough that they were wholly dissatisfied
with the prison regime. *A priori* they must have thought it
doubly bad for young offenders.

The Committee was, however, under no illusions about the
difficulties involved. The existing methods seemed so bad that
they asserted that 'even a moderate percentage of success would
justify much effort and expense devoted to an improvement in
the system'.[4] Nevertheless, some optimism must have been

[1] The Prison Commissioners later made such a study. This showed that
of 50 professional criminals, 11 were under 15 when first convicted and 23
others were under 21. They regarded this as outstanding proof that this
indeed was 'the dangerous age'. *P. C. Report*, 1900–01, p. 13

[2] *Departmental Committee*, para. 29. In particular the Rev. W. Douglas
Morrison, the former Chaplain of Wandsworth, gave strong evidence on
this point. He was well acquainted with penological and criminological
issues. Furthermore he was a leading critic of the prison system, and was
dismissed by Du Cane for the publication of an article in *The Fortnightly
Review* (Vol. 55) entitled 'Are our Prisons a Failure?' Nearly all witnesses
were agreed on this point, even including Du Cane. Some, such as Captain
Hill (Governor of Strangeways), even suggested that habitual criminals
started much earlier than 16. See *Minutes of Evidence* (C. 7702–1).

[3] *Departmental Committee*, para. 84

[4] ibid., para. 84

engendered by the impressive claims of Mr Trevarthen, the head of Red Hill Reformatory. He informed the Committee that he had achieved, with younger offenders, a success rate of 95 per cent.[1] There was also important evidence from abroad. The Committee was in possession of a report on the working of the reformatory at Elmira in New York State, in which it was claimed that 'probably about 80 per cent of the prisoners are reformed'.[2] But it refrained from comment, other than simply stating that different systems 'must vary according to national temperaments and requirements', and 'some of our recommendations, to a considerable extent, will be based upon methods successfully adopted by other countries'.[3] In the absence of any such reformatory movement for 16 to 21 year olds on the continent of Europe, this must have meant Elmira.

Granting that the Committee had isolated the 'dangerous age' and also found reformatory methods to have much to offer, it was still supporting a completely new principle. Up to that time, 16 had been the age of criminal majority. There could be no question of reformatories for adults. They were fully responsible for their actions and so deserved their punishment. To circumvent this problem a new term was invented: the 'juvenile-adult'. The use of this term suggested that these young persons, while too old for purely reformatory methods, were still too young to be dealt with as if they were really adults. For them it was to be the 'half-way house', the 'penal reformatory', the regime with 'penal and coercive sides' as well as 'rational treatment'. But the Committee was not concerned with finding a legal rationale for the separate treatment of this class of offender. (That was not argued until later, when the Commissioners considered the proposals.) Its justification would lie in results, in 'laying hold of these incipient criminals and preventing them . . . from recruiting the habitual class . . . The habitual criminals can only be effectively put down in one way, and that is by cutting off the supply.'[4]

[1] ibid., and see *Minutes of Evidence*, and Sir Algernon West, 'English Prisons,' *Nineteenth Century*, Vol. 39 (1895), p. 150.
[2] Appendix I. Addendum on Elmira (C. 7702-1), p. 526
[3] *Departmental Committee*, para. 30
[4] ibid., para. 29

*Reformatory Methods Debated*

The Gladstone Committee was satisfied that an experiment should be made, but the Prison Commissioners and the public needed more convincing—or at least time to think out the implications of these novel proposals. The Commissioners were not at all clear about what the Committee had in mind. In particular they were unsure to what extent the penal-reformatory was meant to be penal and how far it could at the same time be a reformatory. The two concepts had always been distinctly separated. Indeed, as Ruggles-Brise pointed out, the High Court judges had, at mid-century, been formally consulted as to the possibility of introducing reformatory influences for young offenders and had 'declared reform and imprisonment to be a contradiction in terms and utterly irreconcilable'.[1] In their official observations on the Committee's report,[2] the Commissioners stated:

> At present we are not clear, and we have not had the opportunity of studying the evidence on which the proposal is based, in what respect the proposed penal-reformatory will differ from a prison or even a penal servitude prison. It is conceded that the age to be treated is particularly criminal and dangerous. It is conceded that there must be penal and coercive sides. The institution must be in the country with ample space for agricultural and land reclamation work. We have here a description of Dartmoor, but it will differ from Dartmoor in the adoption of a careful system of classification according to the Redhill methods.

The use of the term 'conceded' shows that the Commissioners were anxious lest a purely reformatory system be adopted. What they wanted was an intermediate classification—not a 'reformatory' but an ameliorated form of 'penal servitude'.

The Commissioners were certainly unclear about who should be sent to the penal-reformatory:

> It does not appear from the report under consideration whether it is intended that first offenders only shall go to the penal-reformatory, or whether it is meant that all criminals under a

---

[1] See *The English Prison System* (1921), pp. 88–9.

[2] *Observations of the Prison Commissioners on the Recommendations of the Departmental Committee on Prisons, appointed by the Secretary of State on the 6th June 1894* (C. 7995), 1896. They pointed out, 'we should be in hearty accord with any *feasible plan*' (my italics). See pp. 27–8.

B.R.—2

certain age shall, in virtue of the 'plasticity' of their natures, be made the subject of the experiment. We infer that the latter is meant, as the possibility of closing one or two prisons is mentioned.

They therefore felt 'by no means certain that public sentiment would be favourable to the idea', especially if comparatively unhardened criminals or first offenders were to receive the relatively lengthy sentence.

The Commissioners were well aware that the Gladstone Committee had been impressed by the Elmira reformatory,[1] the results of which had been described with enthusiasm to the Fourth International Penitentiary Congress held in Paris in 1895. But the Commissioners remained extremely dubious. They must have been influenced by opinions doubting the results claimed and regarding the methods of reformation as a form of extravagant sentimentality and leniency. H. B. Simpson, a Home Office official, described Elmira in the *Contemporary Review* of July 1896 as follows:

> Meanwhile the Elmira system, with its lectures and discussions, its Turkish baths, massage and gymnastics of prisoners, its reading clubs, its daily newspapers, its careful avoidance of anything that may hurt a sensitive prisoner's feelings, or remind him that he has done anything to be ashamed of, must inevitably tend to diminish, on the one hand, the deterrent effect of legal penalties, and on the other to encourage hypocrisy, self-deceit, and a very disagreeable kind of priggishness among the criminals . . . the statistics produced to prove the system to be, on the whole, a success, are as yet wholly inconclusive.[2]

In the *Fortnightly Review* (1895), H. Laslitt-Browne writing on Common-Sense and Crime had stated categorically

> that it [the reformatory method] has been tried elsewhere, and with no very conspicuous success, as at Elmira, in the State of New York, does not necessarily condemn it. The recent disclosures of administrative error in that pretentious establishment may serve as a warning . . . managers ran riot in their extravagant

---

[1] For descriptions of the Elmira system, see Blake McKelvey, *American Prisons: A Study in American Social History Prior to 1915* (1936).

[2] H. B. Simpson, 'Crime and Punishment,' *Contemporary Review*, Vol. 70, July 1896, p. 103

methods of education . . . It is not likely that the authorities charged with the experiment in this country will rush into such excesses as have made Elmira the laughing stock of the whole world.[1]

Indeed the Commissioners were not rushing. In 1897, Mr Ruggles-Brise asked the Home Secretary for permission to accept an invitation first extended to him in 1895 to examine the American methods at first hand.

Ruggles-Brise's reports of his visit leave no doubt that he was very much impressed by the *principles* on which the American system rested. He was not so impressed by the way they were transformed into practice. The three main principles of Elmira—that young offenders could be regarded as potentially good citizens, that reformation would produce better results than imprisonment, and that therefore special measures were needed for their training (i.e., the indeterminate sentence)— were similar to those put forward by the Gladstone Committee. The Commissioners debated their validity.

At Elmira the principle that *up to a certain age* (my italics) offenders should be sent to the reformatory had in practice included offenders in the age range 16 to 30 as 'potential good citizens'—although the average age of the inmates was 22. Ruggles-Brise felt that this age range was extravagant, and meant classifying men as boys: 'the peculiarity and *fault* of the system is that it extends the age of youth as far as thirty and thirty-five' (my italics).[2] He thought that public opinion would not stand for giving grown men a treatment that should be reserved for the young alone,[3] and suggested that the 'truth' lay midway between the English and American systems and advocated an age range of 16 to 21. There seems to have been no other reason for suggesting that 21 be the upper age limit than that it was the age of civil majority.[4] The Gladstone

[1] H. Laslitt-Browne, 'Common-Sense and Crime,' *Fortnightly Review*, Vol. 58, 1895, p. 230. But both Simpson and Laslitt-Browne were in favour of at least *some* reformatory attempts in England, but not for a copy of Elmira.

[2] See the report by Ruggles-Brise on the Brussels Congress of 1900 in *Prison Reform at Home and Abroad* (1924), p. 93.

[3] Evelyn Ruggles-Brise, 'State Reformatories,' in *Report of the Fifth and Sixth International Penitentiary Congress* (Cd. 573), 1901, pp. 91–2

[4] *P. C. Report*, 1898–99, p. 15

Committee had relied on the evidence of Merrick,[1] but Ruggles-Brise based his rationale for separate treatment of adolescents on 'psychological' evidence. He argued that special treatment could only be accepted for particular reasons, and that for 'ordinary crime' (*les crimes proprement dits*) it should be rejected. The 'ordinary offender' was one who was in full possession of his responsibility or 'character',[2] that is, all adults apart from the insane. The case for special treatment for those over 16 and up to 21 rested on the assumption that their 'characters' had not fully formed and therefore not only were they eligible for reform but also likely to benefit from it. Beyond the age when character was 'set' it was assumed that reformatory methods would be hopeless. The evidence for regarding juvenile-adults as 'undeveloped in character' had been presented by W. D. Morrison in his *Juvenile Offenders*, 1896. The argument was that maturity of character depended upon physical maturity, and that because research had shown that the poorer classes were not fully physically developed until the age of about 25 'our existing penal laws and our present methods of administration, in so far as they relate to juveniles over the age of sixteen, are at once cruel and absurd'.[3] Morrison's formula was important as it was repeated on a number of occasions by Ruggles-Brise as a justification for the separate treatment. Furthermore, it had the support of continental scholars. At the Fifth International Penitentiary Congress held in Brussels in 1900, Ruggles-Brise reported: 'M. Garraud [Professor of Law at Lyons University] declared himself in favour of . . . an "indeterminate" sentence up to the age of *twenty-five years; at which age the character may be said to be absolutely and definitely formed* [my italics]. This opinion is interesting in being analogous to that which has found public expression in England.'[4] Further research by Dr Baker at Pentonville of deficiencies in height and weight of the prison population, compared with the average for the general population, convinced Ruggles-Brise that 'the full responsibility for his

---

[1] See p. 2 above.        [2] *Prison Reform at Home and Abroad*, pp. 92 and 94
[3] W. Douglas Morrison, *Juvenile Offenders* (1896), pp. 296–8. Morrison quotes Dr Roberts's evidence before the Secondary Education Commission, and various anthropometric evidence about height and weight. It is of interest that his book was second in a series, the first volume of which had been Lombroso's *The Female Offender* (1895).
[4] *Prison Reform at Home and Abroad*, p. 115

[the young habitual's] actions . . . can be, without danger to society, postponed until the age of maturity, i.e. 21'.[1] But the same evidence could not convince him that offenders up to 25 were capable of being reformed or indeed should be spared the penal consequences of their crimes.

If young criminals lacked 'maturity of character' it followed that they could perhaps be influenced and reformed. What Ruggles-Brise did not agree with was the methods used at Elmira. While paying respect to the 'elaborate system of moral, physical and industrial training of these prisoners, the enthusiasm which dominated the work [and] the elaborate machinery for supervision of parole', he remarked that there was 'much in the system that is extravagant and to English ideas nearly approaching the ridiculous'.[2] The Times on reviewing the report remarked that 'his criticisms are more marked than his praise' and in particular singled out for comment what it termed 'the undue leniency and disregard for deterrent influences'. 'A much less risky experiment,' it concluded, 'is the establishment of probation officers.'[3] One particular fear was that conditions inside the institutions might become better than the alternative for the destitute—the workhouse.

Dr Mannheim has traced the importance of the Poor Law principle of less-eligibility for penal reform.[4] It was thought that conditions in a reformatory should certainly not give any person an advantage over law-abiding people in the community. At a time of low wages, frequent unemployment and limited vocational and educational opportunities, reformatories should not in any way give delinquents opportunities denied to the honest. Alfred Lyttelton illustrated this point in a letter to Ruggles-Brise in 1898:

> Whether we can advance on the lines of the Yankee system, or whether that system will confront us frequently with a most embarrassing problem such as that which met me at Oxford the other day viz: a prisoner telling me deliberately that he had

---

[1] In 'State Reformatories,' op. cit., p. 92. See also the same argument still being used in P. C. Report, 1908–09, pp. 14–15.

[2] P. C. Report, 1898–99, pp. 22–3

[3] Leading article, The Times, 15 May 1899; see also, leading article, The Times, 17 July 1901.

[4] H. Mannheim, The Dilemma of Penal Reform (1940)

broken a pane of glass to get to prison which he infinitely preferred to the workhouse—is one of the most interesting speculations I know.[1]

But it seems that Ruggles-Brise was ambivalent towards Elmira. After describing what he called the 'sentimentality and indulgence and hopefulness towards criminals' in the reformatory system, he went on to remark:

> It is a mistake to suppose that the discipline is lax, or that these places are 'hotels' where the prisoners go to enjoy themselves and have an easy time. The contrary is nearer the truth . . . it is a common thing for the inmates to express a preference for the State Prison. At Elmira a few years ago a strong protest was made in the Press against the severity of discipline administered there.[2]

However, there is no doubt that he did not wish to import a carbon-copy of the American system: the system he recognized as a 'bold experiment', but saw no necessity for 'imitating their methods'.[3]

The third principle was the indeterminate sentence. Under this system the offender would be committed for a maximum period, but within that time he would be released on licence when the authorities considered that he had reformed. This form of sentence was, at least for a time, confused with the 'indefinite' sentence under which no maximum period of detention was laid down and the offender could be kept until he was considered reformed. *The Times*, for example, in discussing Ruggles-Brise's report of the Brussels Congress made this mistake in its criticisms of the American system. Furthermore, it suggested that the 'gravest defect of all' in 'indefinite' detainment was its failure 'to express clearly the condemnation of honest, healthy people of evil deeds'.[4] Yet, at the same time, sentences were being criticized as too lengthy! This indeterminate sentence was, as Ruggles-Brise pointed out, 'at variance with two of the most sacred principles of the English criminal

---

[1] Private correspondence in the hands of the Borstal Division
[2] *The English Prison System*, p. 91; also E. Ruggles-Brise, *Some Observations on the Treatment of Crime in America. A Report to the Secretary of State (156)*, 1899, p. 11
[3] In 'State Reformatories,' op. cit., p. 92
[4] Leading article, *The Times*, 17 July 1901

law—(1) the free discretion of the judge in awarding sentence, (2) the prerogative of mercy vested in the crown'. While he did not think the public would 'tolerate any interference with these principles', he considered that the problem could simply be overcome by extending 'the powers possessed by Judges of sentencing youths under 16 to long periods of detention in a reformatory'.[1] The Commissioners in a special report on their progress up to 1898 stated that they presumed that 'the Secretary of State would not be prepared to sanction any such new departure in prison methods without obtaining an authoritative expression of opinion from not only the highest judicial authorities in the land, but also from Chairmen of Quarter Sessions and other magistrates who are practically conversant with the character of the problem with which we are called upon to deal'. They added that they felt 'convinced that the Committee which has advised this change in our criminal methods, will agree in the necessity of proceeding with great caution, and for obtaining the sanction and authority of the most competent legal opinion before embarking on a procedure which is new to English ideas, and the value of which can only be tested by experiment'.[2] Commenting on the deliberations of the Brussels Congress of 1900, Ruggles-Brise remarked: 'It approached the question of indeterminism with great sobriety and good judgement. It was not misled by the mischievous plausibilities of the American or the fatalistic doctrines of the Italian School.'[3] While the Commissioners agreed on the possibilities of reform, they were not indiscriminately going to apply reformatory methods.

Ruggles-Brise was also very sceptical of the results attributed to Elmira. He mentioned that the managers claimed a success rate of around 80 per cent, but pointed out that the majority of the inmates were first offenders whom he believed would have done equally well under ordinary prison treatment in

[1] In 'State Reformatories,' p. 104

[2] *Statement by the Prison Commissioners of the Action which has been taken up to January 1898 to carry out the Recommendations in the Report of the Departmental Committee on Prisons 1895* (C. 8790), 1898, p. 16

[3] *Prison Reform at Home and Abroad*, p. 92. The Italians, under the influence of Lombroso, believed that persistent criminals could be distinguished by physical characteristics, were a 'throwback' to earlier uncivilized man and thus incapable of reformation.

England. However, in practice Elmira catered not only for first offenders, but accepted all who were thought likely to benefit from the regime.[1] Ruggles-Brise also thought that the 'term of surveillance' of between six to twelve months was too short to allow a proper assessment of results. He considered that results would have been far different if the offenders had been followed up beyond the expiration of their parole licence.[2] On the other hand, he offered no such criticism of the 70 to 90 per cent success rate claimed by Red Hill Reformatory.[3]

The official early history of borstal, as related in Ruggles-Brise's *The English Prison System*, implies that the Commissioners readily accepted the Gladstone Committee's recommendations, and with the aid of the Elmira visit quickly put into effect the proposals. This was certainly not the case. They were not willing to accept the American experience as necessarily valid for England. The report of the discussion on 'The State Reformatory System of the United States' at the Brussels Congress clearly illustrates the European attitude. It reads like part of Henry James's famous theme—the old Europe and the New America:

> The discussion was characterized by a hardly veiled hostility to what is known generally in Europe as the 'Elmira System'; for, though the other States have, in varying degrees, adopted the reformatory system, Elmira remains the type, and pattern, and embodiment of the special and novel institution which the Americans claim to have originated, and which they invite other nations to adopt as an essential feature of any good penal system . . . the rather bulky pamphlets . . . failed to convince the European reader that any new thing had been discovered that was not already in existence under another name in old Europe . . . A

---

[1] See C. E. B. Russell and L. M. Rigby, *The Making of the Criminal* (1906).
[2] In *Some Observations on the Treatment of Crime in America*, op. cit., pp. 12–13. Nevertheless, Ruggles-Brise does point out elsewhere that in reality offenders were only sent to Elmira for serious crime and around 40 per cent had in fact previously come into contact with the law. See 'State Reformatories', op. cit., pp. 87–9.
[3] When the borstal scheme first started there was, however, no period on licence, and even under the Prevention of Crime Act 1908 this period was only originally set at six months. It is interesting that the criticisms made of Elmira were not heard when borstal results were discussed!

certain irritation was apparent throughout the discussion, that the American delegates should force upon the attention of Europe, which had been devoting itself to the study of penal science for the last hundred years, a new form of institution for dealing with crime, which, if the claim made on its behalf can be justified by results, has at any rate not yet been long enough in existence to furnish a certain proof that a new discovery has been made, or that measures were working successfully in America, which European countries were either content to ignore, or too idle to apply. In short the Congress declined to give a vote of confidence to a system which, though abounding in specious theories and promises of reform, was not hitherto fortified by statistical data, which alone can justify prudent men, engaged in the repression of crime, from embarking upon new designs . . . Even discounting a certain reluctance to confess that the Americans had discovered any new thing in penology, not unnatural among the representatives of the older races . . . [they] were prevented, by considerations of prudence, from hastily adopting a new idea, unless they could be satisfied, as practical men, that there was something in the idea which would justify the time, trouble and expense which any departure from the recognised methods would involve.[1]

However, it is clear from the same report that the principle of separate treatment for the age-group 16–21 had been accepted. Yet the Americans were given little credit for it. Ruggles-Brise commented: 'This rather homely, and, as I think, indisputable principle . . . may seem a tame conclusion to derive from the elaborate American system, where the simplicity of the idea is concealed by the complexity of the machinery used.' The adult reformatory, far from being an import from the New World, was conceived of as a natural extension of the long-established European reformatory principles formerly reserved for those under 16.

By 1900 the Commissioners were ready to begin experimenting: but not in imitation of Elmira. *The Times* summed up the essence of the compromise in a leading article: 'if we dwell too much on the deterrent effects of punishment, in America there is at present too much a tendency to think of the criminal as an interesting object to be reformed.'[2] There were to be no 'extravagances' in the new penal-reformatory!

[1] In *Prison Reform at Home and Abroad*, pp. 95–9
[2] *The Times*, 15 May 1899

*The Experiment*

In their report for 1898 the Commissioners suggested that it was a matter for 'very serious consideration' whether the law could be altered to allow sentences of sufficient length so that reformatory influences could be brought to bear on the 16 to 21 year olds.[1] Ruggles-Brise followed this up with a lengthy letter to *The Times* advocating both the raising of the age limit to 18 for reformatory schools and the establishment of a penal-reformatory. He said he believed it should be on the lines of the American system[2] which, with its 'stern and exact discipline, combined with an attempt to "individualize" the prisoner by physical, educational and religious training, is especially adapted for these dangerous young criminals under 21'.[3] But there was little chance of a change in the law until an experiment had proved successful. After all, the Gladstone Committee had recommended that an experiment should first begin 'on a moderate scale'.

Early in 1900 the experiment began on a very small scale. Eight young prisoners were selected from London prisons and transferred to Bedford Prison where they were separated entirely from the other adults and 'made subject to a special system of discipline calculated to influence this very tough material'.[4] The Governor of Bedford reported after three months that 'they have exceeded my most sanguine expectations, with one exception . . . but such a case as this would be rare . . . The scheme is a commendable one and worthy of any trouble and expense the State may incur.'[5] A juvenile-adult 'class' was therefore permanently established. The following year the Commissioners reported that 'the scheme has now taken a practical shape. It has been decided to surrender a portion of the convict prison at Borstal for the detention of this

[1] *P. C. Report*, 1898–99, p. 9

[2] It should be clear from the discussion above on Ruggles-Brise's reaction to Elmira just how far 'along the lines' he was prepared to go.

[3] *The Times*, 22 August 1899

[4] See the Report of the Governor of Bedford in *P. C. Report*, 1899–1900, pp. 19–20. He described the curriculum: 'education, gymnastics, choir, lectures, visits by the chaplain, and working in association "to learn a trade".'

[5] loc. cit.

class.'[1] There were still some convicts at Borstal, but they were in separate buildings out of sight of the youths. Nevertheless, it signified that the new penal-reformatory was very much part of the prison system. No attempt was ever made to establish a large separate reformatory with a population of over a thousand as at Elmira. Selected boys from London prisons who had received sentences of at least six months were transferred to Borstal. It is significant that the first party arrived in chains.

The 'fundamental principles' of the new treatment were outlined as: '(1) strict classification; (2) firm and exact discipline; (3) hard work; (4) organized supervision on discharge'.[2] The institutional regime included strict disciplinary rules, physical drill, some instruction in trades, basic education and a system of grades through which the inmate gained promotion and increasing small privileges by earning marks for hard work and good conduct.[3] The supervision on discharge was aimed not only at helping boys resettle, but in following up cases and collecting evidence so that 'public opinion will be able to judge whether the results of the system, as a new means for the prevention of crime, are so good that what is now being tried only as an experiment and in a small area, should be made of universal application'.[4] These results were to provide the rationale behind the official recognition of the system in 1908.

In 1903 the scheme was extended to young convicts at Dartmoor. These offenders were thought to be the 'worst that can be found in England and Wales'. Again the Governor reported his 'agreeable surprise' with the results of the experiment whereby twenty-six boys were being taught carpentry 'under strict discipline'.[5]

The Commissioners had, from the beginning, emphasized that reformation could not be achieved in a short period. In practice they found this to be the case. After two years' experience they decided only to transfer to Borstal cases which had been sentenced to twelve months and upwards. They had found that 'six months is too short a period for any real impression to

---

[1] P. C. Report, 1900–01, p. 12          [2] ibid., p. 13
[3] The ideas behind this type of regime are discussed in Chapter IV.
[4] ibid., pp. 17–18. The development of supervision and the assessment of results is more fully discussed in Chapters VI and VII.
[5] P. C. Report, 1902–03, p. 85

be made upon a rebellious character'. However, at that time it was quite rare for young offenders to receive such a lengthy sentence. Room was therefore available at Borstal for offenders from all over the country.[1] In particular it was emphasized that sentences needed to be long if the offender was to learn a trade. An article entitled 'The Borstal Scheme' in *The Times*, 1902, drew particular attention to the regulation that 'they shall be specially instructed in useful trades and industries which may fit them to earn their livelihood on release' and urged that the strongest argument for longer sentences was the time needed to learn a trade.[2] Staff at Borstal echoed the sentiment.[3]

The Commissioners and the Borstal Association[4] (which undertook the supervision on licence) pointed out that the regime was one of strict penal discipline, and critics of 'lenient' methods were satisfied that this was so. *The Times* correspondent stated that '. . . any visitor can see that the deterrent influences which must always characterize a sane penal system are by no means neglected'.[5] Alfred Wills (a High Court judge and Chairman of the Metropolitan Prisoners' Aid Society), who opposed lenient methods, wrote: 'A Borstal prisoner is subjected to a very rigorous discipline. He is well, but not over fed, but he is made to work very hard.'[6] Public opinion was evidently convinced that the 'excesses' of the Elmira regime had been avoided, while, at the same time, earnest attempts were being made to reform the youths. Russell and Rigby, in their impor-

[1] *P. C. Report*, 1903–04, p. 19

[2] Trade training in this period is further discussed on pp. 97–8 below.

[3] See articles, 'The Borstal Scheme,' *The Times*, 27 December 1902, and 1 December 1904. See also, for example, the comments of both the Chaplains at Borstal and Dartmoor asking for longer sentences: 'the lads would then be able thoroughly to learn a trade.' *P. C. Report*, 1902–03, pp. 80 and 85. Even the first report of the local visiting magistrates to Bedford in 1900 contained the phrase 'they are to be taught a trade'—see *P. C. Report*, 1900–01, p. 14. Ruggles-Brise in his paper, 'The Borstal Scheme,' delivered to the Budapest Congress 1905, states that the system rests 'on its physical side, on the basis of hard manual labour at skilled trades'—see *Prison Reform at Home and Abroad*, p. 132.

[4] The Association was commonly referred to as the B.A., and this abbreviation will be used below.

[5] In *The Times* article of 1 December 1904

[6] See 'Criminals and Crime,' *Nineteenth Century and After*, Vol. 62, December 1907, p. 882.

tant book, *The Making of the Criminal* (1906), assured their readers that there was 'no undue pampering', while at the same time remarking that it was often due to the '*sympathy* of an exceptional court' (my italics) that many boys had been sent for Borstal's beneficial treatment.[1] When in 1907 steps were first taken to introduce a bill into Parliament, there were no voices of dissent. In fact the Commissioners had produced a system which was thought to herald 'an epoch in the treatment of juvenile crime'.[2]

## The Modified Borstal System

By 1907 there was not only the institution at Borstal, and a small extension of the system starting at Lincoln Prison, but also a wide and diffuse 'modified borstal system'.

The use of the term 'modified borstal' caused a great deal of confusion right up until 1922 when it was replaced by the term 'young prisoner'. The Commissioners had been so pleased by the results of the experience both at Bedford and at Borstal that they decided in 1905 that the principles of the borstal scheme should be extended to all offenders aged 16 to 21 committed to prison. They realized that, 'Having regard to the general shortness of the sentence this will not mean much more than (a) strict segregation from adults (b) physical exercise and drill (c) weekly lectures and addresses in class and (d) special machinery at each prison for the after-care and disposal of these cases.'[3] This system (formally introduced on 1 June 1906) was designed as a 'special effort . . . to reclaim them . . . without prejudice to, or impairment of, the necessary rigour of a sentence of imprisonment'.[4] Despite the fact that over 70 per cent of the offenders had been sentenced to less than one month, the Commissioners reported their satisfaction that 'a considerable impression is being made'. At each prison a special committee was established to help in the aid-on-discharge of these young prisoners.[5] The results of the training sounded most impressive: 'gymnastic exercises have produced remarkable results. The

---

[1] Russell and Rigby, op. cit., p. 126
[2] Lord Yarborough speaking at Lincoln, reported in *The Times*, 29 January 1906.
[3] *P. C. Report*, 1904–05, p. 18, and Appendix 17b
[4] *P. C. Report*, 1906–07, p. 15     [5] See pp. 170–1 below.

lads gain in alertness and self-respect, and an improvement in
moral tone follows naturally upon an improvement in physical
fitness. The puny city-bred lad, after a few weeks of this treatment generally grows out of his clothes . . . [they are] reclaimed
by . . . mental improvement, by training scholastic and
industrial, by lectures calculated to impress youthful minds,
and to evoke the higher moral qualities . . .'[1] Because the Commissioners constantly stressed that sentences were too short for
any real help to be given, some thought that it would be in the
interests of youths to receive longer sentences under the modified system. The Annual Report of the Visiting Committee at
Walton Prison (Liverpool) stressed, for example, that 'the
majority of the sentences were not of sufficient length to enable
the *benefits* [my italics] of the system to be given a fair trial'. In
fact, they wanted longer sentences so that the efficiency of a
new joiners' shop could be tested.[2]

Late in 1907 all those with sentences of over four months
were segregated into a number of prisons acting as 'collecting
centres'. Speaking at the opening of a centre at Wormwood
Scrubs, the Bishop of Stepney said as reported by *The Times*:
'Now the Borstal system was to be applied to all our juvenile
offenders. It was impossible not to be filled with admiration at
the sympathy, the tact, and firmness with which these boys
were trained at the prison . . . under the Borstal system they
were set to a decent trade and given some chance of becoming
decent men when they left.'[3] It is easy to see how the 'modified'
borstal system became confused in the public's mind with the
system of training carried out with longer-term prisoners at
Borstal.

*Legislation*

(a) *Raising the age for reformatory schools.* It will be remembered
that the Gladstone Committee recommended that boys should
not be admitted to reformatory schools until 18 years of age. But
it suggested that first of all 'the satisfactory conditions of the

---

[1] *P. C. Report*, 1907–08, pp. 12–13 and 15
[2] *The Times*, 7 January 1908
[3] Speech to a meeting of the Royal Society for the Assistance of Discharged Prisoners. *The Times*, 23 October 1907

schools would be ascertained . . . [and] the proposals would
have to be looked at from the point of view of the reformatory
managers'. In 1896 the Departmental Committee on Reformatory and Industrial Schools published its report. Many of its
suggestions were subject to dissenting opinions, among them
the proposal to raise the age of admission. The majority report
was in favour of the age limit rise, on the understanding that
either special reformatories should be set aside for the older
youths, or a system of classification devised with a separate
block for the 'adults' in one or two existing reformatories. Most
of the evidence supported this idea.[1] Sir Godfrey Lushington,
the Chairman, and three other members dissented. They 'did
not consider the establishment of an adult reformatory as a
proper remedy'. In particular, they were concerned that the
youths would be 'treated partly like children and partly like
prisoners' and would resent the lengthy reformatory sentence
when the normal alternative was six months' imprisonment.
Sir Godfrey and his colleagues were convinced that this resentment would be so great that neither discipline nor reformatory
influences would change the boys.[2] Of course this objection
could also have been raised against borstal.

The dissenting opinion was upheld in 1908. Mr Herbert
Samuel told the Commons that 'we are not adopting the
suggestion only because we consider it is inadvisable to mix
older offenders with smaller and younger boys and girls, and
because . . . the Home Secretary hopes to introduce a Bill
establishing a new class of reformatories for older offenders'.[3]
The borstal experiment had proved a success, and so the proposal for reformatory schools appeared redundant.

(b) *The Prevention of Crime Act 1908.* A 'State Reformatories
Bill' was introduced in 1907 but there was no time to consider

[1] *Report of the Departmental Committee on Reformatory and Industrial Schools*
1896, Vol. I (C. 8204), paras. 229, 231, 233–t. The proposal was supported
by the Inspectors of Reformatories, Sir Edmund Du Cane, W. D. Morrison,
J. Trevarthen of Red Hill, and others. See Vol. II, *Evidence* (C. 8290) for
evidence of the Council of the Association of Industrial and Reformatory
Schools, Qs. 18280–2. See also the case made for extending the age of
reformatory sentences in Russell and Rigby, op. cit., pp. 337–8.

[2] Departmental Committee, Memorandum D

[3] *H. C. Debates*, Vol. 183, col. 1435, 10 February 1908

it. By 1908, when the bill was again introduced, it had changed its name to 'The Prevention of Crime Bill'. In it there was no mention of the term 'State Reformatory'. The Home Office, anxious not to give the impression that the training at Borstal was like that carried out in the reformatory schools, had substituted the term 'Borstal Institution'.

Herbert Gladstone, now Home Secretary, introduced the proposals he had first made thirteen years earlier. He described them as 'the completion of a definite scheme for dealing with young offenders . . . following upon the Probation Act and the Children Bill introduced this session'.[1] The Act as eventually passed laid down the law governing committal to borstal institutions in Part 1 under the heading 'Reformation of Young Offenders'. It stated:

*Section 1 (i)*
  Where a person is convicted on indictment of an offence for which he is liable to be sentenced to penal servitude or imprisonment, and it appears to the court—
  (a) that the person is not less than sixteen or more than twenty-one years of age; and
  (b) that by reason of his criminal habits and tendencies, or associations with persons of bad character, it is expedient that he should be subject to detention for such term and under such instruction and discipline as appears most conducive to his reformation and the repression of crime;
  it shall be lawful for the court, in lieu of passing a sentence of penal servitude or imprisonment, to pass a sentence of detention under penal discipline in a Borstal Institution for a term of not less than one year nor more than three years.

This power applied only to courts of assize and quarter sessions.

Under the same section of the Act the court was required first to consider a report from the Prison Commissioners as to the offender's suitability for the sentence. It was also stated that the age limit could be raised to 23 by the Home Secretary acting through an order in Council. Other sections provided for the sentencing of refractory reformatory school boys to borstal, the transfer of youths from prison to borstal, and the transfer of 'incorrigibles' to prison. The Act stipulated that boys

[1] Mr Gladstone in *H. C. Debates*, Vol. 189, col. 1121, 27 May 1908

were to be given 'such industrial training and other instruction, and be subject to such disciplinary and moral influences as will conduce to their reformation and the prevention of crime'. At any time after six months the boys could be released on licence and be placed under supervision until six months after their sentence expired. Their licence could be revoked for bad conduct and they could be recalled for three months' further detention.

Two important sections of the original Bill were withdrawn during debate. In Section 1 (2) the Bill had required judges to pass an alternative sentence at the same time as sending the youth to borstal in case he proved unsuitable. The object of this section was to overcome the delay that would have occurred if the court had to await a report on the youth's suitability before sentencing him. The provision received general support *in principle* because it made the detention of a boy in borstal dependent upon the 'expert's' (i.e., the Commissioner's) opinion as to his suitability rather than on the judge's, who was not necessarily competent to make the decision.[1] This section was withdrawn when it was pointed out that the enquiries could be made while the youth was waiting trial at the sessions.

A second and more important provision concerned the age limit for borstal. The Home Secretary was empowered to apply the Act by direct order to 'persons apparently under such age as may be specified in the order'. But the House certainly would not endorse such an 'extraordinary power'.[2] Mr Gladstone agreed that an upper-limit was necessary in order to keep courts from 'the error of committing to Borstal institutions persons so far above the age of 21 that they were totally unsuitable for the institution'. He thought 21 was 'a reasonable age to fix' and that it could be later raised to 23 when more institutions were available.[3]

The wording of the Act made clear that the new institutions

[1] See *H. C. Debates*, Vol. 189, col. 1121, 27 May 1908; Vol. 190, cols. 466–82, 12 June 1908. Debate on this clause brought up the question of the 'indeterminate' sentence fixed by the Commissioners. With only one exception, members supported the idea that those responsible for training would know better than a Judge when to release an offender.

[2] *H. C. Debates*, Vol. 197, cols. 221–6, 24 November 1908

[3] ibid., cols. 225–6

were not for first offenders[1] nor would they be purely reformatory in nature. Only those with considerable evidence of 'criminal tendencies' could qualify for the lengthy 'detention under penal discipline'. The tariff system of sentencing was strongly entrenched, and there had to be good reasons for imposing a form of detention far longer than youths would have received under ordinary imprisonment. The new borstal institutions were, in fact, a form of compromise between the old ideas and the new. Reformation was now admitted as a desirable end, but it could only be administered within the penal system as long as it did not entail a dangerous relaxation of 'stern and exact discipline'. Such a sentence obviously amounted to a heavy penalty, both unsuitable and unfair for the novice in crime. Yet, in practice, the question of who was eligible for borstal was to be a centre of debate for the next forty years.[2]

On 1 August 1909, the Prevention of Crime Act came into force. A new system for dealing with young adults had been born. It was still recognized as being in an experimental stage. But Parliament had given a *carte blanche* to the Commissioners to expand it, and encouragement to the courts to use it.[3] Yet, despite good signs of early progress before 1914, it was not until 1922 that signs of a vigorous attempt to expand and experiment with the system really got under way.

[1] Some commentators had been confused on this point before the Act was passed. The leading article in *The Times* of 13 June 1904 stated that boys were at Borstal 'for gambling, throwing stones or snowballs or playing football in the streets'. A letter the following day from Haldane Porter pointed out that 'the facts are quite otherwise'.

[2] See, in particular, pp. 28–31, 39, 50–7, 70–1 below.

[3] Commenting on the 1908 Bill, the *Justice of the Peace* stated: 'In fact, it might almost be said that the Bill gives to a Home Secretary *carte blanche* to experiment from time to time in the treatment of criminals in the light of the most recent theories of criminologists.' See Vol. 72, 13 June 1908, p. 278.

# II

# The System Expands

*A Hopeful Start*

After the Prevention of Crime Act became law, the new borstal system developed steadily until the beginning of World War I.

In 1911 Feltham was opened as a second institution[1] to cater for the rise in committals. 271 boys had been committed in 1910; in the next year the number was 495. The daily average population of the institutions more than doubled. The system continued to receive very favourable publicity. *The Times* described it as 'the bright spot on the horizon of future prison administration',[2] and the Court of Criminal Appeal as a 'reward for committing a crime'.[3]

In 1914, Mr McKenna, the Home Secretary, in introducing the Criminal Justice Administration Bill made a statement which emphasized that borstal was to be developed as an educational system far removed from its prison roots. He said:

> If we send him to Borstal are we sending him to prison at all? My answer to that is certainly not. I may remind the House at once that the Borstal institution is quite a modern one. We readily admit that. It is by no means yet fully developed. But our object is to provide in the Borstal institution a place where the offender will not be imprisoned, but will only be deprived of his liberty to that degree which is necessary to ensure discipline; where he will be under strict discipline affecting alike his body,

---

[1] In 1907 a wing of Lincoln Prison had been opened to receive boys from the North of England with long enough sentences to undergo training. This prison was not used as a borstal institution after the passing of the 1908 Act.

[2] See article, 'Prison Life and Administration V—The New Departure,' *The Times*, 7 June 1910.

[3] See the comments of the prosecutor in *R* v *Keating* (1910), 5 Cr. App. R. 181. Also *R.* v *Watkins, Smallwood and Jones* (1910), 5 Cr. App. R. 93.

his mind and his character, and where he will be taught an industry.

It is not a prison. It is, or it should be, far more like a school under severe discipline with a strict industrial training.

For we do not intend the Borstal institutions to be anything like a prison, and as we develop in the management of the Borstal institutions, I can assure the House that they will be more and more removed from anything in the nature of a prison, and become more and more purely reformative and training institutions.[1]

Mr McKenna was not alone in his views. Another speaker remarked that 'the place is not a prison at all. It is merely a teaching and training institution. These boys are no more in prison than army recruits can be said to be in prison.'[2]

In view of such a successful start and in virtue of the promises for the future, the Criminal Justice Administration Act extended the powers of courts to sentence young offenders to borstal. The summary courts were, for the first time, allowed to commit suitable offenders to quarter sessions for sentence to borstal—although under limited conditions.[3] An attempt to amend this clause to empower magistrates to sentence boys direct to borstal[4] was, however, defeated by those who

[1] Mr McKenna in *H. C. Debates*, Vol. 61, cols. 197–8, 15 April 1914
[2] Dr Chapple in *H. C. Debates*, Vol. 65, col. 125, 20 July 1914. Only one member spoke against this conception of borstal. Mr Rawlinson said, 'I really think it is playing with words to say that [borstal is not a prison]. I have been over it, and while I believe it is an excellent institution, I regard it as a prison, and a very good form of prison.' Vol. 61, cols. 205–6, 15 April 1914
[3] Under Section 10 (1(b)) the magistrates were not given the same power as the higher courts. Under Section 10 it had to be proved that the youth had been 'convicted of any offence for which the court has power to impose a sentence of imprisonment for one month or upwards without the option of a fine', and also 'previously . . . convicted of an offence or, having been previously discharged on probation [he] failed to observe a condition of his recognisance' as well as that he had criminal habits or tendencies or was associating with persons of bad character. Furthermore, the Act did not apply to summary courts the power of the Home Secretary to increase the age limit to twenty-three years by order in Council.
[4] Similar attempts to extend magisterial powers in this way were again hotly contested when the Criminal Justice Bill was debated in 1938. See pp. 59–61 below.

considered 'this step to give magistrates this tremendous power' as 'monstrous'.[1] Furthermore, the minimum length of the sentence was increased from one year to two, the length of compulsory supervision from six months to one year and the maximum length of recall from four months to one year.[2] In fact the 1914 Act, by increasing the minimum period of detention and extending the length of supervision, made it clear to the courts that the borstal system needed a long period of incarceration to achieve its aim of reform and that it was not to be used simply as a medium-length term of imprisonment. It seems that judges had been loath to commit boys for the full term of three years, probably because this length of sentence was greatly above the normal tariff for ordinary imprisonment. Perhaps they were not convinced that reformation justified such a lengthy deprivation of liberty, or were unwilling to leave to the Prison Commissioners the decision on the actual term to be served. In one study of 120 cases, only 22 were given three years, 26 received one year and the remainder various periods in between, such as fifteen months, eighteen months and two years.[3] The Prison Commissioners insisted that a year was virtually a useless sentence, and that rather than being severe and unkind when giving a boy three years, judges were in reality 'doing the boys and the country the greatest service'.[4]

## Borstal Preferred to Prison

The confusion caused by the use of the term 'modified borstal' continued after 1908.[5] In the Court of Criminal Appeal a boy who had been recommended for borstal training was judged to be ineligible because he had previously been at Borstal. However, the court assured him that he would receive

[1] H. C. Debates, Vol. 65, cols. 115–38, 20 July 1914
[2] These changes are discussed in Chapter VI, pp. 166–7 below.
[3] See E. G. Clayton, 'The Prevention of Crime Act', Nineteenth Century and After, Vol. 68, August 1910, p. 312.
[4] The Governor of Borstal's report in P. C. Report, 1909–10, Part II, p. 212. See also B. A. Minutes, September 1913. The B. A. Committee was in favour of a three-year minimum sentence, but considered periods of two and four years would be a compromise acceptable to the courts.
[5] Ruggles-Brise continued to use this term until his retirement. See The English Prison System, p. 96.

some benefit from the recommendation as he would be sentenced to prison and treated there as a juvenile-adult.[1] On another occasion it ruled that a boy was not qualified for borstal because he had previously received that treatment 'in a modified form' at Wakefield Prison.[2] The difficulty was partly straightened out in 1913 by the case of *J. H. Smith*. Smith had not been sent to borstal because he was medically unfit, but was instead sentenced to two years' imprisonment and recommended for the modified borstal system. The Court of Criminal Appeal was asked to decide whether it was proper to sentence him to a period under the modified system which would have been excessive as ordinary imprisonment. In other words, was the sentence justified by the reform achieved as in the case of a full borstal sentence? The court decided that he would have received this treatment in any case simply because of his age, and that the sentence had been passed under the misapprehension that Smith could have earned an early release as he could have done at borstal. The sentence was reduced to one of four months.[3] But the courts were still unclear on the issue. Part of the trouble seems to have been caused by the rather widespread condemnation of short sentences of imprisonment. It had been said that boys should not be sentenced for short terms because this meant they were not trained. The judges therefore assumed that if a boy had to be imprisoned and was not eligible for borstal the proper alternative was a substantial sentence during which the boy would be trained in prison. In reality the main advantage of modified borstal was the avoidance of contamination with older criminals, but the use of the term 'borstal' made the courts believe that the regime was very similar to that in borstal institutions. Through failure to find a more appropriate name, the Commissioners were mostly responsible for this impression. However, informed sources were aware that 'modified Borstal . . . is in no way to be

[1] *R v Palmer* (1909), 2 Cr. App. R. 146–7

[2] *R v Wright* (1911), 7 Cr. App. R. 52. See also a report for a very similar case where *one month's* modified borstal is said to be a former borstal sentence, in *Justice of the Peace*, 74, 11 June 1910, p. 282.

[3] *R v J. H. Smith* (1913), 9 Cr. App. R. 117; also *R v Lee* (1913), 9 Cr. App. R. 144. See also *R v Thorpe* (1918), 13 Cr. App. R. 176, in which a sentence of three months' imprisonment on a first offender was quashed and three years' borstal substituted.

compared as a departure from ordinary prison standards of life and discipline to Borstal itself'.[1]

The matter was not finally settled until 1919 when Lord Reading in the case of *Oxlade* stated emphatically that two years' imprisonment under the modified borstal system must be regarded as two years' imprisonment, and that because a boy for reasons of his age got the benefit of a modified treatment this should not lead the court to sentence him to a long term.[2] Long-term imprisonment, even under the juvenile-adult rules, was clearly no alternative to borstal detention. Borstal was considered preferable to imprisonment for those physically fit enough to benefit from the training[3] and, furthermore, to be 'in their best interests'.[4]

The idea that the boy gained something positive from borstal, that his sentence far from being a punishment was to his advantage, was largely based upon the widely held belief that boys learned a trade which would help them on their release. The Prison Commissioners were almost entirely responsible for this misconception—or over-statement. A few boys may have learnt the rudiments of a trade which they could pursue on release, but for most the work was ordinary manual labour.[5] On a number of occasions between 1910 and 1919 the Court of Criminal Appeal in making decisions in favour of borstal laid stress upon the advantages of trade training,[6] as did the Home

[1] In 'Prison Life and Administration V—The New Departure,' *The Times*, 7 June 1910. Yet in the same series of articles (IV—'The Youthful Offender') the writer asks for longer sentences: 'the lad who is just entering the ranks of the predatory ought not to be able to get away from his confinement under a year at least.' The description of the juvenile-adult class also gives an impression of rigorous training. *The Times*, 3 June 1910. See also a letter from John Galsworthy and leading article on longer 'modified Borstal' sentences in *The Times*, 23 July 1910.

[2] *R* v *Oxlade* (1919), 14 Cr. App. R. 65

[3] *R* v *Monkhouse* (1919), 14 Cr. App. R. 38

[4] Observations of L. C. J. Avory and J. J. Sankey (1919), 14 Cr. App. R. 84. See also Alexander Paterson, *Across the Bridges* (1911), pp. 189–90, and *R* v *Daniel* (1919), 14 Cr. App. R. 15.

[5] *Borstal in Nineteen Hundred and Nineteen*, p. 3

[6] This belief had been expressed by the Court of Criminal Appeal in 1910 in *R* v *Watkins, Smallwood and Jones*, op. cit., in which the Recorder is quoted as saying 'the chief point [about Borstal] is that they are taught a trade'. Also *R* v *Keating* (1910), 5 Cr. App. R. 181, and Observations on Borstal (1919), 14 Cr. App. R. 84

Secretary, who said, 'we are using the time during which he is detained to teach him a trade . . . we are giving him in the Borstal institution an opportunity which he has never had in his life.'[1] The Commissioners certainly did nothing to give a more accurate picture—in their report for 1919 they even included the Lord Chief Justice's opinion that borstal 'affords them an opportunity . . . in acquiring a trade'. That they were aware of the misconception is apparent from the letter sent by the Committee of the Borstal Association urging them to bring training in line with the Lord Chief Justice's statement or to publicly contradict it.[2]

It appears that even after the 1914 Act the courts were not necessarily convinced that three years was an essential length for the sentence. But the results that were quoted for after-conduct were so impressive[3] that the Court of Criminal Appeal ruled in 1919 that 'in the absence of exceptional circumstances, the term of three years is the right term, because that period of time gives the lads a chance which very often a shorter term does not afford'.[4] It is perhaps not surprising that a number of judges were anxious to extend these 'chances' to a wider variety of offenders not explicitly catered for in the 1908 Act. In these circumstances the question of 'who is eligible?' became a central issue.

### Qualifications for Training

There was certainly a good deal of confusion about who was eligible for borstal. The 1908 Act explicitly stated that the offender must have criminal habits or tendencies or associations with persons of bad character. The problem seemed to lie in the definition of the term 'tendencies', and in the use of the conjunction 'or'. Did the clause mean that an offender with

[1] Mr McKenna, in *H. C. Debates*, Vol. 61, col. 199, 15 April 1914
[2] Letter to Sir Evelyn Ruggles-Brise dated 14 November 1919. See *B. A. Minutes*, November 1919.     [3] See Chapter VII, pp. 205–6 below.
[4] In *R v Revill* (1925), 19 Cr. App. R. 44. Again in this case the court stated that Borstal 'was for his benefit'. See also report of speech by J. Ridley in the *Justice of the Peace*, Vol. 72, 22 February 1908. He was in favour of long sentences . . . 'He had got over his scruples in regard to giving longer terms, because the system was working so well, and a judge had to make up his mind to give the prisoner something which was for his own benefit, although it meant depriving him of his liberty.' In the Court's Observations on Borstal (1919), 14 Cr. App. R. 84, the same sentiments were expressed.

only criminal 'tendencies' was eligible? And how could they be defined or proved? Did it mean that an offender with no criminal habits or tendencies could be sentenced to borstal if it was proved that he associated with persons of bad character? And how close or continuous did the association have to be? These problems were continuously raised until the formula was changed in 1948.

The Act had implied that borstals were not meant to receive prisoners with previous good characters. 'A person of previous good character' was interpreted by a Government spokesman to mean first offenders or a 'novice in crime'.[1] The Commissioners in their report for 1910 reminded judges that these cases were unsuitable as were those at the other end of the scale who had previously been in a reformatory school or at borstal where they have 'had a chance to reform and have failed to profit by it'.[2] But in the same year the Court of Criminal Appeal upheld a sentence of borstal for first offenders convicted of serious burglaries, stating that this in itself was proof of 'criminal habits *and* tendencies'. Furthermore, they did not dissent from the view of the sentencing Recorder in that case who stated that borstal was 'intended for boys who had a clean record up to the present time and had fallen into criminal habits'.[3] Yet the court was not consistent. In two cases decided in 1919 they stated in the first that a youth with no previous convictions who had not been recommended for borstal by the Commissioners should have his borstal sentence upheld because, 'If we could not send him to a Borstal Institution we should have to send him to prison for three or four months. We think it is better in the appellant's interests that the sentence should remain unaltered.'[4] In the second, a borstal sentence on a first offender was reduced to a binding over because, 'In the case of a first offence the court leans against detention in a Borstal Institution.'[5]

---

[1] See statement of Earl Beauchamp in *H. L. Debates*, Vol. 198, col. 682, 10 December 1908. Also, Herbert Gladstone in *H. C. Debates*, Vol. 197, col. 224, 24 November 1908    [2] See *P. C. Report*, 1909–10, p. 8.

[3] *R v Watkins, Smallwood and Jones*, op. cit.

[4] *R v Daniel* (1919), 14 Cr. App. R. 15

[5] *R v Elving and Wallbridge* (1919), 14 Cr. App. R. 24. See also *R v Milner and Atkin* (1920), 15 Cr. App. R. 18.

There certainly seems to have been a tendency to regard a number of comparatively minor delinquencies as indicative of criminal tendencies. The Commissioners in a circular of 1919 again stressed that courts should not commit those whose 'previous character is good' as well as those 'whose offence is one of occasion rather than habit, or where they have respectable friends able and willing to receive them and find them employment when they have served whatever sentence the court may pass upon them'.[1] But in 1921 the Governor of Borstal commented on the apparent divergencies of judicial opinion and illustrated his point by the fact that crimes such as wilful damage, stealing growing fruit and playing football in the street were constantly appearing among previous convictions. For these offenders, he suggested, probation would have been more appropriate, for borstal simply aroused resentment, introduced them to bad companions and started them 'headlong down the road of crime'.[2] One reason for these disparities between the Commissioners' views about the type of boy they wished to receive and the judges' opinions on who should be sentenced lay in the wording of the legislation. The judge was asked to 'consider any report' from the Commissioners on the suitability of the case, but as the Court of Criminal Appeal pointed out, 'he is not bound to come to the same conclusion, he should give his own consideration to it'.[3]

Although the Commissioners wished to exclude ex-reformatory school boys from borstal, the courts insisted on sending many of these cases. In 1919, for example, 99 out of 610 boys discharged had previously been in a reformatory.[4] With only two institutions the dangers of contamination from such recidivists were rightly stressed. But the 'criminally mature' were not the only ones excluded who might have needed special attention. The physically and mentally unfit were 'unsuitable' for the drill, gymnastics, hard work and uniform discipline. Those with bad eyesight, for example, were

[1] Prison Commissioners Circular, 25 November 1919
[2] Remarks of the Governor of Borstal in *P. C. Report*, 1921–2, p. 51
[3] *R v Watkins, Smallwood and Jones*, op. cit. In this case the court disagreed with the prison governor's opinion that the boys were ineligible for borstal.
[4] *Borstal in Nineteen Hundred and Nineteen*, p. 5

not admitted.[1] At the London Sessions in 1910 the Chairman complained that only two out of every ten boys he recommended for Borstal were accepted.[2] And although the position improved slightly with the opening of Feltham, the disabled could not be admitted. The Commissioners expressed their regret that through no fault of their own these boys were denied the benefits of borstal, yet with such limited accommodation and their commitment to a rigid regime they could do little.[3] Plans were laid to open Lewes Prison as a further borstal so that more classification could be achieved, but they were suspended due to the outbreak of war.

## A Period of Stagnation

The real problem lay in expanding the number of institutions and especially in providing a variety of regimes to cater for different types of offender. The Commissioners agreed that converted old prisons were unsuitable, and suggested as early as 1914 that plans should be made to design special *ad hoc* establishments which offered possibilities of land cultivation and strenuous manual labour. In particular it was thought that borstal labour could be used on public works, such as land reclamation.[4] It is interesting that the idea of open institutions in pioneer conditions should have been mooted at this time, as it is usually directly attributed to Alexander Paterson. But for the war the system might have expanded rapidly along new lines. As it was, the war seriously interrupted training, Feltham was closed, and in the aftermath of financial stringency little was achieved to further the bold plans and fine sentiments expounded before the war.

[1] In *R* v *Watkins, Smallwood and Jones*, op. cit. One boy had four months' imprisonment substituted for borstal. Because he had bad eyesight he was 'not a fit subject for Borstal treatment'.

[2] See *The Times*, 26 August, 11 November and 19 December 1910, and reports in *Justice of the Peace*, Vol. 74, 24 December 1910, p. 616, stating that the exclusion of the unfit was 'contrary to the original intention of the legislature', and Vol. 74, 9 July 1910, p. 329, stating that 60 per cent of suitable cases were reported against on medical grounds and asking for an institution for these cases.

[3] See *P. C. Report*, 1909–10, p. 9; and speech by Ruggles-Brise reported in *The Times*, 28 March 1911. See also p. 102 below.

[4] *P. C. Report*, 1913–14, p. 18

By the time Sir Evelyn retired in 1921 the system had at least convinced some external commentators that it had achieved 'a revolution in the prison system and in the attitude of the judiciary and the public to the treatment of the young offender'.[1] Although, in reality, the training carried out in the institutions had changed little during the preceding decade,[2] enough had been accomplished to ensure public support.

## GROWTH UNDER PATERSON, 1922–39

### A New Spirit

From 1922 a new spirit was infused into borstal through the enthusiasm and energy of Alexander Paterson, the new commissioner in charge of borstals, and Sir Maurice Waller, Chairman of the Commission. The 'house system' was inaugurated, men from public schools and universities came forward to give their services in 'changing the lives' of boys, officers discarded their uniforms for plain clothes, summer camps were opened, and increased responsibilities were given to the boys. Although it is not the aim to discuss here the importance of these new ideas of training[3] it is apparent that they gradually increased the prestige of borstal, and further emphasized its detachment from its prison roots.

One of the first reforms of the new Commission was the abandonment of the term 'modified borstal' and its replacement by 'young prisoner's classes'.[4] But a simple verbal change could not immediately clear up a deep-seated confusion. Thirteen years later Paterson was still pleading for 'more discrimination in the use of the term Borstal' and stressing that 'Borstal is not a boys' prison. To collect all prisoners under twenty-one and confine them in a corner of a large jail, and call the result a Borstal institution is a sham and a pretence, a piece of administrative complacency defrauding a credulous public.'[5] Paterson

[1] Article, 'Borstal Ideals: Reformative Work Accomplished,' *The Times*, 29 August 1921

[2] See Chapter IV, pp. 102–3 below, and in particular the criticisms of the Borstal Association of Sir Evelyn's leadership, pp. 171–2 below.

[3] See Chapters IV and V for a discussion of training.

[4] *P. C. Report*, 1921–22, p. 10

[5] In the Introduction to S. Barman, *The English Borstal System* (1934), p. 13. See also similar comments by Lionel Fox in *The Modern English Prison* (1934), pp. 39 and 143.

was determined to establish borstal as a completely reformatory system.

## Trouble at Portland

In 1921 the third institution was opened at Portland in the old convict prison. 'If money had been no object,' said the Home Secretary, 'we should have built our own special building instead of going to the only building available at Portland.'[1] Portland was originally intended only as a temporary expedient, but of all the prisons the Commissioners considered it to be 'owing to its situation, climate and good industrial shops the best place available'.[2] The new borstal received many of the most difficult cases from Rochester[3] and Feltham, who apparently 'took advantage' of a staff only accustomed to the routine of convict prisoners.[4] These difficulties were accentuated and brought to the public notice by the suicide of an inmate and a number of successful escapes. Public opinion was very disturbed. On at least four occasions the Home Secretary was asked in the Commons to instigate a public enquiry;[5] the Howard League called for a Commission of Inquiry, commenting that the boy 'was either insane . . . or preferred death to the treatment he received at Portland';[6] the popular press was given ammunition that it continued to use for the next five years. The Home Secretary visited Portland, and came away satisfied.[7] He found no grounds for the charges of brutality made against the officers, but stopped corporal punishment and the use of close confinement. He concluded that 'the

[1] Reported in *Justice of the Peace*, Vol. 86, 14 January 1922
[2] *P. C. Report*, 1921–22, p. 19
[3] The name Rochester is frequently used for the institution at Borstal in order to avoid confusion. It will be seen that both names have been used by different commentators quoted throughout this book.
[4] *P. C. Report*, 1921–22, p. 20—although it was pointed out that a former member of the 'educational' staff of Feltham had been appointed Governor. *The Howard Journal*, Vol. 1, No. 1 (1921), had stated 'we deplore the decision of the Commissioners to open the institute with a staff of convict warders' (p. 46).
[5] *H. C. Debates*, Vol. 147, cols. 1070–71, 27 October 1921; Vol. 148, col. 200, 8 November 1921; Vol. 150, col. 821–2, 14 February 1922; Vol. 160, col. 831, 20 February 1923
[6] *Howard Journal*, Vol. 1, No. 1 (1921), pp. 45–6
[7] Reported in *The Times*, 14 November 1921

suicide scandals arose from the unfortunate case of the boy
Buckingham. On the evidence as far as I could judge, there was
no doubt that he never intended to kill himself, and that he
expected the warder to come straight into the cubicle and cut
him down. All the other threats of suicide were pure mischief
and not one of them was meant seriously.'[1] One month later,
with the public still unsatisfied, Sir Arthur Conan Doyle was
appointed to report on the situation. Sir Arthur was satisfied
with what he saw, reporting: 'It is a splendid scheme and
works splendidly . . . it is a great idea and greatly carried out.'[2]
But the *Justice of the Peace* was completely unconvinced and
especially dubious of Sir Arthur's credentials for this kind of
investigation. How could he disentangle fantasy from fact, it
asked, for 'he lives in a world of his own'. Of his report in the
*Daily Telegraph* it said: 'It is impossible to treat this sort of thing
seriously. If there are alleged by responsible people, serious
defects in the working of any portion of our prison system, they
should be enquired into and reported upon by persons competent by their training to investigate and report on such
matters.'[3]

A year later both the Commissioners and the Howard
League were satisfied that the major difficulties at Portland
were being overcome, with 'former convict officers [having]
distinguished themselves by their tactful, firm and kindly
handling of the lads'.[4] But the press were not easily convinced.
By 1923 the spate of 'delirious articles denouncing the brutality
and failure of the institutions and the unsympathetic treatment
meted out by the Borstal Association' had led the B.A. to
consider taking legal action.[5] *John Bull*, in particular, gave
regular space to criticisms of borstal. So serious was the effect
of these articles upon the system[6] that the Home Secretary was
asked to intervene. After making representations, he wrote to

[1] Reported in *The Times*, 15 November and 27 December 1921
[2] In the *Daily Telegraph*, 27 December 1921
[3] *Justice of the Peace*, Vol. 86, 14 January 1922, p. 19
[4] *P.C. Report*, 1922–23, p. 29. Also *Howard Journal*, Vol. 1, No. 3(1924), p. 145
[5] *B. A. Minutes*, April 1923. *Evening Standard, Daily Sketch, Reynolds News*
and *Daily Express* all attacked borstal. The Committee noted 'the growing
epidemic of false statements appearing in the Press'.
[6] For more comments on the effect of these attacks on after-care see
pp. 172–3 below.

the B.A. that he had 'every reason to hope that these attacks will now cease'.[1] The attacks did not finally cease, however, until Sydney Moseley, a well-known popular journalist, had been given permission to visit the institutions and encouraged to persuade *John Bull* to let him publish the 'truth'.[2] His book, *The Truth About Borstal*, pleased the Commissioners and the B.A., especially as it was being widely reviewed and so 'getting an audience which would perhaps not be reached by essayists who were afraid of split infinitives'.[3] In August 1926 *John Bull* changed its tune: it now saw borstal as marking 'a new epoch in the moral history of this country'.[4] The *Daily Express*, and other former critics, followed suit with articles favourable to the system.

Criticism, however, was not confined to the popular press. Hobhouse and Brockway's impressive *English Prisons Today*[5] pointed to many flaws in the training regimes, and a number of judges expressed anxiety lest the new methods involving more freedom should produce a flood of escapes. Every escape at this time was therefore bad publicity for borstal.[6] Even so, by 1925 the changes introduced by Alexander Paterson were reaping their reward in the form of a general rise in prestige for borstal training.

[1] Letter from Home Secretary to Wemyss Grant-Wilson: *B. A. Minutes*, 14 May 1923

[2] *B. A. Minutes*, April 1926. See also, *The Private Diaries of Sydney Moseley* (1960), pp. 256–7.  [3] *B. A. Minutes*, April 1926

[4] Quoted in *B. A. Minutes*, October 1926. It was noted that 'press reports published recently appear to have been favourable'. In December 1927 the *Daily Express* published a series of favourable articles. On 14 and 21 September 1929 the popular weekly *Answers* published a favourable report by an ex-inmate under the title 'Borstal: The Truth at Last'. See also article by Sir Percival Phillips, 'Borstal *is* a Success,' *Daily Mail*, 7 May 1929.

[5] Stephen Hobhouse and A. Fenner Brockway (ed.), *English Prisons Today: The Report of the Prison System Enquiry Committee* (1922), p. 126

[6] See report in *The Times*, 5 April 1923: 'The Chairman [of Dorset Q. Sessions] said that the Borstal treatment did not seem to be doing as much good as people had hoped, and the grand jury made the following presentment: "This grand jury record with concern the large number of Borstal boys charged with crime at these sessions, and present that in their opinion enquiry should be made into the methods of control and discipline at the Borstal institution." The Court promised to forward this to the Home Secretary.'

*Judicial Approval*

In 1925 the *Justice of the Peace* stated adamantly that 'Borstal, like probation, is no longer an experiment; it is an established system, a proved success'[1]: an opinion which it voiced again two years later and which was repeated by the eminent magistrate, W. Clarke Hall.[2] Judicial remarks unfavourable to borstal were discouraged. When the Recorder of Shrewsbury said he didn't believe in borstal he 'was spoken to by the Home Office on the subject'. In a public speech the Home Secretary criticized the judge, saying, 'That is a serious remark to be made by a judge in public with regard to these institutions, which with the full assent of the community are being administered in the best interests of the community.'[3] Very favourable publicity was given to the system in 1925 in the columns of *The Times*. Three long articles (written in the unmistakable style of Alexander Paterson) praised the progressive experiments of borstal and the zeal of the B.A. and emphasized the 'manifest disadvantages' of prison.[4] In May 1925 a letter was published in all the leading national and local papers to mark the twenty-first birthday of the B.A.: it stated, 'Borstals combine many of the features of a public school . . . with a long day's industrial training and strict discipline.' The judiciary appears to have uncritically accepted the Commissioner's claims. From 1925 onwards, judicial criticism became the exception, and lavish praise the rule.[5] The Recorder of London called it 'a splendid system'; the Recorder of Middlesex replied to a youth who asked for a chance, 'What better chance can I give you than to send you to Borstal? There you will be trained, fed and clothed at the expense of the State.'[6] Offenders were told that 'Borstal is a public school with

---

[1] *Justice of the Peace*, Vol. 89, 29 August 1925, p. 510

[2] *Justice of the Peace*, Vol. 91, 17 December 1927, p. 963; also *The Times*, 6 January 1927          [3] Quoted in *B. A. Minutes*, October 1925

[4] See the articles 'Borstal Lads,' *The Times*, 4, 5, and 6 August 1925.

[5] See favourable comments of Mr Justice Sankey reported in *The Times*, 6 May 1925, and of Sir James Openshaw (Chairman of Preston and Salford Q. S.): 'I am decidedly of the opinion that the Borstal system is the best reformatory method ever yet conceived anywhere . . . there is a preponderance of excellent results,' *Lancashire Daily Post*, 1 July 1932; and also the Recorder of London, *The Times*, 9 September 1925.

[6] Quoted in *B. A. Minutes*, January 1928

all the advantages you get there',[1] that with its 'enormous percentage of success' it would 'give them a chance in life',[2] or 'teach them a trade'.[3] In strong contrast was the sceptical attitude of the Howard League. In reviewing Sydney Moseley's book, the *Howard Journal* stated bluntly that it considered 'the truth about Borstal as we see it is that its most hopeful feature is the frank recognition by those who are responsible that their work is still so largely experimental'.[4] Here was an unusual situation: the judiciary were more eager in their praise for the reformatory system than the society representing informed opinion on penal reform. This was most probably because the judges were less knowledgeable than the League about the actual workings of the system. Hobhouse and Brockway had stated that 'we are informed that very few of the judges have ever visited any of the Borstal institutions'.[5] The League's cautious attitude appears to have been aimed at those enthusiasts on the bench who thought they were doing the boy a favour by sending him to borstal.[6] This is not to say that the League were not optimistic about the new methods. They were confident that they would reap results superior to the 'comparatively poor results of the old days'.[7] When it is realized that until 1925 the Commissioners had claimed that 60 per cent of their boys were never again convicted[8] it can be seen that the League had high hopes.[9]

[1] Mr Mead, the Marlborough Street Magistrate, reported in *The Times*, October 1929. Also the *Justice of the Peace*, Vol. 96, 3 September 1932, p. 578, reported that 'in the course of hearing a recent case in the Court of Criminal Appeal, Mr J. Swift said that the Recorder that dealt with the case at Quarter Sessions seemed to think that Borstal was a public school'.

[2] Sir Henry Dickens, the Common Serjeant, reported in *The Times*, 19 July 1929

[3] Dr Hamblin Smith in the *Howard Journal*, Vol. 4, No. 2 (1935), p. 185, writing out of long experience, stated that the words 'you are going to a place where you will be taught a trade' are almost common form in pronouncing sentences to borstal detention. See also report of Recorder of Huddersfield on 'trades' in the *Daily Telegraph*, 9 January 1925.

[4] *Howard Journal*, Vol. 3, No. 1 (1930), p. 64      [5] op. cit., p. 426

[6] According to Richard Maxwell, judges often had this attitude. See *Borstal and Better* (1956), p. 104.

[7] *Howard Journal*, Vol. 1, No. 4 (1925), p. 208

[8] For further comments on 'success rates' see Chapter VII, pp. 207–10 below.      [9] See articles in *The Times*, 4 August 1925.

Paterson, in his articles in *The Times*, had not simply been attacking long-term imprisonment—but any form of imprisonment in which there was no positive element of training and every possibility of contamination. He saw borstal as a final means of achieving reformation whereas he believed that one short term of imprisonment almost certainly would lead to another. This view that borstal sentences should be a real alternative to *short-term imprisonment*, when it looked likely that the offender would benefit from training, was an important step forward. Previously borstal had been seen primarily as an alternative to the fairly long sentences of imprisonment that would normally have been passed on those 'advanced in crime'. The acceptance of Paterson's ideas would have meant that borstal was the only reasonable means of dealing with young adults once an institutional committal of some sort had become imperative.

Neither Parliament nor the judiciary or penal reformers were ready to support the system to this extreme. But the Departmental Committee on the Treatment of Young Offenders, which reported in 1927, did go a long way towards agreeing that borstal sentences should be imposed on those who showed signs of needing the training much earlier in their careers than the statutes of 1908 and 1914 allowed.

*The Stimulus of the Departmental Committee on Young Offenders: 1927*

In 1927 the system received a big stimulus when the Departmental Committee on the Treatment of Young Offenders published its report.[1] This committee realized that a sentence of two or three years should not be imposed light-heartedly, but suggested that courts should nevertheless not hesitate to sentence boys to borstal if the only alternative was prison.[2] They based this conclusion on two premises: first, that imprisonment was more likely to do harm than good and, second, that borstal was likely to withdraw a boy from 'the potential recruits for the army of habitual criminals'. Not only was it thought that prison would be harmful because of the possibility of contamination of the youths by older criminals but also that

[1] *Report of the Departmental Committee on the Treatment of Young Offenders*, 1927 (Cmd. 2831)          [2] ibid., pp. 49–50

once a youth had tasted the experience of prison it would lose its deterrent effect and perhaps make him more crime-prone.[1] While the Committee assumed that prison was a complete failure in curing adolescents of their criminal habits, nowhere are there any figures on which they could have based such a view—it was simply an *a priori* assumption about the evils of prison. Only about half of the boys in borstal had previously been in prison[2]: a small proportion of the 2,000 or so boys sent to prison annually. There was certainly not sufficient statistical evidence on which to base a total indictment of imprisonment.

Borstal was preferred to prison because it struck more directly at what was thought to be the root cause of persistent adolescent delinquency. As it was generally believed that the cause of delinquency lay in lax discipline and poor moral training, a system which purported to combat these deficiencies by constructive training aimed at developing social responsibility[3] was viewed, *a priori*, as more successful than a purely deterrent system. In any case, prison sentences were so short[4] as to have little deterrent value.

In keeping with this view was the recommendation of the Committee that there should be a new definition of the type of offender eligible for borstal detention. The new definition would give prominence to the need for training rather than to the existence of formed criminal habits which was the formula under the existing Acts; and, in order to make this clear, they suggested that the sentence should refer to 'commitment for training' instead of to a 'sentence of detention under penal discipline'.[5] This proposal rested on the assumption that the long sentence of up to three years' incarceration would be

---

[1] In 1938 the position was still the same. The Home Secretary quoted the Lord Chief Justice who had quoted a prison officer as saying 'they go in crying and they come out laughing' and added 'in almost all cases imprisonment is the worst possible way of dealing with these uncontrolled, objectionable and sometimes dangerous young people'. *H. C. Debates*, Vol. 342, col. 272, 29 November 1938

[2] Sir W. Joynson-Hicks in a Parliamentary reply: *H. C. Debates*, Vol. 185, col. 1695, 25 June 1925

[3] *Departmental Committee*, p. 86

[4] In 1927 approximately 75 per cent of males aged sixteen to twenty-one received sentences of under three months.

[5] *Departmental Committee*, p. 99

justified if the offenders' reformation were achieved. This assumption had received some support from the Court of Criminal Appeal which had already made it plain that they considered the completion of training more important than the length of the sentence when they had increased two-year sentences to three years—the time they thought necessary to achieve reform.[1]

The Committee was convinced that a proper combination of the probation and borstal systems would provide a means whereby the committal of the vast majority of the 1,700 or so young offenders who were sent directly to prison annually could be avoided.[2] They did not seem to consider it a forceful argument that a borstal sentence was too long for some types of offences[3] or for some types of offenders who could not safely be put on probation. However, the borstal system had not yet developed enough for the Committee's view to be accepted by the Government, the judges or the penal reformers. The Howard League lost no time in attacking the recommendation. Cicely Craven, the Secretary, stated that the proposal to change the formula 'seems to us mere camouflage and for the sake of honesty and clearness of thought' it would be better to retain the current usage.[4] This stemmed again from the League's view that borstal was still largely 'experimental' and that the predominate penal element of the institutions did not justify sentencing on educative grounds alone. But as they did not agree either to the sentencing of adolescents to prison, they suggested that the only solution to the dilemma was to provide a greater variety of institutional regimes.[5] The Committee were of the opposite opinion, contending that the money would

[1] J. Avory, in *R* v *Revill* (1925), 19 Cr. App. R. 44, stated that 'a sentence of less than three years penal servitude is not to be recommended'. In *R* v *Frier* (1927), 20 Cr. App. R. 30, he stated, 'in his own interests we increase the term to a maximum of three years'.

[2] *Departmental Committee*, p. 87

[3] It is interesting to note that when the Home Secretary was questioned in 1925 on borstal sentences passed on two youths who had carried off two farthings, he supported the sentences on the grounds of their previous convictions. *H. C. Debates*, Vol. 182, col. 938, 30 March 1925

[4] *Howard Journal*, Vol. 2, No. 2 (1927), p. 105

[5] *The Times*, 31 October 1927. Report on Howard League Conference on 'The Treatment of Young Offenders'

be better spent on a new borstal institution 'on modern lines', and that any other forms of institutions might be too readily used by the courts in place of the proper use of probation and borstal.[1] They firmly believed, as did at least one eminent judge,[2] that when offenders could no longer be allowed in the open community, the only means of reclaiming them was through a lengthy period of discipline and training.

The Committee made a number of other recommendations which, if accepted, would have had a more practical effect in increasing the use made of borstal. They suggested that the lower age limit should be 17 to correspond with the upper age limit for the juvenile courts and approved schools (except in particularly intransigent cases)[3] and that the upper limit should be raised to 23 under the provision of the Prevention of Crime Act 1908 Sec. 1 (2).[4] The latter proposal was again indicative of the faith which they had in the system. However, nothing was ever done to implement the first of these recommendations, and it was a further ten years before the Home Secretary saw fit to raise the age limit. The Committee also suggested that in the future it would not be necessary for courts to ask the Commissioners whether a boy was suitable for training.[5] During the twenties the Commissioners had lowered two of the major barriers to acceptance for training (admitting boys suffering from a moderate degree of disability and adopting the view that almost no lad would be considered too bad for borstal). If they now accepted the proposal to admit boys without formed criminal habits and weak-minded offenders for whom there were no other provisions, all boys could be committed direct from the courts. Such support for extending institutional training to boys with physical and mental defects

[1] *Departmental Committee*, p. 87

[2] Sir Walter Greaves Lord, Recorder of Manchester, was reported in *The Times*, 2 December 1927, as saying 'my own view is that probation should be tried to its fullest extent, and if that fails, there is one course, and one course only left, and that is to place the offenders where they will be disciplined. That place is Borstal.' Cf. also leading article, *The Times*, 11 August 1927.

[3] As very few boys aged sixteen were sentenced to borstal this would not appreciably have decreased the numbers sentenced.

[4] *Departmental Committee*, p. 102

[5] ibid., p. 100

was important at this time. Five years previously Hobhouse
and Brockway had emphasized that these boys who were most
in need of remedial treatment were in fact ineligible to receive
it under the Commissioners' ruling excluding the borderline
defectives; they had also quoted Standing Order 105 2 (a) in
which it was stated that ex-reformatory school boys should not,
on the whole, be considered suitable for borstal.[1] The Committee firmly supported the view that it was wrong in principle
to deny the benefits of borstal to any specific types of offenders.
Even though this principle was supported by the administration, it could not easily be put into practice with only three
institutions. The viewpoint of the Committee implied the need
for more institutions to enable the wider variety of offenders to
be segregated so that better training would ensue and contamination would be avoided. They were particularly concerned that those who were not certifiable as insane, but who
were obviously of subnormal intelligence and/or unstable
personality, should be treated in a separate institution. Not
only were they an 'embarrassment to the administration'[2] but
it had also been stressed by the medical officer at Feltham[3] that
these cases should be treated on different lines from the
ordinary borstal inmate.

In their zeal to increase the use of the borstal system the
Committee suggested that the courts of summary jurisdiction
should be given the power to sentence boys direct to borstal[4]—
the main reason for this recommendation being that this would
avoid the time spent waiting in local prisons for the sitting of
higher courts. If borstal was to be a complete alternative to
prison it was both ludicrous and fateful to give boys a taste of
prison of up to two months before they reached the sessions or
assizes. But the Committee lacked complete confidence in the
magistracy to use their powers wisely. They insisted that the
limitation should be imposed on the court to prove a previous
conviction or a previous probation order after proof of guilt (as
was currently needed before a youth could be committed for
sentence under the Criminal Justice Administration Act 1914

[1] *English Prisons Today*, pp. 412–13
[2] *Departmental Committee*, p. 108
[3] *P. C. Report*, 1924–5, p. 56
[4] *Departmental Committee*, p. 101

Sec. 10 (1b)) before passing sentence. The Howard League again opposed the Committee, stating that anything tending to encourage magistrates lightly to commit a boy to borstal should be discouraged. This latter point of view held sway not only in 1927 but also during the debate on this issue in the Criminal Justice Bill of 1938.

The views of the Committee had no immediate impact on legislation but did to some extent appear to influence the sentencing practices of the courts. The Home Office was content to issue a circular in 1928 suggesting that justices should satisfy themselves that no other course was available before committing a youth to prison, but making no specific mention of the use of borstal sentences.[1] In fact, there appears to have been a partial reaction to the optimism of the Committee. Sir Vivian Henderson, the Parliamentary Under Secretary for Home Affairs, reminded the House of Commons that a two- or three-year borstal sentence might be severe for a small offence, but refused to agree that alternative short-term institutions could be successful.[2] The *Justice of the Peace* stressed that although borstal was beneficial it also 'seemed drastic'[3] because of the long period of detention. It feared also that too high praise of borstal would lead magistrates to make too ready use of the system.[4]

This Committee was most important in drawing attention to the borstal system at a time when more institutions were needed to cater for the increasing number of committals. An examination of the available statistical material shows that it also had an effect upon the sentencing practice of the courts at least for a couple of years. But apart from an increase in committals in 1928 and 1929 the courts did not start to sentence an increasing *proportion* of boys to borstal until the late thirties when the system had proved that it could deal effectively with the problem of contamination by classifying different types of offenders and providing appropriately different regimes.

[1] Circular of 20 July 1928 entitled *Young Offenders*, reprinted in *A Handbook of Probation*, ed. Mrs L. Le Mesurier (1935), p. 319
[2] *H. C. Debates*, Vol. 217, col. 1624–7, 21 May 1928. He stated that he believed short sentences had been shown not to work.
[3] *Justice of the Peace*, Vol. 91, No. 33, 13 August 1927, pp. 605–6
[4] *Justice of the Peace*, Vol. 92, No. 26, 30 June 1928, p. 434

*Variations in the Crime Rate, 1926–35*

Fluctuations in the level of crime in the early thirties appear to have favoured the development of the system. The number of youths aged 16–21 found guilty[1] of crimes rose by 38 per cent between 1929 and 1932, and then fell by 15 per cent over the next three years. This rise and fall in the total number of offences was reflected in the numbers appearing before the higher courts.

(*a*) *The use of borstal and imprisonment in relation to the crime rate.* Although there was a gradual increase in the numbers sentenced to borstal from 1926 to 1929, the greatest rise in the inmate population came in 1931 and 1932. In six years the number of committals to borstal for indictable offences had increased from 539 to 952. The proportion of offenders aged 16–21 sentenced to borstal by the higher courts increased from 34 per cent in 1926 to 38 per cent in 1930, perhaps as a result of the Young Offenders' Committee, but at the time that the greatest number were sentenced the proportion had fallen to 35 per cent.[2] The increase in the number of committals appears therefore to have been due to the rise in crime and not to any changes in judicial practice.

In the years 1933 to 1935 the numbers sentenced to borstal fell by over a third. This fall was again mainly due to the variation in the crime rate. In fact, during two of these years

---

[1] It is possible to use two different measures with which to compare crime rates in these years, either the number *convicted* of indictable offences, or the number *found guilty*. The latter measure compares with the number convicted as given in the *Criminal Statistics* after 1948, as prior to the Criminal Justice Act it was possible for an offender to be found guilty under the Probation of Offenders Act 1907 and sentenced without a conviction being recorded. Detailed statistics are given in Appendix I of *The Borstal System: An Historical and Empirical Study of some of its Aspects*, the author's unpublished University of Cambridge PH.D. dissertation.

[2] Two different measures can be used to assess variations in the proportional use of borstal by the courts: either the proportion of the total number found guilty, or of the total number appearing before the higher courts. For the purpose of the argument above, it seems more reasonable to compare the practice of the higher courts in succeeding years, as the majority of borstal boys were sentenced direct by these courts. A difficulty lies in the fact that separate statistics are not given for males and females; however, the number of females is low.

the higher courts sentenced a slightly higher proportion of cases to borstal.

The number imprisoned dropped in the years immediately following the Young Offenders' report, but rose to a peak in 1932. This was followed by a large fall, both numerical and proportional, in the following years. Apart from the increase occasioned by the rise in crime, imprisonment was used less frequently throughout the thirties than in the late twenties. In 1926 only 27 per cent of the youths who received an institutional sentence (either prison or borstal) for an indictable offence were sentenced to borstal: the proportion had increased to 41 per cent by 1929 mainly because of the decrease in imprisonment. There were slight fluctuations around this level in the next six years, but no definite increases in the relative use made of borstal.

(b) *The need for new institutions*. It was this rise in committals after 1925 that led to pressure for a new institution. In 1926 the Commissioners had warned that the question of providing a fourth institution 'may have to be faced before long',[1] and by the time the Departmental Committee reported this had become a necessity.[2] The issue of overcrowding was raised in the Commons, where it was pointed out that although the recommended population for the three institutions was 720 it had been allowed to rise to 1,060. The Home Secretary in replying to questions stressed that he was in favour of a new institution but stated that financial considerations made this impossible.[3] Six months later he appealed to private charity to provide £100,000 with which to build the institution.[4] This was followed during 1928 by increasing pressure on the Government, both in Parliament and in the press, to provide the institution from public funds. It was certainly strange that the Government should consider borstals so different from other penal institutions that they could ask private enterprise for assistance. The Howard League clearly considered that it was wrong to make prison-building dependent on charity,[5] a view

[1] *P. C. Report*, 1924–25, p. 23
[2] *Departmental Committee*, p. 107
[3] *H. C. Debates*, Vol. 209, cols. 1542–3 and 1558–9, 28 July 1927
[4] *The Times*, 12 January 1928
[5] *Howard Journal*, Vol. 2, No. 3 (1928), p. 183

which was supported by a number of Opposition spokesmen in the Commons during an attack on the policy of the Home Secretary, Sir William Joynson-Hicks.[1] In his defence, Joynson-Hicks stated that in fact it was not true that young persons were being sent to prison instead of borstal because of insufficient accommodation[2] and later even went so far as to urge the judiciary to show that they were definitely going to send more boys to borstal so that he should *have* to find the essential accommodation.[3] It appears that while in 1928 Joynson-Hicks considered that the situation did not warrant such drastic action, his opponents thought that the position was already impossible. There can be little doubt too that the latter were right. The Prison Commissioners stated that overcrowding was so bad that the essential elements in borstal training were being smothered,[4] and *The Times* even claimed that not just one institution was needed but many—whilst a more restrained leading article spoke of the demand as 'fully justified'.[5] Classification and separate treatment of different types of offenders were non-existent. As one observer pointed out: ' "Highbrows" and "morons" find themselves subject to almost identical treatment.'[6] Eventually, after more demands in the Commons and from elsewhere[7] for a solution to the problem, Joynson-Hicks announced that the Chancellor of the Exchequer had agreed to provide the money for the new institution.[8] The reputation of borstals had so increased during the twenties that the question of expanding the system could become one of major public importance. So great was the belief that here was a means to solve the crime problem that the Home Secretary in his appeal for financial help spoke of a possible donor as having his name 'immortalized for ever'.

[1] *H. C. Debates*, Vol. 217, cols. 1586–7, 1605 and 1633, 21 May 1928
[2] *H. C. Debates*, Vol. 213, col. 1018, 16 February 1928
[3] Addressing a conference of Visiting Justices for Prisons: reported in *The Times*, 24 July 1928
[4] *P. C. Report*, 1926, p. 11
[5] *The Times*, 11 August 1928
[6] 'Crime and Cure II: Borstal at Work—A State Economy,' *The Times*, 11 August 1928
[7] See letter from the B.A. to the Home Secretary (23 November 1928) asking him to 'evoke statutory powers, not charity'. *B. A. Minutes*, 1928
[8] *H. C. Debates*, Vol. 225, col. 524, 14 February 1929

Writing in the *Sunday Times* of his 'Hopes for Good Results', he declared: 'If, as I am confident is the case, the foundations on which we build are sure, then the Home Secretary of twenty years hence will have the pleasure of closing a large number of our present prisons.'[1]

The decision to make the new borstal a new type of institution could not, however, solve the immediate accommodation problem. A completely new open borstal was to be built at Lowdham in Nottinghamshire. Not until 1930 did any boys begin to go there in the work parties which were to build it. In 1930 the daily average population was thirty-four and only in 1932 did the number exceed 100. The campaign for a new institution had been fought and won in 1928 on the assumption that it would ease overcrowding, yet it was four years before it made any significant contribution to the solution of the problem.

Between 1928 and 1932 the problem of accommodation became more acute; the steady increase in the borstal population had to be fitted into the existing institutions. The only new accommodation was the addition of a fifth house at Portland; but the reception centre at Wandsworth which first began operations in 1926 also kept at least a hundred of the daily average population out of training institutions. With such a strain on resources there was inevitably a 'waiting list' for borstal places. Borstal was the alternative to imprisonment; yet many boys waited in local prisons before they could be moved to a borstal. This question was raised more than once in the Commons, but it was claimed by successive Home Secretaries that no boy waited longer than six months in Wandsworth[2]— although there was never a statement on how long they waited in local prisons first. One Home Secretary, in particular, seemed optimistic that the plans for one more institution would meet the needs of the Commissioners. J. R. Clynes, Home Secretary in the Labour Government of 1929, stated that he did not anticipate any increase in the number of juvenile offenders.[3] It is not his optimism which is so difficult to

[1] *Sunday Times*, 19 May 1929
[2] *H. C. Debates*, Vol. 227, col. 1076, 25 April 1929; Vol. 248, col. 572, 12 February 1931
[3] *H. C. Debates*, Vol. 231, cols. 2199–200, 14 November 1929

understand so much as his implied suggestion that he was satisfied with the sentencing practices of the courts. He must have been well aware that most opinion favoured an expansion in the use of borstal and that the proportion of boys sent to borstal was in fact gradually increasing, while the proportion sent to prison was decreasing.[1]

The rise in adolescent crime in 1931 and 1932 was extremely valuable to the borstal system, for it meant that new institutions had to be provided quickly to cope with the accommodation problem. Camp Hill Prison was opened as a borstal at the end of 1931 and by 1932 had a daily average population of 287. Bagthorpe Prison near Nottingham was taken over in 1932 to be used especially for the older 'tougher' types. The allocation centre was transferred from Wandsworth to Wormwood Scrubs in 1931 where there were better facilities for this work and for segregating the boys from other prisoners, and the former prison became a recall centre and correctional institution for the system. By 1933 therefore there were six training institutions and two others serving specialized functions.

(c) *An advantageous fall in crime.* The numbers sentenced to borstal dropped as the crime rate decreased from 1933 to 1935. This variation in the crime rate gave breathing space to the system: the new institutions which had been founded to cater for the high numbers sentenced in 1932 were now available for a smaller population. The reduction of pressure meant that attention could be paid to the problem of classification, more experiments introduced and more individual attention given to each boy.[2] This further improved the reputation of the borstals, particularly among those who previously had been wary of the dangers of contamination.[3]

In 1927 there had been a long struggle before the Government had given funds for a new institution despite all the

[1] Speech on laying the foundation stone at Lowdham, reported in *The Times*, 28 July 1930

[2] At Portland where Rodney House was closed in 1935 the Commissioners stated that the 'reduction . . . by making possible a greater measure of individual attention . . . has been attended by a definite improvement in training'. *P. C. Report*, 1934, p. 31

[3] *H. C. Debates*, Vol. 225, col. 2145, 28 July 1931. Mr Cadogan stated, 'you have beginners with old hands . . . the smart young motor bandit and forger associating with the hooligans.'

evidence of need. Yet in 1934, when the borstal population was falling, financial assistance was given to open a small experimental institution on the East Anglian coast: a clear indication of the importance attached to the borstal experiments.

The new borstal at North Sea camp was completely open, and provided training for 'trustworthy' boys under pioneer conditions. Thus not only did the increase in institutions reduce the danger of contamination but also made a new and positive contribution by providing diverse types of regimes for different types of offenders. In some minds the borstal system was already a proven success.[1] The decrease in receptions remedied the usual criticism that boys had to wait in local prisons and the reception centres for months before reaching the institutions,[2] and the Commissioners insisted that their classification procedure was so practicable that contamination was reduced to a minimum.[3] In fact, in view of all the praise and the impressive claims of the authorities, it is surprising that the use of borstal did not increase very substantially during these years.

*The Increase in the Use of Borstals, 1936 to 1938*

The crime rate began to rise again in 1936 and by 1938 the number of committals had risen above the 1932 peak. The immediate increase in total borstal committals in 1936 appears to have been almost wholly due to the effect of the Order in Council which raised the borstal age limit to 23. The Commissioners had been convinced that the practice of segregating the older offenders and training them in a separate institution had proved a success.[4] The continued increase in the number of committals in the following years prior to the war was also due to the rise in the level of crime combined with the practice of the courts in sending a slightly higher proportion of offenders to borstal. The courts seemed to be increasingly convinced that

---

[1] See review in *Cambridge Law Journal*, Vol. 5 (1933–35), p. 285, of Albert Crew, *London Prisons of Today and Yesterday* (1933).

[2] *H. C. Debates*, Vol. 279, col. 1865, 30 June 1933

[3] *P. C. Report*, 1930, p. 31

[4] *P. C. Report*, 1935, p. 21, and *The Times*, 24 April 1936; also *H. C. Debates*, Vol. 324, col. 1365, 4 June 1937

if an institutional sentence was appropriate then it should be borstal. By 1938, 49 per cent of all institutional committals were borstal sentences. The pattern had changed quite remarkably since 1926.

### Borstal as an Alternative to Imprisonment

(a) *The attitude before 1932.* During the late twenties the Prison Commissioners repeatedly stressed in their reports, mainly it seems for the benefit of the judiciary, that in many cases they considered a borstal sentence would have been more appropriate than the sentence of imprisonment actually passed. They particularly felt that a sentence to borstal should follow a failure after a prison sentence.[1] A Government spokesman went further than this and suggested that it was wrong for courts to send boys only after several terms of imprisonment had been tried, as he thought that this made them more difficult to reclaim than if they had been sent straight to borstal for the first offence.[2] His evidence probably came from the Borstal Association who, in its annual reports, issued figures to show that a higher proportion of cases became successes among those not previously sentenced to institutions than of those who had previously received some institutional sentence.[3] It had also

---

[1] *P. C. Report*, 1928. A selection of such cases from the report for 1927, pp. 17–19, are:

*Case 7*—Aged 19, bound over for stealing a watch, ten days later sent to prison for fourteen days for stealing money, and four months later sent to prison for two months for stealing cigarettes, etc.

*Case 10*—When aged 16 bound over for housebreaking; at age 20 again bound over for housebreaking, six months later one month's imprisonment for stealing a bank book and for false pretences; when just under 21, twelve months' imprisonment for housebreaking and larceny.

*Case 11*—Aged 20, in May 1927 bound over for stealing from an automatic machine; in June seven days' imprisonment for loitering with intent, etc. In October bound over for shopbreaking; in November two months' imprisonment for theft. In the next year two other prison sentences.

[2] *H. C. Debates*, Vol. 255, cols. 2125–6, 28 July 1931. See also Vol. 264, col. 1175, 15 April 1932, for other comments.

[3] In the handbook, *Borstal in Nineteen Hundred and Twenty One*, separate figures were given for those who had previously been in prison, reformatory or industrial school and for those who had never before been in an institution. The figures for the boys discharged in 1921 showed: First experience

been shown that boys committed when under 18 were more successful on release than those over 20 years old.[1]

The judiciary were more wary, and constantly stressed the importance of following the statutory requirements for a borstal sentence. It was maintained that the borstal sentence could not be passed where there was no evidence of criminal habits or tendencies or association with persons of bad character.[2] A boy with no previous convictions and only a casual association with a criminal was not qualified under the Act. It was this qualification, not the need for training, which was of paramount importance. Mr Justice Swift pointed this out astutely—'It may be, or it may not be—I do not know—that the best thing for them ought to be Borstal discipline. That we need not speculate upon, because the conditions of the Act of Parliament which provides Borstal discipline for young people are not existent in this case.'[3] And although Mr Justice Avory made a break with the traditional view by pronouncing that the very nature of the offence could justify the court in drawing the inference that a boy had criminal tendencies,[4] it was still thought that in general there was a need to prove a criminal history or continued association with persons of bad character.[5] In the early 1930's the Court of Criminal Appeal had decided not to permit youths with particularly bad records to be sent to borstal,[6] so adding to the numbers excluded. It

---

of institutions, 84 per cent reported as satisfactory. Previously in an institution, 73 per cent reported as satisfactory.

In *Borstal in Nineteen Hundred and Twenty Nine*, and in following years, figures were given which showed: first experience of institutional treatment, 71 per cent successes; to prison prior to Borstal, 55 per cent successes; to prison and reformatory prior to Borstal, 49 per cent successes.

[1] A study of boys discharged between 1909 and 1914 showed that 84 per cent of those under 18 were not reconvicted compared with 63 per cent of those over 20. See W. Healy and B. S. Alper, *Criminal Youth and the Borstal System* (1941), p. 222.

[2] *R v Stenson and Winterbottom* (1930), 22 Cr. App. R. 18

[3] *R v Connell and Irving* (1930), 22 Cr. App. R. 102–5

[4] Reported in the *Justice of the Peace*, Vol. 95, No. 10, 7 March 1931, p. 146

[5] Discussion in the *Justice of the Peace*, Vol. 95, No. 16, 18 April 1931, p. 251. See also *R v Walding* (1931), 22 Cr. App. R. 178.

[6] *R v Kneale* (1931), 23 Cr. App. R. 73

was not until more institutions were opened and the Commissioners could satisfy them that contamination was rare that both very bad boys and relatively good boys became eligible.

(b) *A change in attitude.* The Departmental Committee on Persistent Offenders which reported in 1932,[1] while not concerning itself primarily with borstals, stressed that it considered imprisonment would increase the chances of recidivism, while borstal would definitely decrease them. There was no real evidence on which to base this conclusion. It is true that the Court of Criminal Appeal once reversed sentences of imprisonment and substituted borstal sentences after calling Mr Alexander Paterson to give evidence of the merits of the system,[2] but this was only in effect a further opinion. Nevertheless prisons were thought to be bad *a priori* and borstal was the only available alternative if probation could not be tried.

According to the Recorder of Leeds, the Court of Criminal Appeal had suggested that borstal should be used in preference to prison.[3] The *Justice of the Peace* noted that the judiciary were increasingly reluctant to use prison sentences[4] as did *The Magistrate*, which called the attention of new magistrates to the need to examine all alternatives before committing a youth to prison.[5] The Lord Chief Justice even went so far as to say that he doubted whether prison was the right place of commitment for anyone under the age of 21.[6] In Parliament some members were ready to support the suggestion that legislation should be introduced to ban young persons from prison altogether.[7]

The first moves to try to alter the statutes so that a wider variety of offenders could be sentenced to borstal were not very

[1] *Report of the Departmental Committee on Persistent Offenders* (Cmd. 4090, 1932), para. 13
[2] *The Times*, 14 June 1932
[3] *The Times*, 5 July 1933
[4] *Justice of the Peace*, Vol. 98, No. 52, 29 December 1934, p. 846
[5] *The Magistrate*, Vol. III, No. LVIII (May–June 1935), p. 903
[6] Quoted by Basil Henriques in a letter to *The Times*, 5 June 1935
[7] *H. C. Debates*, Vol. 303, cols. 532–3, 20 June 1935:

    *Mr Lovat-Frazer*—Can the Home Secretary promote legislation to ban young persons 17–21 being imprisoned—in view of the widespread condemnation of the practice?

    *Sir J. Simon* (*Home Sec.*)—The decision to use alternatives (Borstal or probation) must be a matter for the discretion of the court.

successful. In 1932 Mr Justice Avory suggested that it was 'worth consideration whether the strict limits should not be relaxed',[1] but when Lord Polwarth made a plea for the definition to be changed so that it would be based on the need for training, the Lord Chancellor stated that he thought the statutes covered nearly all cases for which borstal was appropriate.[2]

There is some evidence to suggest that not everyone was convinced that borstal was a tremendous success.[3] The reviewer of J. W. Gordon's *Borstalians*[4] in the *Howard Journal* states: 'I asked a railway porter the other day what he thought of Borstal, without hesitation he said, "That's where the future criminals of England are trained, aren't they?" . . . opportunities to confirm this impression come daily to the newspaper reader, chances to combat it never.'[5] In a public statement pointing out that of over 10,000 men in convict and local prisons only 600 were ex-borstal boys, Alexander Paterson repudiated what he called the 'common statement' that prisons were full of ex-borstal lads.[6]

Perhaps a more subtle influence operated through a slight reaction to the exaggerated claims of many of borstal's champions. In particular, the claim that borstal was really a 'public school' was clearly difficult to believe. 'How much nearer could the organization be to that of a public school?' asked the *Daily Mail*, after stating that 'men educated at Eton, Harrow, Repton, Charterhouse and the Universities are the masters at the Borstal Institutions'.[7] Dr Methven, the Governor of Borstal, had been reported as telling magistrates 'that a distinct tradition was growing up amongst the boys, and they looked

[1] *The Times*, 2 March 1932
[2] *H. L. Debates*, Vol. 87, cols. 156–8 and 168, 29 March 1933
[3] Mr Bingley at the Marylebone Police Court was reported as saying, 'Borstal is supposed to reform everyone but I doubt it very much in my experience.' *The Times*, 18 March 1932
[4] See further comments on the Borstal Association's repudiation of the facts given in this book, p. 177 fn. 5 below.
[5] *Howard Journal*, Vol. 3, No. 3 (1932), p. 102. This book was widely and generally favourably reviewed. It was seen as an antidote to the 'horror and awe' of borstal aroused by 'public misinformation from the popular press'. See *The New Leader*, 1 July 1932.     [6] *The Times*, 30 July 1933
[7] Articles by F. W. Memory in the *Daily Mail*, 5 and 7 November 1928

B.R.—5

forward to a time when the traditions of Borstal would be at least equal to those of Eton and Harrow. . . . The Borstal "blue" feels just as much pride in his colours as if he had won a Varsity Blue by his sporting prowess.'[1] In the circumstances it was perhaps not surprising to find criticisms of 'mollycoddling', of boys getting better treatment inside than their non-criminal contemporaries: less eligibility once again was called for.[2] The *Sunday Pictorial*, in an article entitled 'He Who Doesn't Get Smacked', even suggested that 'Borstals are public schools which the middle classes can't afford', and that boys should not be 'made adoptive sons of the State . . . and generally mollycoddled through life by fussy sentimentalists at the public expense'.[3] But probably the *Justice of the Peace* was correct in pointing out: 'We have yet to meet anyone who wanted to go there.'[4]

As the borstal system improved in the facilities it offered for training, and the new experiments in open institutions with their accent on the teaching of self-discipline proved successful, it became more reasonable to emphasize the positive advantages of training and justify the imposition of the long sentence. Some even went so far as to see the institutions as places of 'education and assistance for young persons who have had a bad start in life'[5]—as places where the punishment fitted the criminal and not the crime.[6] The idea that the borstals aimed

[1] Reported in an article, 'Borstal Blues,' in *Answers*, 4 August 1928
[2] Criticisms in *Nottingham Guardian* and *S. Wales Echo*, 6 July 1932, quoted in *B. A. Minutes*, 1932
[3] *Sunday Pictorial*, 3 July 1932
[4] Reports in the *Justice of the Peace* stressed the pervasiveness of this attitude:
'We hear criticism directed against the Borstal system from time to time because it is made so attractive that it presents no deterrent aspect. We believe the criticisms to be unfounded.' Vol. 94, No. 6, 28 February 1930, p. 82
Report of the Chairman of Quarter Sessions saying that a lad 'would be almost as kindly treated as if he were at a public school'. 'There has been enough misunderstanding about the "public school element" in Borstal treatment.' Vol. 94, No. 17, 26 April 1930, p. 266
[5] Statement by Mr Justice Humphreys at Durham Assizes, reported in the *Justice of the Peace*, Vol. 101, No. 27, 3 July 1927, p. 422
[6] Leading article in *The Times*, 3 January 1938. Also article in *Answers*, 4 August 1928, 'Borstal is no longer a place of punishment, it is a place of education.'

at individualization of treatment was the antidote to the fear of depriving a boy of three years of his liberty after conviction for a petty crime.[1]

In all events, it was generally agreed that three years was a serious sanction. While many were willing to agree that prison was not the right remedy for those who could not be trusted on probation, they were unwilling to accept a law which could lead to the indiscriminate passing of long sentences. After the Home Secretary and the Young Offenders' Committee had spoken out against short-term institutions in 1927 little more seems to have been said about alternatives to borstal and prison until Claud Mullins, in an article in *The Magistrate* in 1936, stressed the need for 'something in the nature of a borstal for a limited period' to get over the impasse of having prison and probation and borstal as the only alternatives for first offenders.[2] He stated that the Metropolitan Magistrates had supported this idea. The Magistrates' Association in their 16th Annual Report followed this up by recommending a new type of sentence to be known as 'young offenders' detention' which would be for a minimum of three months and a maximum of twelve, followed by twelve months' supervision.[3] There is no indication anywhere what type of institutions these would be, except that they would try to provide some kind of positive training for those who would normally have gone to prison.

(c) *A statistical evaluation of the use of borstal and the alternatives.* The only way in which it is possible to get some perspective on the relationship between the use of imprisonment and borstal and to what extent other alternatives were desirable is to examine the statistical material. From this it can be seen to what extent imprisonment was being used for offenders who were well advanced in crime and to what extent it was used for offenders who would have been ineligible for borstal under the existing statutes. The only data available for statistical comparison are the previous convictions of boys sentenced either to borstal or prison, and the length of the sentences passed.

[1] See impression given of 'individualization of treatment' in S. Barman, *The English Borstal System* (1934).
[2] *The Magistrate*, Vol. IV, No. LXV (January–February 1936), p. 991
[3] Reported in *The Times*, 19 October 1937

A comparison of the previous convictions of offenders sentenced to either prison or borstal in the years 1928[1] to 1935[2]
shows that the percentage of borstal boys with no previous
convictions increased slightly from 7 to 11 per cent. The
proportion of young prisoners with no previous criminal record
was 40 per cent in 1928, 46 per cent in 1932 and 38 per cent in
1935—the lowest it fell was to 34 per cent in 1933. There was
only a very slight increase in the proportion of borstal boys
without previous convictions in 1931 to 1933 when the committal rate was at its peak, which further substantiates the
point that the increase in committals was not due to a change
in judicial practice.

The majority of boys who were sentenced to imprisonment
were committed from magistrates' courts.[3] Many among them
had been convicted of a non-indictable offence and so would
have been ineligible to be committed for sentence to the higher
courts (as would those who had no previous convictions) due to
the restrictions imposed by Section 10 of the 1914 Act. It is
evident then that at least between 30 and 40 per cent of boys
sentenced to prison could not have been sentenced to borstal
under the existing statutes.

The Prison Commissioners had no rules to exclude any
offenders guilty of particularly bad offences, or minor offences[4];
but magistrates and judges may well have considered some
offences only to merit a short term of imprisonment, and others
to merit a stiffer and longer sentence than that provided by
borstal. In a period when the severity of sentences closely
reflected the seriousness of the offences the length of prison
sentences given may tell us something about the types of
offences for which they were imposed. In 1926 only 18 per cent

[1] Figures were not available in the *P. C. Reports* before this year for
borstal receptions.

[2] Figures after this for borstal boys include some aged 21–23 for whom
comparative material for boys imprisoned is not available.

[3] In 1937 when the figures were first available, 166 boys 16–21 were
imprisoned by higher courts, while 670 for indictable and 518 for non-
indictable, offences were dealt with in this way by the lower courts. It is
not improbable that the same pattern existed in earlier years.

[4] *P. C. Report*, 1930, on p. 32 states that 'Borstal is, generally speaking, to
be preferred to prison both for youths who have repeated serious crimes
against property and for those who have been guilty of violent practices.'

of the boys imprisoned were sentenced to more than three months, and 4 per cent to more than six months. The proportion sentenced for over three months increased annually so that in 1935 the proportion serving very short sentences had dropped to 68 per cent. But over these years the proportion sentenced to more than six months never rose above 8 per cent. Even more revealing is the fact that under 2 per cent continued to receive sentences of over twelve months. Imprisonment as a means of deterrence appears to have been little used. The small number of sentences over six and twelve months shows that long terms of imprisonment were not being imposed as a general alternative to borstal.[1] The lengths of sentences were often so short that the majority of offenders did not even become segregated into the special institutions where some semblance of treatment was given. Not only did they receive no positive training but were open to contamination by older criminals in local prisons. The drop in the proportion of very short sentences was probably a response to the widespread condemnation of this practice and the general campaign to eliminate these conditions.

Throughout the years 1926 to 1938 magistrates seemed to be reluctant to increase the numbers which they committed for sentence—even during the increase in crime in 1931 and 1932. It is clear that they did not really consider that borstal was a reasonable alternative to prison for most of the types of offenders who appeared before them. The increase in the rate of committal of boys to borstal in 1937 stemmed almost entirely from the higher courts. Part of this was due to the rise in the age limit to 23 in 1936, which did not affect the magistrates' courts power to commit for sentence, and part to a genuine change in the practice of the courts.

It was in place of very short sentences, for which borstal could not be used as an alternative due to both statutory limitations and the feeling on the part of judges that it should not be imposed unless really necessary, that a short-term alternative was needed.

---

[1] See W. Healy and B. S. Alper, *Criminal Youth and the Borstal System* (1941), p. 220. In their comparison of lengths of imprisonment they do not mention that a substantial proportion of the sentences were for non-indictable offences or non-payment of fines.

*The Criminal Justice Bill 1938*
When it had been proposed by the Departmental Committee in 1927 that the formula which governed sentences to borstal should be widened there had been considerable opposition. But during the thirties the system had changed to such an extent that the old statutory phraseology was completely outdated. As Paterson pointed out, 'It is difficult to associate such a phrase as "penal discipline" with the Borstal system as it operates today at Lowdham Grange.' For borstal, he claimed, was in reality a 'training school for adolescent offenders . . . pursuing educational methods'.[1] There can be little doubt that the proposals in the Criminal Justice Bill to provide a new and wider definition for borstal detention and new alternatives to short-term imprisonment would have been accepted but for the outbreak of the war.

(a) *A proposed change in the statutory basis.* Sir Samuel Hoare, the Home Secretary (later Lord Templewood), summed up the change in attitude when he said, 'In our view what is important is not the character of the offence or the period of imprisonment with which the offence is punishable, but the age and character of the offender himself . . . The question [of borstal] depends upon the character and habits of the offender.'[2] The basis of the new statute was to be the need for training rather than proof of the existence of criminality: the sentence was to be known as 'borstal training'. The formula as it finally appeared after the committee stage specified that the court should be 'satisfied that by reason of the offender's character or habits or associations with persons of bad character . . .' before passing the borstal sentence. The word 'criminal' had been dropped both because of its limiting effect and, as the Home Secretary stated, because it 'has created confusion in the minds of certain courts'. The Bill went further in removing the limitations placed on summary courts before committing a boy for sentence to a higher court; they no longer had to find him guilty of an offence for which they had power to impose a sentence of

---

[1] In the Introduction to S. Barman, op. cit., pp. 11 and 13
[2] *H. C. Debates* (Standing Committee A), Session 1938–39, cols. 471–2, 9 March 1939

imprisonment of one month or upwards (or prove that he had been previously convicted or discharged on probation). The Home Secretary evidently thought that this would increase the number of cases which the magistrates could send for sentence.[1]

The summary courts were also put on an equal footing with the higher courts by making it possible for them to pass sentences on boys up to 23. The only other major change was that the two-year sentence was abolished so that all boys received the same sentence. It had been clear for years that the two-year sentence reduced some of the incentive to earn early release, created a sense of unfairness in the institutions and shortened the period of after-care. In practice it probably made little difference, as the courts had usually imposed the maximum sentence during the thirties.

The Magistrates' Association was the only body to speak out against the new formula. They considered that there were too few safeguards for such a severe penal sanction.[2] Their concern, however, was probably more for the possible actions of their members than with the policy of the higher courts. Similarly in Parliament, where there were glowing references to the advantages of borstal, warnings were given that magistrates might use their power too readily. But these warnings were mainly the result of the proposal, originally in the Bill, that summary courts should be allowed to sentence boys direct to borstal. By the second reading this proposal had been dropped, and the concessions to make it easier for magistrates to commit boys for sentence replaced it.

(b) *The magistracy and the borstal sentence.* The proposal to extend to the summary courts the power of sentencing direct to borstal was based mainly on the desire to eliminate the time spent

[1] The Home Secretary stated that the 'limitation often works badly'. ibid., col. 326. For years it had been debated whether the offence which actually constituted the breach of the recognizance was sufficient for qualification for committal, or whether this could only be ordered for an offence following a breach of recognizances on some other occasion (see a letter to *The Times*, 1 November 1935). This point was not legally debated until *R* v *Biller* (1938), 1 All. E. R. 501, in which it was held that there did not have to be a further offence after the breach. The point was only finally settled in 1944; *Martin* v *Noland and others* (1944), 2 All. E. R. 342; also *R* v *Dibble* (1945), 30 Cr. App. R. 151.

[2] Reported in *The Times*, 3 February 1939

waiting in prisons on remand (until the remand centres also proposed in the Act were functioning) but it was also seen as a natural continuation of the powers already available to sentence boys to approved schools. In the House of Commons the majority of speakers raised objection to the proposal on the grounds that the length of the sentence made it too great a responsibility to impose on magistrates, and that such a sentence should be reserved for the more dignified higher courts. It was felt that any move which might lead to a haphazard infliction of the punishment should be avoided,[1] and that the use of such a power by the magistrates was likely to create a sense of injustice[2]: the House was unwilling to accept that borstals were at all comparable to approved schools. On the other side it was believed that as quarter sessions usually sentenced to borstal most of those committed by the magistrates for the sentence, this proved that the latter used their powers sensibly.[3] And yet as the system expanded magistrates did not make any greater use of their powers to commit to the higher courts for sentence.[4] Sir Donald Somervell, the Attorney-General, explained this in the debate by saying, 'There may be a tendency for a court to feel anxious to impose a sentence which it can impose itself . . . there is a certain feeling "Oh we think we can deal with this matter" and it may be that this is to some extent a disadvantage which would be removed if the magistrates were given this power.'[5] This statement bore its own indictment of the summary courts which the *Howard Journal* seized on in its reply: 'If magistrates do not use their powers to commit to quarter sessions because they prefer to act alone and sentence to imprisonment, they would be self condemned as unfit to exercise either jurisdiction.'[6] Even the Magistrates' Association could not agree with the proposal as

[1] The debates can be followed in *H. C. Debates,* Vol. 342, cols. 276–374, 636–726, 29 November 1938; also *H. C. Debates* (Standing Committee A), Session 1938–39, 9 March 1939.

[2] *Howard Journal*, Vol. 5, No. 3 (1939), p. 150

[3] Sir Leo Page in a letter to *The Times*, 4 January 1939

[4] Whereas between 1926 and 1938 the numbers committed to borstal by higher courts almost trebled, the numbers committed by magistrates' courts remained almost the same.

[5] *H. C. Debates*, Vol. 342, cols. 373–4, 29 November 1938

[6] op. cit., p. 150

it stood; they asserted that the right must be given to appeal to the Court of Criminal Appeal instead of the sole right to appeal from summary courts to the Appeals Committee of the Quarter Sessions.[1] In face of the criticism from all sides in Parliament the Home Secretary asked leave to withdraw the proposal.

(c) *New alternatives.* The Bill aimed at limiting the use of imprisonment in two ways. Magistrates were required to give reasons in writing before imposing a prison sentence; also, new alternatives were provided. It was proposed that once these alternatives became fully available, imprisonment of persons under 21 would be totally prohibited.

Compulsory attendance centres were to be established for those allowed to remain at home, where the offender might spend up to sixty hours of his leisure time in periods of not more than three hours.[2] Those who needed to be taken from their homes or who had no homes were to live 'under disciplinary conditions' in Howard Houses.[3] While all the youths' activities would be well supervised, they would at the same time have full-time jobs outside the House. Sentences here were for a maximum of six months, followed with six months' after-care and presumably were meant for the criminally unsophisticated. It was thought that this type of institution would be able to free itself from the stigma attached to penal institutions, and would provide the right kind of training for those who would respond to a 'shorter period of supervision in a suitable home'.[4] This was the answer to the belief that 'a large amount of crime in this country is due to the conditions in which the offender is living. He has not got a home or, if he has a home, it is an unsuitable home and there is no control to check him.'[5] It is most illuminating that in 1938 the provision of a home environment was thought to be the answer whereas by 1948 lack of discipline was presumed to be the problem and the detention centres were set up to give a 'short, sharp shock' as the remedy.

Unfortunately the Bill had to be abandoned just before the final stages were completed. It was another ten years before the

[1] Reported in *The Times*, 3 February 1939
[2] Section 12 (1)            [3] Section 13 (1)
[4] *Report of the Departmental Committee on Social Services in Courts of Summary Jurisdiction*, 1936 (Cmd. 5122), para. 93
[5] Sir Samuel Hoare: *H. C. Debates*, Vol. 342, col. 278, 29 November 1938

statutes were altered so that a wider variety of offenders could be sentenced to borstal training, and new alternatives (other than prison) provided for those who were not in need of this training.

*A Review of the Progress up to the War*

In 1938 Sir Samuel Hoare made a resumé of the progress made by the borstal system. He said he thought that there were three main reasons for the increase in cases sent to borstal. The first was the great interest stimulated by the passing of the Children and Young Persons Act in 1933, the second was the increase in the age limit, and the third was the increase in the population after World War I.[1] It has been shown that the increase was due to a more complicated process than this, and in fact not due in essence to any of these three factors. The Young Offenders' Committee was certainly far more important than the 1933 Act, which did not directly refer to borstal and appeared not to excite any opinions about the use of borstal either in Parliament or in the press. The rise in the qualifying age was responsible only in part for the increase after 1936, and the rise in the numbers convicted in 1938 was due to an increase in the crime rate per 100,000 of the 16 to 21 age group and not just due to an increase in numbers in this age group.

In fact, the increase in the prestige of the borstals was almost entirely due to an admiration of the training carried out in the institutions under Alexander Paterson. There can be little doubt that Paterson was aided by the marked fluctuation in the crime rate during the thirties. Without the rise in crime it is doubtful whether so many institutions would have been opened; without the fall in crime, opportunities for experiment, improved classification and relaxation of discipline would have been far fewer.

The Government's faith in the system is shown by the promptness with which it established two new open institutions when the rate of receptions again rose sharply in 1938. By the outbreak of the war the borstal system was acclaimed everywhere as an outstanding success.

[1] *H. C. Debates*, Vol. 332, cols. 937–8, 1 March 1938

# III

# Recent Developments

## INTERLUDE: THE WAR YEARS

ON 2 September 1939, two-thirds of the borstal population was discharged, leaving only those who had not served six months; five of the institutions were closed and taken over for use by the War Office or as adult prisons; many of the long-experienced staff were drafted for service. The carefully built-up institutional traditions were immediately shattered, and in consequence the borstals became unsettled and were unable to provide training comparable to pre-war years.[1]

The courts were forced to consider three factors in sentencing boys to borstal during the war: whether or not the training received justified the length of the sentence, how much accommodation there was in the institutions, and whether long-term reformatories were justified in wartime. All of these factors were influential in leading to a cautious attitude towards borstal and a more frequent use of imprisonment in these years.

Statistical evidence[2] shows that there was a great increase (both proportional and numerical) in the use of imprisonment during the war, and a slight decrease (proportional but not numerical) in the use of borstal. In 1939 the number aged 16 to 21 imprisoned for indictable offences was 897; in 1942 it was 2,527. This accounted for 7 per cent of the total number convicted in this age group in 1939 and 13 per cent in 1942. At no time during the war were fewer boys sent to borstal than in 1939, but the slight increase in numbers was due to an increase in crime—the proportion sent to borstal of the total number convicted showing a slight decline.

[1] *P. C. Report*, 1939–41, p. 50
[2] See Annual *Criminal Statistics* and *P. C. Reports*. Detailed figures are available in Appendix I of the author's unpublished University of Cambridge PH.D. dissertation.

63

The courts sentenced a far higher proportion of young persons to institutions during the war than in 1936 to 1939, but the increase was entirely due to the more frequent use of imprisonment. It is not possible to compare the records of offenders receiving imprisonment with those sentenced to borstal, but the figures for both higher and summary courts show that the former increased their use of imprisonment as well as the latter. In 1938 the courts of assize and quarter sessions sentenced to imprisonment 7 per cent of persons aged 17 to 21 convicted before them; by 1946 this proportion had risen to 19 per cent. At the same time the proportion sent to borstal decreased slightly from 37 to 35 per cent. At the magistrates' courts there was a similar pattern with the proportion imprisoned increasing from 7 to 13 per cent, and the proportion committed for sentence decreased from 3 to 2 per cent.[1] The increase in imprisonment at magistrates' courts may well have been due in part to the disorganization of the probation system, and to the difficulties of properly organizing supervision under wartime conditions.

Probably one of the most influential factors in causing the higher courts to use long terms of imprisonment in place of borstal was the practice of the Commissioners of releasing boys relatively early in their sentences. They did this for two reasons. Firstly because they felt that a boy should not be kept a day longer than necessary and should be released to aid the war effort[2] and secondly because of the overcrowding caused by the shortage of institutions. This policy made it clear that the Commissioners were less concerned about the niceties of reform during the war, and at the same time made the judges suspect that if they wanted to pass a long sentence borstal was not so appropriate as prison.

When 1,677 boys were released in 1939 the remainder fairly easily fitted into the institutions which were left, but as committals continued at the same rate as before the war there was soon an acute accommodation problem. In 1941 the Commissioners managed to re-occupy some of the buildings vacated in 1939 to 1940, but there was still insufficient accommodation: in that year the daily average population of the institutions

[1] *Criminal Statistics*, 1946, pp. viii and ix
[2] *P. C. Report*, 1942–44, p. 58

was 1,212 but there were still some 245 boys waiting in local prisons to be transferred. Little could be done during the war,[1] and so the increase in committals due to a rise in crime in 1942 continued to outstrip the space provided.[2] The only expedient open to the Commissioners was to licence boys early in the belief that this was a lesser evil than allowing boys to remain in local prisons waiting for a place in borstal. There were two reactions to this solution. On the one hand the *Justice of the Peace* supported the Commissioners' choice,[3] while on the other members of the judiciary considered that shorter sentences neither gave time for reformation nor were sufficient punishment. One judge was reported to have said:

> I am getting cases in which people have all sorts of chances and they are sent to Borstal, but Borstal seems as capable of holding them as a sieve of holding water, and in far too short a time they are allowed out again and are making fresh depredations. Some of my brother judges are beginning to wonder whether it is safe to send them to Borstal.

The same report stated that a recorder had declared that he preferred to send these boys to prison, where if they behaved themselves they could earn a proper remission of sentence.[4] The same criticism was made throughout the war years,[5] and may well have been a major factor in limiting the use made of borstal.

In 1945, however, the rate of committal to borstal increased in proportion to the total number convicted, and as a proportion of the total number sent to institutions. This led to an even greater pressure on the institutions. In that year there was a daily average population of 1,788 and as many as 618 waiting in local prisons. The increase in the use of borstal, coincident with the end of the war and the increase in crime, was a reaffirmation by the judiciary of the principle of long-term reformatory treatment. The end of the war meant that new staff could be recruited, new institutions opened and training

[1] *H. C. Debates*, Vol. 370, col. 1685, 10 April 1941, and Vol. 373, cols. 721–2, 17 July 1941
[2] *H. C. Debates*, Vol. 379, cols. 371–2, 23 April 1942
[3] *Justice of the Peace*, Vol. 105, No. 16, 19 April 1941, p. 218
[4] Reported in *The Times*, 24 March 1943
[5] Mr Muff in *H. C. Debates*, Vol. 406, cols. 55–6, 29 November 1944

re-organized on the pre-war basis. But the fact that in 1945 none of these conditions was actually realized, shows that the courts were anxious to return to their pre-war practice irrespective of the state of the system at the time. They presumably believed that everything would soon return to normal. It shows clearly that the borstal principle was firmly established: in the 1920's there had been no certainty that an increase in committals would lead to an increase in the number of institutions. Now the borstal system was a proved success, claims for its achievements were even greater than ever. It was claimed in the House of Lords that 'the fact that borstal succeeds in some 80 per cent of the cases, roughly speaking, is a marvellous testimony to the system'.[1] In such a climate of opinion the judiciary could be sure that borstal would not be allowed to suffer for lack of space in the post-war penal system.

Although the war years had brought about an increase in the incidence of imprisonment of adolescent offenders, and the borstal system had suffered in its internal organization, the principle of long-term institutional training had not suffered permanently. Imprisonment was more expedient in wartime than a reformatory system. Once the war ended the scales were again reversed.

## POST-WAR PROBLEMS: 1946–62

### The Need for New Institutions: The Dartmoor Controversy

In 1945 there was an increase in committals to borstals, but insufficient accommodation. The Commissioners' first attempt to remedy this situation led to a storm of protest. They decided to find accommodation wherever possible rather than fall back on the early release system which had been so controversial during the war.[2] They proposed that part of Dartmoor Prison should be used as a borstal institution. The Home Secretary and the Commissioners stated that they took this step with reluctance but saw it as the only practicable remedy[3] in face of the large numbers waiting up to four months in local prisons

---

[1] Lord Roche in *H. L. Debates*, Vol. 131, col. 349, 29 March 1944
[2] *P. C. Report*, 1945, p. 45
[3] Reported in *The Times*, 27 September 1945

before transfer to the allocation centre at Wormwood Scrubs.[1] It was made clear that the use of Dartmoor was only a temporary expedient until building materials could be spared.[2] The *Justice of the Peace* supported the move, stating that it thought that public opinion would certainly be favourably impressed by this measure to rid the local prisons of boys waiting transfer.[3] Public opinion, at least that segment of it which had knowledge of the penal issues involved, was not impressed. The Howard League refused to believe the 'no alternative' plea and stated categorically that Dartmoor was entirely unsuitable: 'history, tradition, geography and meteorology' were against the institution.[4] *The Times* went further and stated openly that it considered that the use of Dartmoor would be in opposition to the spirit of borstal: 'no surroundings could be better calculated to develop in the minds of boys there the sense that they are branded and set apart from their fellows . . . that is the impression above all others that the founders of Borstal were determined must not be made on the characters of the young offenders.'[5]

The main point of interest about this controversy is that it posed the question of whether there was a fundamental distinction between prisons and borstals. It has been shown already that borstal came to be used more frequently when, by reason of the training it offered, it justified the imposition of the long sentence. Dartmoor was not acceptable as an institution where this type of training could be carried out for it embodied so many of the worst features of prisons that it would have been difficult to distinguish a sentence served there from ordinary long-term imprisonment. The Recorder of Liverpool was reported to have refused to send boys to borstal because of the danger of their going to Dartmoor.[6] It stood, as *The Times* said, for 'moral contamination and social isolation' which were contrary to the reformative ideals on which training had been developed in the open institutions before the war. This was the

[1] Mr Ede, *H. C. Debates*, Vol. 415, col. 2312, 15 November 1945
[2] Ede, reported in *The Times*, 12 October 1945
[3] *Justice of the Peace*, Vol. 109, No. 40, 6 October 1945, p. 469
[4] *Howard Journal*, Vol. 7, No. 1 (1945–46), p. 10
[5] *The Times*, 3 October 1945
[6] *The Times*, 26 November 1945

crux of the matter: borstals had to be free of prison traditions and provide an entirely unique type of regime.

The opening of Dartmoor did not solve the accommodation problem, but the controversy ensured that additional space had to be found in more suitable places. It is to the Commissioners' great credit that within twelve months they had opened four new institutions in country houses and old army camps as well as one closed institution. In April 1946 there were 3,391 boys under sentence but only 2,358 in institutions[1]; by 3 December, the number in prison awaiting escort to reception centres was only 27.[2] It has been suggested that judges and recorders had been wary about committing boys to borstal because of the long wait in local prisons[3]: the prompt action of the Commissioners must be seen as a reflection of their desire to differentiate the borstal system entirely from the prison system—to avoid as far as possible the contaminating and depressing influence of prison life. The Commissioners had reaffirmed their faith in the open system of the thirties. The willingness of the courts to sentence boys to these institutions showed an overall confidence in the future of borstal.

The main criticism made by judges during the war had been aimed at the procedure of early release, and although this may have continued,[4] even after the new institutions had been provided, the main centre of criticism after the war was directed at the increasingly large number of escapes. Sir Lionel Fox had admitted that '. . . for a substantial proportion of our young men . . . a substantial framework of security and physical control is necessary'.[5] Camp Hill was the only one of the five institutions opened in 1946 which had any security and if the Commissioners had been entirely free to choose the type of accommodation they wanted they might have decided to have less 'open' accommodation in spite of their theoretical attraction to it. From 1947 onwards questions were frequently

[1] The Lord Chancellor in *H. L. Debates*, Vol. 141, cols. 267–68, 15 May 1946

[2] Mr Ede in *H. C. Debates*, Vol. 431, col. 273, 12 December 1946

[3] Lord Calverly in *H. L. Debates*, Vol. 141, col. 263, 15 May 1946

[4] Comments in *Howard Journal*, Vol. 7, No. 1 (1945–46), p. 64

[5] In 'Borstal since the War,' *The Magistrate*, Vol. VII, No. VI (November-December 1947), p. 82

asked in the Commons about the numbers escaping: the main point of them all being that boys were being put into a position of trust which they only abused. Although the Home Secretary expressed his confidence in the borstal governors there is no doubt that it was a serious problem for the Commissioners. In the past when absconds had been rare, it had been said that escaping was simply due to 'the spirit of adventure'.[1] The Borstal Association had been scathing in its criticisms of those who complained about escapes. In 1924, for example, it complained:

> Even a Judge has been found to remark that 'It is an awkward thing to send a lad to a Borstal Institution if he can run away,' but no one has explained how farm work and outdoor games and most of the things which distinguish a Borstal Institution from a prison can go on without affording opportunities for escape. There is consolation in the fact that escapes are few—probably fewer than desertions from many regiments—and that they seldom afford more than a brief spell of liberty.[2]

Now there was no longer this consolation. At the end of the war the formidable increase in absconds was seen as a definite blot on the system, even though it was thought to be temporary and due to the shortage of staff.[3] The war was still near enough at hand to provide a reasonable explanation for the difficulties being experienced.[4] The complete acceptance of the reformatory principle in the Criminal Justice Act of 1948 spoke well enough for the faith placed in the system.

## The Criminal Justice Act 1948

The Criminal Justice Act 1948 affected the use of punitive measures for adolescents in two main ways: on the one hand it widened the category of offenders who could be sentenced to borstal, and on the other it limited the power of magistrates to impose prison sentences and provided new alternatives.

[1] Viscount Brentford (formerly Sir William Joynson-Hicks): 'A Practical Talk to Magistrates,' *The Magistrate*, Vol. II, No. XXVII (April-May 1930), p. 386

[2] *Borstal in Nineteen Hundred and Twenty Four*, p. 6

[3] Lord Templewood in *H. L. Debates*, Vol. 144, cols. 419–20, 27 November 1946

[4] Leading article in *The Times*, 6 August 1948

(a) *Statutory alterations in the borstal formula.* Most of the changes made in 1948 were those which would have been made ten years earlier but for the war. The sentence was made a standard one of three years (which simply confirmed judicial practice) to be imposed when the court was satisfied 'having regard to his character and previous conduct, and to the circumstances of the offence' that the offender was in need of training.[1] Unlike the draft for the 1938 Bill this section left out any reference to 'associations with persons of bad character' but it did for the first time draw attention to the 'circumstances of the offence'. This it seems was inserted to make clear to the judiciary that although the sentence should rest upon the need for training, it was still a severe punishment which should not be lightly imposed. The summary courts were also enabled to commit offenders to quarter sessions for sentence under this formula. This was a concession to those who still wished to extend to magistrates the power of sentencing direct to borstal[2] (not that this was ever considered seriously in the way it had been in 1938).

These changes were met with approval by those who wished to see a reformatory sentence passed at an earlier stage in a youth's criminal career.[3] It was now easier to impose the sentence for the first offence.[4] And yet, even among those who were well-known penal reformers, there were those who stressed doubts about extending the courts' power. Lord Templewood suggested that under the formula boys might be sent who were not really criminals at all[5]; Miss Margery Fry reminded magistrates of the length of the sentence and the consequent need for basing it on a stringent test and not upon an easy decision.[6] The *Justice of the Peace* even went so far as to suggest

[1] Section 20, Criminal Justice Act 1948
[2] See proposals in Committee: *H. L. Debates*, Vol. 156, cols. 307 and 310–13, 3 June 1948.
[3] *H. C. Debates*, Vol. 444, col. 2165, 27 November 1947
[4] The Council of the Magistrates' Association supported this change in the law; see *The Magistrate*, Vol. VIII, No. LXXI (January-February 1948), p. 87.
[5] In 'The Outlook for Penal Reform,' *Howard Journal*, Vol. 7, No. 3 (1948–49), p. 167
[6] In 'The Effect of the C. J. Act on the Borstal System,' *Journal of Criminal Science*, Vol. 2 (1950), p. 60

that 'we think there is no reason for regarding this as indicating a change in the class of offenders considered suitable for such a sentence'[1]—a conclusion which ignored completely the arguments and developments which had at last led to such a change.

In one way the Act reduced the types of offenders eligible for borstal. The experiment started in 1936 to include boys aged 21 to 23 in the system had not proved a success and so the age limit was again set at 21. In a way it is strange that this decision should have been made in 1948, for ten years earlier Parliament was willing to give magistrates power to sentence these older boys, and in the meantime there had only been the experience gained from the highly untypical war years. Nevertheless, the Home Secretary stated that they did not fit effectively into the community of younger and less mature offenders.[2] But as they had mostly been segregated into one institution it seems more likely that they had failed to respond to the type of appeal which had proved successful with the younger boys. For these older offenders the more adult system of Corrective Training also introduced in the Act was thought to be more appropriate.

The judicial anxiety over early releases also affected the Bill. In its draft form it included the proposal that the minimum sentence should be twelve months. The main reason for this move appears to have been to allay the suspicions of the judiciary that the lengthy sentences they thought they were imposing were being cut administratively behind their backs.[3] So much publicity had been given to early releases that it was necessary for the Home Secretary to assure the House that the average period of training was around eighteen months,[4] and

[1] *Justice of the Peace*, Vol. 112, No. 33, 14 August 1948, p. 505
[2] *H. C. Debates*, Vol. 444, col. 2140, 27 November 1947
[3] In *The Times*, 20 January 1948, the following report appeared: At Southend Quarter Sessions yesterday, the Recorder (Mr J. Flowers, k.c.) expressed surprise that M. P., 19, whom he sentenced to a month's imprisonment for theft, had so soon been released on licence from the borstal Institution to which he had been committed at the Northants. Quarter Sessions last year. A detective said that it was a thing that had 'dumbfounded the police for long enough'. He added, 'We expect to keep these youths for a reasonable time after committal but before we know where we are they are back in crime again.'
[4] *H. C. Debates*, Vol. 444, col. 2140, 27 November 1947

for Lords Llewellin and Chorley to show that, of those released in under twelve months, the majority had done well.[1] One of the main points for resisting such a high minimum was that there were undoubtedly cases who responded exceptionally well (or perhaps never had been really in need of lengthy training) and who both deserved and benefited from early release.[2] Eventually a compromise was reached at a nine months' minimum sentence: an assurance to the courts that borstal was in most cases a reasonable alternative to long-term imprisonment.

(b) *Limitations on the use of imprisonment and new alternatives.* The imprisonment of young persons was dealt with in the Act by impressing on magistrates that they should only use it when no other course was open to them and by providing them with two new alternatives. The legislation limited the haphazard use of imprisonment by requiring magistrates to give reasons in writing for their decision to sentence a youth to prison and to 'obtain and consider information about the circumstances'[3] in all cases. The summary courts were also prohibited from sentencing anyone under 17 years to prison: but as the numbers aged 16 imprisoned in previous years had been very low this made little difference to the general use of imprisonment. Provision was made under Section 17 for the Secretary of State to abolish the use of imprisonment by summary courts when he was satisfied that alternatives were available.

The short-term measures provided by the Act were detention centres and attendance centres. In the former the regime was to be one of strict discipline to provide a 'short sharp shock' to the unsophisticated hooligan. They were obviously meant to deal with those who were not persistent offenders, as boys who had previously been sentenced to prison or borstal were excluded from those eligible. The Act did not embody any proposals to strictly compare with the Howard Houses of the 1938 Bill, when a lack of a decent home rather than a lack of discipline was thought to be at the basis of the problem of delinquency. Probation Hostels were the nearest alternative but they did not provide the strict regime which the Houses

---

[1] *H. L. Debates*, Vol. 156, cols. 846–8 and 1088–9, 15 and 22 June 1948
[2] See comments in *Howard Journal*, Vol. 7, No. 4 (1948–49), p. 203.
[3] Section 17 (2), Criminal Justice Act 1948

would have done.[1] Attendance centres were obviously meant as a short punishment for those who did not need the help of probation or deserve the punishment of the detention centres.[2] Neither type of institution was meant to divert any of the borstal population, but they may have had some effect in this way among judges who had previously used borstal in preference to prison in the absence of these alternatives.[3]

(c) *The effect of the Act on the courts.* The Act brought about an immediate, and spectacular, drop in the numbers of young offenders sentenced to imprisonment. Even excluding those committed for non-indictable offences, the number fell from 1,873 in 1948 to 860 in 1949. Although the number sentenced to imprisonment again increased to 1,743 by 1961 this was entirely due to the rise in the crime rate. The proportion of boys sentenced to borstal also increased after the Act, both in relation to the total number of convictions and to the use of imprisonment. However, in the years since 1953 the proportion dropped in terms of both these indices. It seems that the opening of the first senior detention centres deprived the borstals, and not the prisons, of some of their population. Until early in 1961 there were only two senior detention centres, both continually full to capacity. With the creation of three new centres, the courts made the most of the opportunity to use them. At the same time as more detention centre places became available, the proportion of boys sentenced to borstal, of the total number sent to any of the institutions, fell more than the proportion sent to prison.

Although the prison statistics show a great increase in the numbers sentenced to borstal, especially since 1957, this has been entirely due to the rise in the crime rate. The proportion receiving borstal sentences of the total number convicted of indictable offences has in fact been slowly, but steadily, falling. This has been particularly true for the higher courts which have sentenced, since 1954, a lower proportion of the convicted boys to borstal than in most pre-war years.

It should be remembered, however, that in all the post-war years more use has been made of borstal in relation to

[1] Leading article in *The Times*, 5 November 1947
[2] F. H. McClintock, *Attendance Centres* (1961)     [2] See p. 89 below.

imprisonment plus detention than in any of the pre-war years. What characterizes the fifties is the fall in the prestige of the borstal system. The detention centre has become to some extent an alternative to long-term training, and the use of sentences of imprisonment of greater length than the detention sentence has persisted as a real alternative to borstal.

## The Borstal Principle in Decline

(a) *Borstal and changing penal practice.* The 1948 Act gave the courts freedom to sentence to borstal a wider variety of offenders. It was an expression of the optimism of the thirties that all those who were in need of training should be able to benefit from it: in principle it emphasized the advantages of a borstal sentence over any other alternatives. The borstals were now the most important element in the penal system for young offenders. Implicit in the Act was the hope that borstals would entirely replace the use of imprisonment for terms similar in length to those served by borstal boys. It was also hoped that magistrates' courts could commit more offenders to the higher courts for sentence to borstal in place of short-term imprisonment. For those who were clearly not in need of such lengthy training the Act had established detention centres to replace the apathetic regimes of local prisons with a 'shake-up' course for the young hooligan. But although these centres could perhaps modify a too-ready-use of borstal, they were never meant as a real alternative: both types of institutions were for different types of boys. There was certainly nothing to suggest that detention centres were to be part of a graduating course to borstal.

In the years that followed, the climate of opinion, and the effects of the courts' practices, were to change the scene. In 1959 the Government published the White Paper, *Penal Practice in a Changing Society*,[1] which outlined a number of proposals designed to rationalize penal practices for young offenders. These proposals were further discussed, and enlarged on, in the Home Secretary's Advisory Council's publication, *The Treatment of Young Offenders*,[2] and later substantially embodied in the

---

[1] *Penal Practice in a Changing Society—Aspects of Future Development* (England and Wales) (Cmd. 645, 1959)

[2] *The Treatment of Young Offenders:* A Report of the Advisory Council on the Treatment of Offenders. Home Office (1959)

Criminal Justice Act 1961. They were: (i) to ensure that detention centres would completely replace short-term imprisonment: in fact, to fulfil the original intentions of the 1948 Act; (ii) to combine the borstal and young prisoners' centres so that there would be a single indeterminate sentence of between six months and two years; (iii) to provide imprisonment for three years or more for the more serious offenders and offences, and sentences of imprisonment of eighteen months or more for the failures of the indeterminate sentence.

While there was nothing novel in the first proposal as it stood, the discussion which preceded the passing of the Act[1] showed quite clearly that the detention centres were considered by the Government to be a particularly appropriate way of dealing with the crime problem. Their advantages were constantly emphasized while at the same time no defence was offered against the critics of borstal. Nor was borstal given any of the praise formerly lavished upon it. The second proposal was, as the White Paper described it, 'more novel and far reaching'.[2] In fact it merely combined what had in practice become one system. But, in emphasizing that prisons and borstals could be conceived of as one united system, it fundamentally altered the image of borstal. This proposal, and the way in which it was received, was a natural consequence of a loss in the prestige of borstal in the post-war years. The system had failed to cope successfully with post-war youth and had been forced to adopt measures which emphasized some of the negative aspects of the system, such as the need for closed institutions and discipline. In a period of a fast-rising crime rate more emphasis had been placed on the severity of penalties. This had led to the belief that brisk and exacting regimes, such as those at detention centres, were the correct antidote to increased lawlessness. As Mr Butler pointed out, one of the principal aims of the 1961 Act was to 'increase the severity of

---

[1] See *H. C. Debates*, Vol. 630, cols. 562ff., 17 November 1960, Vol. 638, cols. 310ff., 12 April 1961; *H. C. Debates* (Standing Committee B.), 1 December 1960–14 February 1961; *H. L. Debates*, Vol. 230, cols. 1059ff., 1 May 1961, Vol. 231, cols. 393ff., 15 May 1961, Vol. 232, cols. 66ff., 12 June 1961.

[2] op. cit., para 41

the penalty'[1]—an implication that a course of training was not the appropriate sentence for many boys. The results of research, along with the annual statistics of the Commissioners, had also played an important part in this fall from grace, for they pointed to the high failure rate of borstal: these figures alone might well have shattered some of the dreams of pre-war penal reformers.[2]

The last of the proposals made explicit the view that some young offenders could not benefit from a wholly reformatory regime or that their crimes were too severe to allow them to serve sentences of only two years. For the first time alternative long-term sentences to borstal had been mentioned in an Act of Parliament. The failures of the reformatory system were to receive sentences of eighteen months' imprisonment or longer: they were to be classed as beyond reformation by borstal methods. Although the courts had always used long sentences for the more serious offenders this had been considered by penal reformers (from the Gladstone Committee on) as undesirable because of the need to consider reformation as the prime object of the penal system for young offenders. The proposals of the White Paper and the Criminal Justice Act, on the other hand, supported current judicial practice in asserting that some young offenders deserved long sentences in penal establishments.[3]

The borstal system in the years after the war lost some of the attributes which formerly distinguished it from the prisons. As the Ingleby Committee stated: 'The Borstal system was established under the Prevention of Crimes Act 1908, to provide suitable training for adolescents in conditions other than those in prison.'[4] By 1961 this distinction was by no means so clear-cut: the prison and borstal systems had been fused together. The new system was not a result of the abolition of imprisonment, but a natural result of the growing similarity of the

[1] Mr Butler in a speech to the Women's Advisory Council of the Conservative Party. Reported in *The Times*, 20 April 1961

[2] These figures are reviewed on pp. 212–15 below.

[3] Within the prison system as such, it is, of course, official policy that the reformation of the offender should be the object, not his punishment. Nevertheless, punishment is the object of *some* sentences.

[4] *Report of the Committee on Children and Young Persons* (The Ingleby Committee) (Cmd. 1191, 1960), para. 350

regimes of the closed borstal institutions and the young prisoners' prisons. The fundamental distinction between the respective roles of imprisonment and borstal was destroyed. Above all, the post-war years have seen a remarkable fall in the prestige and public favour with which the reformatory principles of the borstal system were formerly held.

(b) *Criticism of the open system.* A steady growth in absconding immediately after the war, combined with complaints of indiscipline, put the Commissioners in a dilemma.[1] While they were anxious to maintain a particular emphasis on training in open conditions, they were at the same time aware of the need to consider public anxiety over excapes. By 1950 they were forced to make what was to be a critical decision on the problem of what to do with persistent absconders. There were several alternatives: either to return the boy to borstal via a punishment centre; to allow him to be sentenced to prison by the courts; or to open a special institution to deal specifically with these and other difficult cases. In fact, the Commissioners usually did not allow absconders to serve terms of imprisonment but transferred them back to borstal; they were also relatively unsympathetic to the idea of a special institution. But the practice of transferring back to borstal absconders who were imprisoned for offences while free had aroused criticism,[2] and received the condemnation of the Court of Criminal Appeal which had upheld the practice of passing a reasonable prison sentence for crime committed during an escape.[3] The Commissioners were not anxious that the courts should always decide on the fate of these boys, and when Lord Templewood publicly supported the idea of a special institution the issue was more or less settled.[4] Since the Commissioners were unable to

[1] In 1927 the number of escapes (absconds) was 3·6 per cent of the daily average population of borstals. In 1935—5·0 per cent, 1938—9·2 per cent, 1945—27·9 per cent, 1948—41·3 per cent, 1950—42·0 per cent. Since 1950 there has been a gradual but steady decline (1956—29·0 per cent, 1962—19·1 per cent). Nevertheless, it still remains a substantial problem.

[2] See Lord Schuster's comments, *H. L. Debates*, Vol. 156, cols. 317–20, 3 June 1948.

[3] The Court has reacted strongly to the Commissioners' action in returning boys to borstal; see *R v Grimshaw* (1945), 30 Cr. App. R. 184.

[4] *H. L. Debates*, Vol. 156, col. 8178, 15 June 1948. Also *The Times*, 2 July 1948

reduce absconding they capitulated to opinion—an opinion most fully and emphatically endorsed by the Committee which had been appointed to examine the problem of discipline in borstal. This Departmental Committee set up to review punishments in borstals and other institutions had also commented unfavourably on the relaxed regimes of many borstals and suggested that because the offenders were tougher than in pre-war days they were in need of more discipline.[1] The institution opened at Hull Prison in 1950 was particularly for those 'who have received a second Borstal sentence' and for other hardened offenders, where they would receive training based on a stiff discipline because of their inability to respond to 'the normal and freer system of training in other Borstals'.[2] But it was also intended for some persistent absconders. In fact, the most difficult groups were to be segregated so that they could be dealt with by measures more suited to their behaviour. *The Times* commenting on this decision stressed that escape-proof borstals would shatter the 'fundamental concept of the present system' but added that the Commissioners had to reduce persistent absconding to satisfy public opinion.[3]

The problem of absconding, and the difficulty of finding any alternative other than imprisonment for borstal failures, had produced a 'penal borstal' more akin to the young prisoners' centres than to the open borstals. Although the Commissioners had established this institution in preference to sending boys to prison, they had in fact narrowed the distinction which had previously been maintained between prisons and borstals.

Despite the opening of Hull, complaints about absconding continued. The main concern was that boys who were not trustworthy were being sent to open institutions. Although it was hoped that this was a temporary setback—due to the effect of the war—and that boys would later settle and become more like the 'trustworthy pre-war type', the Commissioners were forced to consider the re-organization of their system.

---

[1] Articles in *The Times*, 17 and 18 September 1951

[2] *Report of the Committee to Review Punishments in Prisons, Borstal Institutions, Approved Schools and Remand Homes. Part II, Borstal Institutions* (Cmd. 8265, 1950–51), paras. 61–3. For a short discussion of the effect of the Committee's recommendations on ideas of training see Chapter V below.

[3] *P. C. Report*, 1950, p. 64

There was clearly now no foundation for the earlier optimism which had envisioned the day when there would no longer be a need for any closed borstals. It was frankly admitted that there were too many open institutions, and plans were made to establish small secure borstals in the future.[1] Fear of antagonizing judicial and public opinion led the Commissioners to agree that this question of security was of prime importance. With an increasing emphasis in the following years upon the problem of providing adequate discipline and on the need for closed institutions to deal with the progressively difficult population, the difference between prison and borstal became even more indistinguishable.[2]

What is perhaps even more important is that the belief that progressive reformatory methods could be justified by the results they produced had received a severe blow. It is always difficult to justify progressive penal methods. But during the thirties the Commissioners had been able to point with a great deal of pride to their open borstals with their low absconding rate and fine spirit. After the war this was no longer possible; the open system and progressive methods could not be justified by results, and the stress was on the need for more discipline— apparently the progressive system would not work. This is not meant to suggest that all the borstals became disciplinary establishments or that the Commissioners completely stopped experimenting with methods, but simply that the atmosphere was not as favourable to a reforming movement as it had been in the thirties. The borstal principle could no longer be accepted as an article of faith, justified by its good work.

(c) *The new emphasis on discipline.* In the thirties the hope had been expressed that short sentences would eventually cease to exist; that once an offender had failed to respond to non-institutional sanctions, steps would be taken to secure his rehabilitation by methods which would inevitably involve the long process of institutional training. The concept of training

---

[1] See *Report of the Select Committee on Estimates: Session 1951–52, 7th Report,* Q.2322; also *P. C. Report,* 1952, pp. 75–6; and *H. C. Debates,* Vol. 512, cols. 131–2, 2 March 1953.

[2] On the closure of Hull in 1961 boys of this type were sent to Northallerton and then in 1962 to Hindley Borstal. It is particularly illuminating that at this institution the officers wear uniforms.

had implicitly contained the notion of a long-term process. The detention centres provided in 1948 were intended as a punitive measure to replace the normal functions of short-term imprisonment: they were not meant to replace borstal by an alternative training regime.[1] In the following years the idea that training must necessarily imply a long-term process was attacked by those who saw discipline, in its own right, as a form of training. Probably the most important factor in affecting a return to an emphasis on discipline was the rise in the crime rate in the second half of the fifties.[2] The alarm caused by this increase, and in particular by the notion that most of it was taking the form of crimes of violence, led to renewed demands for more stringent methods for dealing with delinquents. It was thought that a high proportion of these offenders neither needed prolonged training nor would respect probation,[3] the only appropriate remedy being a course of rigid discipline or a dose of the birch. It is clear from the debates on the Criminal Justice Bill that many were in sympathy with the notion that detention centres were the 'civilized alternative to the birch . . . to be the means, almost the principal means, of protecting society against dangerous young men and against violence.'[4] Borstal was not once mentioned as the correct remedy for these youths. Before the war, the only alternative to prison had been borstal: the 1948 Act provided for the first time an institutional means of dealing with those not yet in need of long-term training. During the fifties they came to be thought of as an ideal form of punishment for the 'delinquent generation'. The regime of the detention centres, while not employing techniques normally associated with the idea of training and treatment, was thought to provide just that form of disciplinary training which the young hooligan needed.

[1] But see Margery Fry's observation that these centres might make the judiciary more cautious in their use of borstal; in 'The Effect of the Criminal Justice Act on the Borstal System,' *Journal of Criminal Science*, Vol. 2 (1948), p. 60.

[2] See L. T. Wilkins, *Delinquent Generations* (1960), which highlights the problem of the increase in adolescent crime during the late fifties.

[3] It is interesting to note that whereas in 1938 magistrates' courts placed 45 per cent of 17–21-year-olds on probation and fined 18 per cent, the figures for 1963 were 20 and 50 per cent respectively.

[4] Mr Deedes in *H. C. Debates*, Vol. 630, col. 635, 17 November 1960

In this case punishment had become synonymous with training. The Lord Chief Justice insisted that discipline and punishment must remain the purpose of these centres; that they should not be allowed to 'become again places of training, of remedial treatment and not primarily of punishment'.[1]

The quest for discipline had spread to the higher courts. Far from imprisonment waning as a method of punishment, they began to use it more frequently in the fifties while at the same time resorting less often to the use of borstal. It was considered that those in need of punishment and discipline should receive the more serious and onerous sanction of imprisonment rather than be sent to the more relaxed borstal institutions. In 1946 the higher courts had sentenced 46 per cent of 17 to 21 year olds convicted of indictable offences to borstal and only 7 per cent to prison. In 1960 the figures were 28 and 13 per cent, respectively.[2] It is clear that there had been a most definite drop in the proportion of borstal sentences and a corresponding increase in sentences of imprisonment. The Court of Criminal Appeal, in a number of judgements, had made it clear that they considered sentences of between nine months' and two years' imprisonment to be more appropriate for an offender convicted of some serious offences 'needing discipline'.[3] The Advisory Council had pointed out that very few boys were sentenced by the courts to terms of imprisonment of over six months in 1957 —but that was in fact one-third of the total imprisoned.[4] With the increase in the crime rate in the following years the numbers sentenced to over six months' imprisonment almost doubled.[5]

[1] Lord Parker in *H. L. Debates*, Vol. 230, col. 1105, 1 May 1961

[2] These figures are taken from *Criminal Statistics*, 1961, Ch. VI. They refer to both males and females. These statistics show the gradual decline in the use of borstal by these courts since the war, although by 1963 the proportion had risen slightly to 32 per cent.

[3] For example, *R v Harris* (1958), *Cr. Law Rev.* 318; *R v Gomez* (1958), *Cr. Law Rev.* 405; *R v Rowland* (1958), *Cr. Law Rev.* 318. For a review of the policy of the Court of Criminal Appeal since 1948, see D. A. Thomas, 'Sentencing Young Offenders: The Effect of the Criminal Justice Act, 1961,' *Cr. Law Rev.* (1963), 536ff

[4] In the post-war years the proportion receiving sentences of over six months has been almost four times as great as before the war.

[5] *The Treatment of Young Offenders*, para. 49. In 1957 only 387 youths under 21 were sentenced to imprisonment for more than six months. In 1961 the number was 738. Since August 1963 the courts have lost their

The Council also failed to note that the higher courts sentenced a substantial proportion of boys to prison for less than six months as an alternative to borstal. This was true even after the opening of more detention centres in 1961, although by 1963 they were making very much more use of detention.[1]

Perhaps one of the most important factors in the revitalization of the prison regime has been the specialized work carried out at the young prisoners' centres. The Commissioners had made every attempt to separate young prisoners from adults. The critics of imprisonment could therefore no longer say that this form of punishment would necessarily lead to contamination. One of the principal objections to imprisonment was thus rendered obsolete. As the Advisory Council said, 'there is really little difference between the principles of training in young prisoners' prisons and those in borstal institutions'.[2] On the other hand, these centres had a regime based far more on disciplinary principles than on the ideas of progressive responsibility and personal contact traditionally associated with borstal. To quote the Commissioners, 'all young prisoners' centres are geared to a brisk tempo, designed to exact the fullest physical and mental effort, in an atmosphere of strict discipline'.[3] Yet, the borstal system, with its increasing emphasis on closed institutions and the need for increased discipline, was becoming, in parts, more like these centres. By 1960, Sir George Benson, a former champion of the borstal system, was in fact able to say that there was little difference between closed borstal and prisons: in substance the systems had become integrated.[4]

The proposals of the White Paper and the Advisory Council were based on the common-sense view that there was no point in differentiating between two systems which had in practice

---

power to sentence 17 to 21 year olds to imprisonment, due to the implementation of the Criminal Justice Act 1961.

[1] In 1961 approximately 300 youths were sentenced to imprisonment for *under* six months by the higher courts. No comparable statistics are available for later years, but in 1963 the higher courts sentenced 11 per cent of 17 to 21 year olds to detention centres, compared with 5 per cent in 1961.

[2] *The Treatment of Young Offenders*, para. 49

[3] *P. C. Report*, 1960, p. 48

[4] Sir George Benson, *H. C. Debates*, Vol. 630, col. 597, 17 November 1960

fused together. Lord Denning was able to say, 'I have looked at a centre for young persons under twenty-one, with their strict regime. It is a very fine thing for bringing them back to sanity; and that, in effect, will be the general system of borstal training.'[1] Mr Butler never ceased, in discussing the role of borstal, to stress that it was to be a 'severe' punishment. He stated that there would be more closed borstals and a wider variety of institutions 'particularly for boys who need to be in a secure establishment' and that there would be a 'brisk and exacting . . . intensive regime of training' which would ensure a 'short but severe attendance at borstal'.[2]

In numerous public statements and throughout the debates on the Act, Mr Butler and his supporters stressed that the new Act was one which would not 'make the way of transgressors softer and more agreeable': in fact one of the principal aims was to 'increase the severity of the penalty'. The emphasis on deterrence, and the fear that the new proposals might in some way be thought inferior to the birch, prompted the Advisory Council to preface its proposals with a long explanation justifying them as at least equally severe as existing methods.[3]

(d) *The influence of research.* Despite the Advisory Council's most extraordinary dismissal of research,[4] there is no doubt that research results have had some influence on the movement of opinion away from long-term reformatory sentences towards short-term sentences, although not towards the detention centres as such.

---

[1] Lord Denning, *H. L. Debates*, Vol. 230, col. 1121, 1 May 1961
[2] *H. C. Debates*, Vol. 630, col. 571, 17 November 1960
[3] op. cit., para. 14
[4] ibid., para. 17 states, 'The proposals may also be criticized on the ground that reforms of this kind should be made only in the light of greater knowledge based on research. No specific research was carried out before the proposals were formulated, but we do not think that this is a reason for not making the proposed changes. They are based on principles which would not be affected by the results of further research into the effects of different methods of treatment, and we do not think that their introduction should be delayed while such research is carried out. At some future date the results of any research that is carried out may, of course, suggest some modification of the present proposals.' See also the comments of J. P. Martin and Hermann Mannheim in *British Journal of Delinquency*, Vol. 10, No. 3 (January 1960), pp. 217 and 219–20.

It was after 1953 that doubts about whether borstal was a particularly successful means of dealing with adolescent delinquents began seriously to spread. Earlier, references to the 'vast progress made in the half-century'[1] had referred to changes in the methods of dealing with the offenders in the institutions and not to any increase in the 'success rates' since the 1920's. In fact, the reconviction rates had never been seriously examined. Various claims made over the years had all given roughly the same success rate (estimates of between 65 and 80 per cent of boys not reconvicted)[2] despite the variations in the type of training carried out by the institutions. The statement had simply been made that imprisonment led almost inevitably to reconviction, and borstal to reform. Mr Benson, for example, speaking in the debate on the Criminal Justice Bill in 1948, had stated that, 'If they [the critics, look at the statistics] they will see how marvellously successful Borstal is. Not three out of 10 [as in borstal] but nearly seven out of 10 return [to prison]. In other words, Borstal which aims at reform and which repudiates punishment is twice as successful as imprisonment for youngsters between 16 and 21.' He was, however, drawing upon pre-war figures.[3] After the war it became increasingly noticeable that results were not so good as in pre-war years. The most prevalent explanation attributed this to the unsteadying influence of the war on the boys and to lack of experience among the staff.[4] The assumption was that once the war years were in the background results would return to pre-war level. However, this was clearly a misinterpretation of the problem. The boys became increasingly more difficult to handle and success rates continued to fall.[5] In these circumstances there was obviously a particular need for research.

The first major research project involving sophisticated statistical analysis to be born out of the post-war interest in

[1] *The Times*, 18 September 1951
[2] The results of the system are discussed fully in Chapter VII below.
[3] Mr Benson in *H. C. Debates*, Vol. 444, cols. 2293–4, 28 November 1947. He went on to say, 'We have tried deterrence, we have tried mixing deterrence with reform, and it is only when we can concentrate on reform that we shall get results.'
[4] See, for example, leading article, 'Fifty Years of Borstal' in *The Times*, 20 December 1958.
[5] See Chapter VII below.

criminology was a study of the results of borstal training. It is
of great significance that the first major expenditure on research
should have been directed at the borstal problem and that it
should have been officially financed and published by the
Home Office.[1] The Mannheim-Wilkins prediction study, published in 1955, showed that the borstal system failed in a
substantial number of instances, particularly among the more
hardened cases in the closed institutions. The study emphasized the problem posed by the failure rates of closed
borstals and showed that long terms of training did not
produce better results than shorter terms. The failure rate it
disclosed came as something of a shock—*The Times* described
it as a 'problem which ought to evoke much heart searching'.[2]
Also it cannot have failed to have had some influence on the
attitudes of the courts. As a more positive result the research
provided other research workers with a tool whereby they could
measure the effectiveness of different forms of treatment. The
prediction technique enabled for the first time a comparison to
be made between the results of long and short sentences.
Throughout the debates on the relative merits of long-term and
short-term institutional treatment it has been emphasized that
the offender should only be subject to a long course of reformatory treatment if the results were far superior to those of short
sentences. Even after the war Mr Benson claimed that borstals
were much more successful than prisons. In 1954, however, he
took another look at the evidence and came up with a completely different answer. He stated that while after a three-year
sentence 47 per cent of the borstal boys were not reconvicted,
after three months or more in a prison 68 per cent were not
reconvicted. This startling conclusion led him to say that
'either the figures are wildly misleading . . . or the Commissioners will have to revise their perennial advice to the
courts to prefer Borstal to imprisonment'.[3] It is certainly

[1] H. Mannheim and L. T. Wilkins, *Prediction Methods in Relation to
Borstal Training* (1955). For a discussion of this prediction study see the
symposium in *British Journal of Delinquency*, Vol. 6, No. 2 (September 1955).
Also in the same issue, R. L. Morrison, 'Predictive Research, A Critical
Assessment of its Practical Implications,' p. 99

[2] *The Times*, 16 November 1957

[3] George Benson, 'Report of the Commissioners of Prisons 1953,' *Howard
Journal*, Vol. 9, No. 2 (1954), p. 142

difficult to account for the difference between 1948 and 1954: if it is not due to a misinterpretation of the figures at the earlier date, it must be attributed to the more careful selection of young persons for imprisonment at the latter date, combined with the after-care they received. With the aid of the Mannheim-Wilkins prediction technique, Sir George Benson set to work to compare borstal boys with young prisoners. He used the prediction classification device to match borstal boys and young prisoners and concluded that (allowing for the fact that there were more difficult offenders in the borstal population) it was impossible to distinguish between the results of short-term imprisonment and of borstal.[1] At a later stage he compared both these groups with boys at a detention centre and reached exactly the same conclusion.[2] The idea that all methods of treatment and punishment produce similar results has been a hard pill to swallow[3] but an increasing number of studies produce similar evidence.[4]

Once the Commissioners had accepted as valid the results

[1] Sir George Benson, 'Prediction Methods and Young Prisoners,' *British Journal of Delinquency*, Vol. 9, No. 3 (January 1959), p. 192

[2] *H. C. Debates*, Vol. 630, cols. 598–9, 17 November 1960, and Standing Committee B, cols. 214–15, 15 December 1960. It should be noted, however, that Sir George used the Mannheim-Wilkins formula in making comparisons despite those authors' contention (p. 146): 'Nor, of course, can they be applied to any other form of treatment than Borstal training.'

[3] Sir R. Manningham-Buller in *H. C. Debates* (Standing Committee B), col. 224, 15 December 1960 stated that he could not be converted to Mr Benson's view for 'that is very depressing'. Lord Templewood had also asserted that a review of penal experiments would show that 'we are on the right lines' and that experience showed that different forms of treatment did matter—'at least helped certain offenders lead a better life': *The Times*, 5 November 1958.

[4] For example, L. T. Wilkins, 'A small comparative study of the results of probation,' *British Journal of Delinquency*, Vol. 8, No. 3 (January 1958). For American evidence see: H. Ashley Weeks, *Youthful Offenders at Highfields* (1958). The recent Home Office booklet, *The Sentence of the Court* (1964), showed that for offenders with previous convictions, borstal, fines and discharges were equally slightly more effective than 'expected'—detention centres and imprisonment were worse. See p. 50.

This is not the place for a critical assessment of the research on comparing the results of treatment, but it should be pointed out that such *overall* comparisons between different methods are very suspect. The results may simply be due to:

(i) the relative crudity of present prediction methods, which may fail

derived from the Mannheim-Wilkins research, the gates were open for a complete re-evaluation of the time factor in training.[1] The results of the research were in fact embodied in the proposals of the White Paper and of the Advisory Council under the guise of the 'experience of the Prison Commissioners',[2] in the proposal for reducing the maximum length of the borstal sentence from three years to two and the minimum from nine months to six.

These results were a severe blow to the dearly held principle that training needed time, and further moved the balance of favour in the direction of the detention centres. If these centres could produce results similar to those of borstal in a shorter time, and at a substantially smaller cost,[3] they were naturally

---

adequately to take account of real differences in the types of offenders given different treatments. Particular factors involved are the inappropriateness of regression analysis for heterogeneous populations, and the present inadequacy of the records, on the basis of which such comparisons are made. Among recent evidence is the heterogeneity of the Mannheim-Wilkins prediction groups, see T. C. N. Gibbens, *Psychiatric Studies of Borstal Lads* (1963), pp. 192–6 and 205–6. See also the author's study of homeless boys in his PH.D. dissertation, op. cit.

(ii) that while *overall* results are the same, the treatments are both having successes and failures with different types of offenders so that results balance out to look the same. For example, if treatment 'A' gives very good results for offenders with characteristics 'xyz' but bad ones for offenders 'abc', while on the other hand treatment 'B' gives moderate results for both 'xyz' and 'abc', the *overall* rate of success for each treatment could be the same. The particular appropriateness of treatment 'A' for offenders 'xyz' would be masked. For results which show such a situation, see J. D. and M. Q. Grant, 'A Group Dynamics Approach to the Treatment of Non-Conformists in the Navy,' *Annals* (March 1959), p. 126. Also, S. Adams, 'Interaction between Individual Interview Therapy and Treatment Amenability in Older Youth Authority Wards,' in *Inquiries Concerning Kinds of Treatment for Kinds of Delinquents*, California Board of Corrections, Monograph No. 2 (1961). On the question of the research problems of comparing the effectiveness of treatments see the author's 'Research on the Effectiveness of Punishments and Treatments', prepared for the Second Conference of Criminological Research Centres, Council of Europe, Strasbourg (1964). *Mimeo.* Also L. T. Wilkins, 'Criminology: An Operational Research Approach,' in A. T. Welford (ed.), *Society, Problems and Methods of Study* (1962).

[1] See Chapter V, pp. 156–7 below.  [2] op. cit., para. 53
[3] Mr Mayhew in *H. C. Debates*, Vol. 630, col. 626, 17 November 1960; also comments of M. Grunhut in 'The Human Element in Prison Administration,' *Howard Journal*, Vol. 10, No. 1 (1958), p. 30

to be preferred.[1] From the 1948 Act until the Advisory Council made its suggestions and the Bill was debated, only two senior detention centres had been in operation. Even though the results of research at a centre emphasized its limited value,[2] the Commissioners (and the Advisory Council) were ready to expand the system as a matter of principle. Despite the fact that these centres had still 'to justify their existence'[3], especially with a wider variety of offenders, the Government were sold on the idea. It can only be assumed that the strict nature of the regime was thought *per se* to be the correct remedy for adolescent crime. The centres already in existence had never been seriously regarded as experiments. As Lady Wootton pointed out, commitment to the detention centre principle, without having first clearly worked out what the institutions were for, might simply result in the substitution of the detention centre for prison with all the same objections.[4]

Figures for 1961, when the new detention centres were

[1] This argument was used in particular by the late Sir Basil Henriques in his suggestion to set up Youth Centres on the lines of those used in Boston for many years. It was stressed that considerable saving could be achieved by training boys in the community through the use of school premises as compulsory evening centres. See *The Times*, 24 March 1961, and leading article 11 April 1961.

[2] *The Treatment of Young Offenders*, para. 29. See also the warning of Dr Grunhut on the problem of sentencing a wide variety of offenders to detention centres, in 'After Effects of Punitive Detention,' *British Journal of Delinquency*, Vol. 10, No. 3 (January 1960), p. 193. See also A. G. Rose, 'Training for Young Offenders' in *Penal Practice in a Changing Society: A Critical Examination of the White Paper Policy* (I.S.T.D. 1960), pp. 7ff. See also leading article in *The Times*, 11 April 1961.

[3] See a letter from Dr W. H. Allchin in *The Times*, 24 September 1958, and the ensuing correspondence on detention centres. Also leading article 'Cause and Cure Uncertain,' *The Times*, 11 August 1960, which states, 'At a time when the government propose virtually to abolish imprisonment for young offenders, it is disconcerting, for example, to learn that there is little to choose between borstal and imprisonment from the point of view of recidivism. The challenge is still there.' George Benson, commenting on the detention centres in 1954, had observed that 'this suggestion that the new detention centres are likely to be preferable to imprisonment is, of course, pure surmise' and added that five years' experience might well not be enough when it was remembered that forty-five years of borstal experience had still not proved the efficacy of this type of punishment. *Howard Journal*, op. cit., p. 143.

[4] *H. L. Debates*, Vol. 230, col. 1154, 1 May 1961

opened, showed that nearly 60 per cent of the boys sentenced to them had three or more previous convictions and that 30 per cent had five or more. It is clear that the courts were considering that this form of punishment was appropriate even for offenders well advanced in their criminal careers. There has also been a fall from 22 per cent with no previous convictions in 1955 to only 14 per cent in 1961.[1] These institutions are being used for offenders for whom a borstal sentence was considered essential in the late thirties. It has been recognized that a great increase in the detention centre population will necessitate a wider variety of regimes to cope with those who either are not in need of or cannot benefit from discipline. But in fact there is no classifying system available to ensure that these boys will go to an appropriate institution. A boy is simply committed to the centre serving the court which sentenced him—if a vacancy is available. No one has fully considered what will happen to the results of these centres if they continue to receive a substantial proportion of the more difficult cases formerly being sent to borstal. It appears that the closed borstals' poor performance compared with open institutions may well be due to the contaminating effect produced by a predominance of the worst type of inmate.[2] Detention centres might produce the same results as borstal for the more hopeful cases but could they do so if they had to deal with a higher proportion of more difficult boys? The comparisons so far made between borstal and detention centres have not taken this factor into account.

(e) *The intentions of the Criminal Justice Act 1961.* The Act made one other major alteration in the powers of the courts to sentence boys to borstal. The minimum age was reduced from 16 to 15 years. It was felt that there were some offenders who were so completely unsuitable for approved schools that they needed closed training. The Durand Report on the

[1] It is of great interest to note that the proportion of those with no previous convictions sentenced to any form of institution has fallen in recent years. In 1957 it was 15 per cent and in 1961 10 per cent. In 1952 12 per cent of receptions into borstal had six or more previous convictions; by 1962 the proportion was 48 per cent. Clearly, boys at the latter period were being sent to borstal later in their criminal careers.

[2] See Mannheim and Wilkins, op. cit., pp. 109–13. Also J. P. Martin's review in *Case Conference*, Vol. 2, No. 7 (November 1955), p. 27.

Carlton House disturbances in 1959 had recommended that closed provisions should be made for approved schools to be able to deal with these troublesome boys,[1] but the Home Office refused to agree on the grounds that these would fundamentally alter the character and image of the approved school. The age had not been lowered so as to provide more boys with the benefit of borstal but to extend its discipline to an age-group formerly dealt with by the more educative approved school regime. Critics were readily aware that this section of the Act, combined with the integration of the prison and borstal systems, meant that serious penal sanctions were now to be applied to even younger offenders: such was the effect of the rising crime rate and the early sophistication of some young criminals. Some observers could not help but feel that to introduce them into the environment of borstal would only worsen the problem.[2] Borstal and approved schools were now alternative forms of punishment for an increased number of young offenders. It was unlikely, however, that borstal would be frequently used for the 15 and 16 year olds. The juvenile courts were not given the power to sentence direct to borstal, but they could send a boy straight to an approved school. Although it was perhaps quite rightly stressed that this situation was illogical when approved school sentences were often longer than the borstal sentence, it is clear that the Government were anxious to reserve borstal only for the most serious offenders. The fact that juvenile courts would have to commit a boy to a higher court would in itself restrict the use of borstal for this age-group.

Here there is an interesting parallel. The Home Office solved the problem posed by difficult offenders in approved schools not by establishing closed schools and so altering the character of the system but by allowing these boys to be treated under the entirely separate regime of borstal.[3] It felt that there

[1] *Disturbances in the Carlton Approved School on 29th and 30th August 1959*, Report of Inquiry by Mr Victor Durand, Q.C. (Cmd. 937, 1960), paras. 69–71

[2] See *H. L. Debates*, Vol. 222, col. 490, 30 March 1960; also Lord Chorley in *H. L. Debates*, Vol. 230, cols. 1139–40, 1 May 1961.

[3] Even so, they have established closed blocks for absconders and other difficult cases at certain classifying schools, and this is regarded by some as a retrograde step.

was a 'fundamental difference between borstal and approved school . . . in regime, atmosphere and tradition'.[1] When the Prison Commissioners had been faced by a similar dilemma earlier in the fifties they had capitulated, and so brought about a process which led to the destruction of the peculiar character which had been associated with borstal.

Of course, it could be contended that prisons have disappeared and been replaced by borstals, but this is not so. Borstal had been conceived of not simply as a type of prison under an enlightened regime, but as an institution that would eventually shed its prison associations.[2] The borstal sentence had been based in the 1948 Act on the principle that it should be imposed when the offender was in need of training. A sentence to imprisonment was on the other hand considered appropriate when punishment and discipline were the primary objectives. The new Criminal Justice Act, by joining prisons and borstals together in one system,[3] altered the traditional role of the borstal sentence and confused it with an entirely different role—that of punishment. Boys under this Act were to be sentenced to custodial training for a variety of purposes, only one of which might be training. Although it was stated that everyone was now agreed that the training of young offenders was the purpose of the penal system, the continued use of imprisonment in place of borstal during the last few years has shown that the courts also have other considerations still in mind.[4]

In effect, however, the Act has made a number of potentially important changes. Besides making possible a more integrated

[1] Mr Renton, commenting on the suggestion that summary and juvenile courts should have the power to commit offenders direct to borstal in *H. C. Debates* (Standing Committee B), col. 84, 1 December 1960. This view was not shared by the Ingleby Committee who saw borstals and approved schools as alike in many ways and who recommended that juvenile courts should have the power to commit direct to borstal, paras. 502–03. See also, *The Times*, 28 October 1960. Compared with 1938 there was little serious debate on this issue.

[2] The former young prisoners' prisons will still maintain all their apparatus under the new system. For example, officers will still wear their uniforms—discarded in borstal for over thirty-five years.

[3] This part of the Act came into force on 24 June 1964.

[4] See the discussion in D. A. Thomas, op. cit.

system for dealing with young offenders with the advantages of a freer exchange of ideas and wider possibilities for experiment, it has taken some of the sentencing powers from the courts and placed them with the Commissioners. They are now able to decide, on more adequate evidence than that available to the courts, which type of regime is the most suitable for the offender and when his discharge is most appropriate. Some boys who formerly were in need of discipline but were committed to borstal can be sent to the tougher establishments; some formerly sentenced to imprisonment may well be found to be more likely to benefit from the freer regime of an open borstal. It is most probably true that the executive is in a better position to decide on these matters than are the courts.

Perhaps nothing has been lost but the idealism embodied in the name of borstal. By 1960 borstal was no longer a term describing a unique and progressive experiment in the treatment of young offenders. Although it may not be exactly true that 'the government are becoming so punishment minded that they are trying to turn Borstal into a sort of glorified detention centre to satisfy certain types of public opinion and are not regarding it as a place for constructive training',[1] the emphasis on closed institutions combined with the fusion with young prisoner centres, had produced a system which was not consistent with the predominating spirit of the pre-war years. The problems of post-war youth, a rising crime rate, an emphasis on discipline and not least the results of research, had overshadowed the optimism under which borstal flourished in earlier years.

[1] Mr McColl in *H. C. Debates* (Standing Committee B), cols. 209–10, 15 December 1960

# IV

# Training in 'The Golden Age'

*The Idea of Training*

Although the term 'borstal training' did not appear on the
statute book until 1948, the system has always aimed at providing a regime in which a positive approach to changing the
attitudes of offenders has been much more important than the
custodial element. In the borstal system 'training' has meant a
conscious effort to influence the attitudes and behaviour of the
inmate. In this sense the term has no emotive content and is not
necessarily opposed to the idea of discipline: it is possible for
discipline not to be the object of punishment in itself but a
means for changing attitudes. In this sense borstals have
always been training institutions. For example, although the
regime of the Ruggles-Brise period with its strict discipline was
markedly different from the regime of Paterson's open institutions of the thirties, the difference was mainly due to a change
of opinion about the best means of changing attitudes, and not
to there being a desire for discipline as an end in itself in the
earlier period. What have changed, then, are the concepts
which affect the system of training, and it is these that will be
explained in this chapter and the next. To understand the
changes that have taken place in training since the early years
of the century it is necessary to look beyond the different
elements used in the system at various periods, to the ideals
and viewpoints which lay behind them.

The idea of treatment is frequently linked to that of training.
Training does not imply treatment, although both terms have
been frequently used as though they were synonymous. The
use of the term treatment in connexion with the rehabilitation
of criminals stems from the widely held opinion that delinquent
behaviour is symptomatic of, or at least somehow closely linked
to, the problems of personal maladjustment. In the borstals
various efforts have been made to deal with the problems of

individuals, either through the friendly help and advice of one of the staff, or more rarely through a psychiatrist. Treatment may sometimes be part of the training process, but borstals have never been in any sense centres for individual treatment.

The factors which are part of the training process must be distinguished from any aspect of the sentence which might be purely deterrent. *In theory* a retributive or purely punitive element is absent from the sentence, and the length of training is not determined by considerations of general deterrence. The use of disciplinary measures is always justified by their value in 'character training' and not by their effectiveness as deterrents. It must be admitted though that for some boys the very length of the sentence might be the most important factor in bringing about their reform; but this would be incidental to the real or supposed object of the institutions. The positively applied reformatory elements must be distinguished in theory, at least, from the deterrent element which is rooted alone in the length of the sentence.

Broadly speaking, the main change in training methods has been from measures aimed at instilling discipline through external controls to the partial development of methods aimed at changing the attitudes of inmates through personal example, group opinion and attempts to develop self-discipline.

No attempt will be made in this chapter or the next to describe in detail the regimes of different institutions at various periods, but the reader is referred to Appendix A which summarizes information on the institutional growth of the system and to the full literature on this aspect.[1]

---

[1] Summaries of the type of regime in operation at the institutions are available in S. Barman, *The English Borstal System* (1934); W. Healey and B. S. Alper, *Criminal Youth and the Borstal System* (1941) (for a description of the system in 1939); A. G. Rose, *Five Hundred Borstal Boys* (1952) (for a description of the institutions during the war); L. W. Fox, *English Prison and Borstal Systems* (1952) (for a description of the institutions up to 1951); Winifred A. Elkin, *The English Penal System* (1957) (brings some of the developments up to date); also *Prisons and Borstals* (Home Office, 1945, 1950, 1957 and 1960). There is another study under process of publication in the U.S.A. bringing these descriptions up to date. Descriptions are also available in *Reports of the Prison Commissioners*; attention is particularly drawn to the comments of Governors and Chaplains at the back of the Reports. See also the *Borstal Association Reports* for 1938 and 1947.

This study is more concerned with the ideas behind the training than with the mechanics of the system.

## Training under Ruggles-Brise

In 1901 the 'fundamental principles' of the new institutional treatment were outlined as '(1) strict classification; (2) firm and exact discipline; (3) hard work'.[1] Twenty years later Sir Evelyn Ruggles-Brise still wrote of 'stern and exact discipline, tempered only by such rewards and privileges as good conduct with industry might earn'.[2] There had in fact been no change in the general principles of training.

The training was based upon a specific concept of the type of boy it had to deal with, and on the sort of boy which the institutions should aim to release. The boys were described as 'the worst products of the evil influences of the London streets . . . dangerous young criminals . . . rebellious characters . . . hardened in vice . . . reckless, wayward, and uncontrollable young lads . . . stubborn, unruly and criminal youth . . . misdirected youth rebelling against the law . . . the young hooligan advanced in crime perhaps with many previous convictions'.[3] The young man was to be turned into a 'strong well-set-up, handy English lad qualifying him to enter the ranks of honest industrial labour'.[4] It was believed that the young offender suffered from either 'physical degeneracy or bad environment'[5] and lacked the 'strength of character' essential to hard work and industrial discipline. His shiftlessness, laziness and disrespect for authority could be cured by placing him in a regime very similar to that which kept the army in good order. This system of external controls, and the insistence on the need to recognize authority both spiritual and temporal, stemmed from the hierarchical nature of British society in the era up to the end of the First World War. An effort was made to convince youths of the need to recognize authority in industry and to respect the established patterns of life.

[1] P. C. Report, 1900–01, p. 13          [2] The English Prison System, p. 93
[3] The first quotation is from the first Annual Report of the London Prison Visitors' Association, 1901, p. 5. All other quotes are from various Prison Commissioners' Reports between 1899 and 1910. The last quote is from The English Prison System, p. 99.
[4] ibid., p. 99          [5] P. C. Report, 1897–98, p. 22

Training placed particular emphasis on strictness of discipline and the earning of privileges through good conduct. In this way it was thought the boy would learn that through working hard and behaving well he could secure a few pleasures and comforts. Once this principle was appreciated by the boy within the institution it was assumed that he would see its relevance to his situation outside. Other important elements of the regime were physical training, work in a 'trade', educational influences and moral 'exhortation' and persuasion.

The idea of affecting a cure through strict discipline and a brisk regime, with gymnastics and early rising, was based upon the assumption that the offender needed 'physical' as well as moral reform.[1] Ruggles-Brise had been impressed at Elmira by what he called the 'physical method' as an instrument of reform. He agreed to a certain extent with the Elmira 'principle', expounded in England by W. D. Morrison,[2] that physical degeneracy was at the root of the criminal character. The Elmira regime set out to 'fit the organism for its normal and healthy functions, increasing the amount of nervous energy, and by this means strengthening the character': a military organization was also included 'to inculcate manliness of bearing and movement and feeling'.[3] It had been noted that young prisoners were in fact underweight and physically underdeveloped. At the same time it had been agreed that development of 'character' must await full physical development. The briskness of the discipline, the hard work and the exercises were considered an antidote to 'shiftiness', the symptom (and cause?) of crime. Writing in 1910 on the system, an enthusiastic correspondent of The Times noted 'the difference in carriage and bearing of the inmates from prisoners living in ordinary prison conditions . . . the shifty eyes have grown steady . . . heads are held erect'.[4] The improvement was thought to be due to an increase in 'self-respect' brought about by the

[1] ibid., p. 23. See also, leading article on 'Hooliganism' in The Times, 30 October 1900. It stated that hooligans are often physically and morally dégeneré.        [2] See pp. 8–9 above for a description of this idea.
[3] E. Ruggles-Brise, Some Observations on the Treatment of Crime in America: A Report to the Secretary of State, 1899, p. 12
[4] Article: 'Prison Life and Administration V, The New Departure,' The Times, 7 June 1910

physical development produced by the rigorous regime. In his recommendation of the system to the House of Lords in 1914, the Lord Chancellor described the regime of early rising, before-breakfast gymnastics and work with enthusiasm: 'He gets up at 5.30 a.m.—it is an early hour, but it is found that the process of reformation is assisted by early rising.'[1] No critics could say the regime was 'soft': it was clearly aimed at developing the 'character' and inculcating obedience.[2] 'It must be recognized,' stated the Commissioners, 'that hard work, stringent discipline and order are the fundamental conditions of any change in the habits and character of these wayward lads.'[3]

Work was from the very beginning an essential part of training. If the disciplining proved successful, the inmate still had to find work on release and to be able to compete with other free labour. Most of the boys had poor work records, either because of involuntary unemployment or through an inability or lack of desire to work. There were two cures in borstal. First the boys were made to work hard every day in an attempt to make them both efficient workmen and steady workers by habit. Secondly, some were supposedly 'taught trades', in the hope that skilled work would both give them more self-respect and shield them from chronic unemployment. Russell and Rigby had stated authoritatively that 'the trade most likely to be useful [to the boy] is chosen'.[4] The Home Secretary told the Commons in 1914: 'We are using the time during which he is detained to teach him a trade so that he can go out into the world afterwards and earn an honest living. We are giving him in the Borstal institution an opportunity which he has never had in his life.'[5]

The Commissioners did nothing to persuade anyone that the situation was otherwise. In strong contrast, the B.A. stated bluntly: 'Borstal does not pretend to teach a trade; [It could

[1] H. L. Debates, Vol. 17, col. 245, 29 July 1914
[2] See also, Alfred Wills (a High Court judge), 'Criminals and Crime,' Nineteenth Century and After, Vol. 62, December 1907, p. 882. Also a leading article in The Times, 30 June 1902, said, 'One cannot but regret that many a youth brought up at the police court is not taken firmly in hand and given a military training.'
[3] P. C. Report, 1910–11, p. 24
[4] Russell and Rigby, op. cit., p. 125
[5] Mr McKenna in H. C. Debates, Vol. 61, col. 199, 15 April 1914

though] make an undeveloped but teachable lad into a strong and handy workman, and give to him that protective pride in himself which comes with a sense of mastery of some part of a craft.'[1] There can be little doubt that, at the most, only a small proportion of the boys received any adequate or lengthy trade training. The Governor of Borstal appeared particularly sceptical about its efficacy. He claimed that few would take an interest in learning a trade and stick to it because of their inherent inconsistency. At the same time he raised doubts about whether the minds of the inmates were being forced beyond their capacity, and concluded that 'the best form of work is hard labouring . . . only by constant watching and admonition [do] they begin to see that there is another side to life . . . What they require, and get, as far as possible is a severe course of drill, gymnasium and hard work, together with strict attention to discipline.' As this all took some time there was little left for proper trade instruction.[2] It can be seen that the disciplinary aspects of work training were predominant over the vocational.

One other side of work-training was the early development of farming. The Gladstone Committee had recommended that the penal-reformatory should 'be situated in the country with ample space for agricultural and land reclamation work',[3] although it had given no reasons for this idea. Borstal Prison was particularly chosen because of its opportunities for cultivation and farm work, and from the early days this became an essential part of borstal work-training. In the thirties this aspect was extended even further.[4]

Discipline and the spirit of the institution were maintained and fostered by the progressive grade system. Under this system a boy had to earn marks for good conduct and hard work. When he had gained a particular quantity of marks taking at least nine months to reach, he passed into the 'special grade' where he received various privileges including a better diet and a larger gratuity. In the special grade an 'appeal was made to higher and better instincts', and the boy was 'placed in

[1] *Borstal in Nineteen Hundred and Nineteen*, p. 3
[2] *P. C. Report*, 1913–14, Pt. II, p. 107
[3] Gladstone Committee, para. 84; and *P. C. Report*, 1906–07, p. 24
[4] See pp. 127–8 below.

a position of trust and allowed the healthy and manly recreations indulged in by [his] fellow-creatures in free life'.[1] Punishment was mainly by loss of marks.[2] The effort needed to attain the privileges was said to 'create a wonderful spirit of emulation' among the inmates.[3] The psychological idea behind the cure was one of conditioned-response: that the boy should learn that he could only gain the rewards at the end of the 'very severe ordeal which the Grade system entails'[4] by behaving well. In practice the resulting process looks very much as if it were founded on a theory of deterrence, and it was, in so far as it acted at the crude level of the pleasure-pain principle. Although it is very difficult to distinguish between aim and method, there was still a very tenuous distinction between the method, which was to inflict unpleasantness in order to stimulate good conduct, and the aim, which was to develop 'character' and teach boys to obey orders and recognize the 'right side' of life.

The revelations of Lieutenant-Colonel Rich, Governor of Borstal between 1919 and 1922, give a vivid description of the discipline employed. He wrote that when he arrived at Borstal the punishment cells were full, but that he soon brought order. He would stand no 'boorish-impoliteness' from the boys: 'In order to stuff into the heads of my lads some elementary notions of politeness I had them brought under strict military discipline. I impressed upon them, for instance, that when addressing an officer it was their duty to stand to attention, salute and call him "sir".' He considered that 'one wholesome thing from the beginning was the uniformed officer. The uniform kept it constantly before the lad that he was in a penal establishment, and not merely in a "home".'[5] No wonder the B.A. complained that borstal was not developing away from

---

[1] P. C. Report, 1910–11, p. 24

[2] Other punishments were close confinement in a cell and dietary punishments. Corporal punishment could only be awarded for an attack on the staff. The Governor of Borstal at one stage asked for this power so that 'we could treat these inmates as masters of Public Schools treat our sons.' P. C. Report, 1913–14, Pt. II, p. 108

[3] Extract from Governor of Borstal's report in P. C. Report, 1902–03, p. 77

[4] P. C. Report, 1910–11, p. 24

[5] Article, 'Bad Boy's Paradise,' by Lt.-Col. C. E. F. Rich, Sunday Dispatch, 17 July 1932

the prison system as the Home Secretary had promised in 1914.[1] It is perhaps significant that a year after Ruggles-Brise retired, Colonel Rich was transferred from Borstal.

But even though strictness was a cardinal principle, efforts were apparently made to influence the prisoner by education and personal exhortation. The Governor, tutors and chaplain were particularly involved in trying to instil moral ideals. The special-grade boys were allowed to associate in the schoolroom for chess, draughts and spelling games; they were not allowed to talk on other subjects. The Governor gave them 'lectures and addresses in the school room on subjects calculated to convey wholesome moral lessons to them'.[2] The chaplain in particular played a large part, for it was definitely considered that the criminal was a sinner, and a change of heart must come through a recognition of Christian virtue.

Although education was provided for the illiterate,[3] much of the educative influence in the early days came from lectures intended to impress the listeners. As an example of the sort of lecture considered desirable the chaplain inspector wrote:

A young barrister lectured . . . on 'The wonders of the deep sea'. I had not thought this title promising, but the lecturer so handled his subject that he quickly had his audience listening to him with eyes and mouth wide open. He wound up with a brief and telling 'moral' and sent all the lads, I am certain, back to their cells with thoughts directed into new and wholesome channels. One or two, I fancy, had caught a glimpse of 'The light that never was on sea or land'.[4]

An attempt was, however, also made to make the personal influence of the staff an important factor in training. The

[1] For a discussion of this correspondence, see pp. 171–2 below.

[2] P. C. Report, 1902–03, pp. 78–9. In the early days at Dartmoor, boys were given Roman history for moral instruction. See Russell and Rigby, op. cit., p. 123.

[3] In 1910, the Kent Higher Education Committee provided two teachers for four evenings a week at borstal. Reported in The Times, 29 April 1910

[4] P. C. Report, 1908–09, p. 39. This referred to a class of juvenile-adults in Pentonville, but is a good illustration of the contemporary view on the value of lectures. See also Chaplain of Feltham's Report, P. C. Report, 1913–14, Pt. II, p. 112.

Prison Commission stated that 'the personal element is the essential'.[1] Sir Evelyn wrote:

> But of all the human factors making for reformation, the greatest is the personal influence of good and manly men . . . It is on this factor, therefore, that next to religion, the State places its reliance . . . the whole of the staff . . . should be chosen as men of strong and superior character, men . . . who take a keen personal interest in the training and rehabilitation of those placed in their charge. And every member of these staffs, from the highest down to the last joined, is expected to take, and does take, his part in the actual work of influencing and forming character, by watching the inmates under his charge, getting to know something about their lives and their surroundings; and while always maintaining firm control, speaking kindly words of help and advice and encouragement from time to time when suitable opportunities occur.[2]

The expansion and application of this principle was eventually to change the whole emphasis of the system. In 1919 a most important innovation was made. The schoolmasters were supplemented by 'tutors' who were given the rank of Deputy Governors and placed in charge of sections or wings of inmates. They were particularly charged to 'individualize' the boy, to observe him closely and be his friend and counsellor. Men were selected for their special qualifications in this sort of work, but they were also expected to be an 'adjutant to the Governor in maintaining a strict discipline, and a due observance of order and method in every particular'.[3] Although this was the first stage of the development of the 'House system' along public-school lines, the custodial and disciplinary aspects of the system were still being emphasized when Ruggles-Brise retired in 1921.

By the time that Ruggles-Brise retired, little progress had

---

[1] *P. C. Report*, 1909–10, p. 10. See also *Borstal in Nineteen Hundred and Twelve*, p. 9, suggesting that officers need 'such character as will radiate a constant and strong influence'.

[2] Quoted in *B. A. Annual Report*, 1914, pp. 6–7. See also *The English Prison System*, p. 99.

[3] *The English Prison System*, p. 98. See also the report that due to the changes 'a remarkable improvement in tone has already resulted', *P. C. Report*, 1919–20, p. 11.

been made on the lines of the first principle he had laid down twenty years earlier, that of strict classification. Within the institutions great care was taken to avoid contamination through the separation of different 'grades', but there was no system of classifying boys of different types to different institutions. In any case, until 1921, when Portland Prison was opened as a borstal, there were only two institutions.[1] In these circumstances only very limited classification between the wings of each institution could be carried out. All that could be done was for the Commissioners to lay down what types of offenders they were willing to admit. As the statute made it necessary for any court before passing sentence to receive a report from the Commissioners on the suitability of the offender for training, it was easy for them to exclude certain classes of offenders as unsuitable. Physically and mentally handicapped boys were excluded.[2] As Hobhouse and Brockway pointed out in their Prison Enquiry, these boys were often among those who most needed institutional treatment, but with only two institutions they would have been an embarrassment to the administrators. It would have been impossible to maintain a regime based on strict discipline and uniform treatment. There is no evidence to suggest that the boys allotted to either institution differed in any particular way; indeed the allocation had to be made on the governor's recommendation at the local prison, which must have made any classification almost impossible.

The slow progress, especially after the war, had not been received with equanimity throughout the borstal service. The B.A. visitors noted the prison character of borstal. In the institutions some boys were only working as little as twenty-four or twenty hours a week[3]—boys came out 'slacker in that important habit of work than they went in'.[4] They called for an eight-hour working day as an essential part of training. Mr Ellis, a superintendent of a Jewish approved school, provided

---

[1] Borstal and Feltham. Plans to open Lewes in 1914 had been stopped by the war.

[2] See pp. 30–1 above and relevant notes.

[3] For further comments on B.A. criticisms see pp. 171–2 below.

[4] Quote from a letter from the B.A. to Ruggles-Brise dated 4 November 1920. See *B. A. Minutes*, November 1920.

a complete condemnation, stating that officers should not be dressed as warders, borstals were too large, officers were of the military type and so unsuited for the work, supervision was too close and detailed in early stages, trade instruction was hopeless —'a lad who spends two years in the bootmaker's shop would scarcely be fit to take up a repairer's job in a remote country village'—a psychologist was needed, and lastly that it was clear the Prison Commissioners were not the proper persons to run borstal.[1] While Sir Evelyn still described the inmates as 'young hooligans advanced in crime', the B.A. insisted that 'few are criminals or hardened. Most of them have suffered from the failings of others.'[2] By 1920 they were described as 'boys . . . of spirit whose lives are poor and dull and street bound'.[3] It was this attitude which was behind the developments under Paterson from 1922 onwards.[4]

*New Ideals*

In 1921, the new Chairman of the Commission, Sir Maurice Waller,[5] wrote of the need to link industrial training more closely with the requirements of the outside world, to segregate offenders of different precocity and temperament into different institutions, and most important to 'arouse intelligence and the sense of responsibility by the gradual extension of trust, partial liberty and limited forms of self-government'.[6] A wind of change was blowing strongly in the direction of borstal.

The following year, Waller appointed Alexander Paterson as Commissioner with special responsibility for borstal. Paterson has been described as a 'missionary'. He brought to his tasks not only an enormous reforming zeal but also a very wide experience of working-class life. At the age of 21, after graduating at Oxford, he went to live at the Oxford Medical

[1] *B. A. Minutes*, January 1921
[2] *B. A. Annual Report*, 1915, p. 16; also *Annual Report*, 1919, p. 11
[3] *Borstal in Nineteen Hundred and Twenty*, p. 5
[4] This is not perhaps surprising. Alexander Paterson had for some years both before and after the war been active in the Association as Assistant Honorary Director. See also pp. 171–2 below.
[5] He retired in 1927, and was succeeded by Sir Alexander Maxwell.
[6] M. L. Waller, 'New Points in the Borstal System,' *The Magistrate*, Vol. I, No. 1 (1921), p. 8

Mission in Bermondsey where he developed the Oxford and Bermondsey Club for boys. For twenty years between 1906 and 1926 he lived in one of the worst slum tenements in East London and there he had opportunity enough to study the sort of environment from which many borstal boys came.[1]

Alexander Paterson was the man whose conviction and initiative were immediately to change the spirit of borstal training and inspire the bold experiments of the thirties. He was convinced that the military style of discipline would have no permanent effect on delinquent adolescents and that the system should move only towards methods of instilling in the boys a sense of self-discipline. In a now famous passage he wrote:

At the back and at the bottom of this Borstal System of training there lies a fundamental principle. There have always been bad lads and the supply will never cease entirely. Once upon a time the method employed to deal with them consisted simply in the use of force. The lad was regarded as a lump of hard material, yielding only to the hammer, and was, with every good intention, beaten into shape. Sometimes there were internal injuries, and the spirit of the lad grew into the wrong shape, for sometimes the use of force produces a reaction more anti-social than the original condition. There ensues a second method which has flourished for fifty years in many schools and places where boys are trained, and might be termed the method of pressure. The lad is treated as though he were a lump of putty, and an effort is made to reduce him to a certain uniform shape by the gentle and continuous pressure of authority from without . . . In course of time, by perpetual repetition, he forms a habit of moving smartly, keeping himself clean, obeying orders and behaving with all decorum in the presence of his betters. They are in themselves very useful qualities, and it is hoped by those who use this system that, after some years of constant admonition and daily habit, all lads will retain the same pleasing shape when no longer subject to the pressure of those in authority. But the springs of action lie deeper than the laws of habit or the voice of the mentor are likely to reach, and character is determined ultimately not by the outside shape that has been fashioned, but by powers within that possibly have not been touched. It happens, therefore, sadly often that the lad who has been merely subjected to the

[1] See Gordon Hawkins, *Alec Paterson: An Appreciation*. Private circulation.

pressure of authority from outside will, when exposed to different influences of free life, assume quite another shape. In other words having been treated like a lump of putty, he will behave like a lump of putty and respond successively to the influences of each environment.

The third and most difficult way of training a lad is to regard him as a living organism, having its secret of life and motive power within, adapting itself in external conduct to the surroundings of the moment, but undergoing no permanent organic change merely as a result of outside pressure. So does Borstal look at him, as a lad of many mixtures, with a life and character of his own. The task is not to break or knead him into shape, but to stimulate some power within to regulate conduct aright, to insinuate a preference for the good and clean, to make him want to use his life well so that he himself and not others will save him from waste.[1]

Hobhouse and Brockway had argued that boys were 'in rebellion against restrictions which choked the life in them' and that it was self-discipline which the boy needed most rather than mechanical obedience.[2] It was this principle that Paterson sought to make the basis of the system.

Paterson considered that much crime was due to boys being shut off from the wholesome amusements and interests available to more fortunate children. Furthermore, he regarded much crime as akin to the boyish misbehaviour which among the middle classes would never be dealt with by court action.[3] He believed that a great deal of delinquency could be reduced by good housing, education and regular employment.[4] In particular, he was distressed by the effect of unemployment and the consequent 'street corner society' on the morale of the young:

> Material which could have been shaped into good men has now softened, mildew and poison have invaded the system. Each new recruit to the group, drawn there in the first week of unemployment because the only company for the workless lad

---

[1] S. K. Ruck (ed.), *Paterson on Prisons* (1951), p. 97
[2] *English Prisons Today*, pp. 416–18
[3] The descriptions of the boys in the B.A. handbook *Borstal in Nineteen Hundred and Twenty* clearly illustrate this point of view: 'Unhappily, whilst others bird-nested or trespassed on not unfriendly orchards, these youngsters ran up against something much less open to explanation or apology,' p. 3.
[4] See S. K. Ruck, *Paterson on Prisons*, p. 58.

during the daytime is bad company, swallows his inhibitions with his pride, yields to the lower tone he finds there, and becomes accustomed to idleness. A lodging house takes the place of home, and standards of conduct grow daily less distinct. Such is the soil from which spring the great majority of young criminals.[1]

But it was not unemployment alone that was at fault. The boy could resist the evil temptations with the aid of self-discipline. 'A weakness of inhibition, arising from lack of early training at home, is contrasted with a desire for those things they have neither the patience nor the opportunity to earn, and emphasized by surroundings which do not exercise their vitality or give any scope for their capacity.'[2] Training, therefore, was conceived as an attempt to strengthen inhibitions by teaching self-discipline and appealing to the 'goodwill' of the boy. This approach rested on the liberal philosophy of non-determinism: not only that all are entirely responsible for their actions (unless insane), but that all are aware of the value of good (that is, socially approved) actions and of the wrong of criminal action, and are able to make a choice between them. The circumstances from which the criminal had come were admittedly unpleasant, but his desire to commit crime could have been controlled by self-discipline. This assumption rested on the belief that unconscious motivation was rare in crime,[3] that each boy 'at heart' wanted to act right and that only his irresponsibility through lack of a consciously controlled will-power stopped him from doing so. If these boys had been 'born under a happier star they might have been among the best'.[4] Paterson was, in fact, a great believer in the good in every 'British lad'. He wrote in 1925 that 'Borstal training is based on the double assumption that there is individual good in each, and among nearly all an innate corporate spirit which

---

[1] *The Principles of the Borstal System*, pp. 5–6

[2] ibid., p. 6. See also Cyril Burt, *The Young Delinquent* (1925), which emphasized the effects of in-discipline and unemployment.

[3] The Medical Officer of Borstal commenting on psycho-analysis stated: 'It is only a very small proportion of cases which require an investigation of the subconscious mind to get at the real causes of crime. My experience in examining some hundreds of these lads has been that conduct is very largely influenced by the dominant desires of the moment.' *P. C. Report*, 1922–23, p. 70

[4] See *Borstal in Nineteen Hundred and Twenty*, p. 5.

will respond to the appeal made to the British of every sort to play the game, to follow the flag, to stand by the old ship'.[1]

This quotation shows clearly what type of attitudes the system aimed at producing. The fundamental aim of the system had not changed since the time of Ruggles-Brise: the boy was still to be trained to be a normal conforming member of decent working-class society.[2] The middle-class conception of the good working man was one who accepted his position with good grace and, if he were a skilled man, perhaps with some pride. The twenties were years of unemployment and industrial bitterness but, despite the growth of the working-class political movement, they did not bring any great changes in the social structure. The lack of educational opportunity, the relatively low wage levels, and unemployment meant that the majority of the working class had few possibilities for a rise in their social and material welfare. The idea of 'service' from the working class was firmly entrenched in the minds of the *bourgeoisie*. Paterson, writing a New Year letter to borstal boys, said 'work is sometimes a bit monotonous, but to work for others is never dull . . . that we shall so learn to become masters of ourselves that we may be fit to be the servants of others'.[3] Presumably there was something wrong and selfish in just working for a living as an end in itself. Paterson went so far as to say 'it becomes necessary . . . to infect him with some idea of life which will germinate and produce a character, controlling desire and shaping conduct to some more glorious end than

[1] Article, 'Borstal Lads,' *The Times*, 4 August 1925; also report on 12 July 1930

[2] An interesting example of the values taught to boys is seen in the attitude towards trade unions. In the first issue of *The Borstalian* (Rochester's magazine, later called *Phoenix*) boys were warned by an anonymous writer 'to give trade unionism a wide berth, for it will be the worker's ruin and a curse to the country' (*Borstalian*, Vol. 1, No. 1, July 1923). In the same year (1923), the Borstal Association commented on two young married ex-inmates from Bolton who had marched with the unemployed on London, and expressed satisfaction that they were 'thoroughly dissatisfied with their organization which had led them false hopes and left them adrift' (*B. A. Minutes*, January 1923). Trade unions were perhaps not in favour with those who stressed 'service', 'playing the game' and individual responsibility.

[3] Quoted in Sydney A. Moseley, op. cit., pp. 77–8

mere satisfaction or acquisition'.[1] In these circumstances, those who were responsible for training deviant members of the working class emphasized those elements in which they might have pride—hard work, skill, honesty and patriotism.

Hard work remained as an important element of the system,[2] but in order to encourage the change in the delinquent —through self-discipline—new elements were added to the training regime. The staff of the institutions gave up their uniforms for plain clothes; matrons were appointed; the institutions were organized into 'houses' along public-school lines; new men were brought in from the universities and public schools to be housemasters; the regime gave the boy more scope to exercise his responsibility; outside activities were encouraged, and the educational element was broadened beyond the basic learning of the three R's. Despite the 'liberal-izing' of the regime there was no intention to 'pet or pamper' the inmates. As the Home Secretary said: 'We do not give them a moment in which to get into mischief or to be idle.'[3] The emphasis was still upon discipline and the learning of 'general morality', but the methods had been changed. The staff and the house system became a dynamic element in the effort to change criminal ways.

Previously, the work of 'tutors' and chaplains had been directed towards 'moral exhortations', but now the personal example of the staff and the team spirit of inter-house rivalry were used as a dynamic element in effecting attitude change.[4]

The house system was instituted with three main aims: (i) to get smaller groups for more individualization; (ii) to make the task of house monitor more possible of fulfilment by an average boy, that is to increase the opportunities to exercise responsibility; and (iii) to encourage the *esprit de corps* of small groups. Each institution was to have four houses, each with 'its

---

[1] *Paterson on Prisons*, op. cit., p. 97. See also Alexander Paterson, *Across the Bridges* (1911), p. 171.

[2] Developments on the work side of training are discussed below. See pp. 124–6ff.

[3] Quoted in an article, 'Borstal *is* a Success,' *Daily Mail*, 7 May 1929

[4] 'Inter-house rivalry, coupled with the influence of housemasters, is one of the main factors on which we rely to develop the right spirit.' *P. C. Report*, 1922–23, p. 29

own measure of self-government'.[1] The houses enabled a system of monitors and prefects to be developed who could have minor responsibilities: 'The responsibilities they carry have a good effect upon them, and they rise to it, as a rule, in much the same way as happens at public schools.'[2]

Paterson believed the success of the house system rested upon securing the right kind of staff. He wrote: 'The Borstal system has no merit apart from the Borstal staff. It is men and not buildings who will change the hearts and the ways of misguided lads. The foundations of the Borstal system are first the recruitment of the right men.'[3] The advertisement in *The Times* for housemasters asked for men 'of sound general education, able to hold their own with all ranks'.[4] Paterson used his contacts with the universities to recruit staff, and was highly successful. Gordon Hawkins suggests that Paterson's unique contribution was not so much in making changes but 'in finding and inspiring the men through whom the change was to work'. 'It is true,' Hawkins says, 'that he was instrumental in recruiting into the newly created grade of Borstal Housemaster many who would perhaps otherwise have not joined the Prison Service and whom he infused with something of his own ardour and enthusiasm.'[5] By 1928, 'the staff [had] been replenished from the public schools and the universities with men of character and education'.[6] At the officer level, too, attempts were probably made to try to meet the earlier criticisms of the B.A. that the subordinate staff 'should not be of the same class and outlook as inmates as is at present frequently the case'.[7]

The institutions wanted to turn out a strong dependable type with the public-school man's sense of honour and loyalty, and the means to achieve this was by a transference of standards and conduct from the housemasters into the group: 'He has to

[1] Circular issued by the Commissioners, 18 December 1922, urging the adoption of the house system
[2] *P. C. Report*, 1921–22, p. 21
[3] *The Principles*, p. 17. See also Fox, *The Modern English Prison*, p. 182, 'The greatest care is therefore taken to select men of the right type with a definite vocation for work of this sort'.
[4] *The Times*, 3 January 1923          [5] Gordon Hawkins, op. cit., p. 19
[6] *The Times*, 11 August 1928
[7] In the memorandum from Grant-Wilson to Waller dated 21 November 1921. See *B. A. Minutes*, 1921.

be with his lads early and late, sharing in and guiding all their pursuits, and making himself a leader of thought and action in every direction.'[1] The housemaster was to act as 'father-substitute' and adviser, but above all he was to stand as an example of upright and good living. As one observer remarked, the men were from 'the well-to-do class quietly showing that a gentleman can do what is asked of him'. He was greatly impressed by 'the quiet example of good men who are manly, gentle without being weak, tolerant without being uncertain'.[2] These new officers were 'introducing public school ideals',[3] infusing in their charges that *esprit de corps* and thought for others which they themselves learnt on the slopes of The Hill or the playing fields of Eton';[4] they were, in particular, 'imbued in a special degree with the spirit of playing the game'.[5]

The disciplinary staff were also encouraged to drop the symbol of the prison past—their uniform. In the summer of 1923, officers at Feltham began to wear plain clothes at week-ends and although the staff at Portland, dealing with the tougher element, hesitated for a time prison uniform was completely dropped in 1924. The Commissioners were pleased to report that discipline had not suffered and that with officers now appearing 'more like masters in a school', the change would help 'to promote the real spirit of a training school'.[6]

The attempt to transport middle-class social values to working-class youth was implicit in the house system. The Home Secretary hoped that boys would leave the institution 'having gained in the sense of honour which is the proud possession of our public school boys'.[7] The system had, in fact, assumed that the public-school man's sense of values would naturally commend themselves to the group, and that through the pressures of the group the values would be reinforced. The 'good' in every lad would recognize the inherent superiority of

---

[1] *P. C. Report*, 1923–24, pp. 23–4
[2] See 'Impressions of Borstal,' a series of reports on lectures delivered by A. C. L. Morrison, Chief Clerk of the Metropolitan Juvenile Courts, *Justice of the Peace*, Vol. 95, 31 May 1930, p. 351.
[3] According to the Governor of Portland. See *P. C. Report*, 1922–23, p. 72.
[4] See article in the *Daily Mail*, 5 November 1928.
[5] *Report of Prison Officers' Pay Committee* (Cmd. 1959), 1923, p. 15
[6] *P. C. Report*, 1922–23, p. 25
[7] Reported in *The Times*, 29 April 1925

the housemaster's beliefs and actions; the 'innate corporate spirit' would 'play the game'. The inmates were not, however, asked to be middle class themselves; they were exhorted to fulfil the *bourgeois* image of the 'honest workman'. The Governor of Rochester in the first issue of the institution's magazine *The Borstalian* reminded the boys of the importance of being satisfied with their position in society:

> Without being angels we can all be sportsmen . . . it means someone who can be depended upon to play the game, to own up when he is in the wrong, to take his punishment like a man, and to play for his side and not for himself. My advice to you all is then, be sportsmen, play the game, and when you owe pay to the last farthing . . . Whatever work or game you take up can be performed or played to the best of your ability . . . It's no use asking a carthorse to win the Derby, but he can win a ploughing match with equal credit. So realise your own limitations and don't set out to equal those whose lives lead to higher spheres than those of your own . . .[1]

Although religious conversion was no longer the only means of reform, it was certainly not pushed into the background.[2] The first housemasters were the chaplains of the institutions, and religion was undoubtedly the inspiration of many who saw this work as a vocation. Among the influential, religion was still seen as 'the first line of defence against crime—which after all is sin in another form'.[3] To the need for religion had been added the need for social responsibility.

To fit into the plan, education was given a wider meaning. Games-playing on an inter-house basis became an integral part of 'character-building'.[4] But beyond this boys were encouraged to pursue 'cultural' activities—'to discover and develop a love

[1] *The Borstalian*, Vol. I, No. 1, July 1923. It is possible, however, that this was the purely personal attitude of Colonel Rich.

[2] The Home Secretary, in appealing for a new chapel at Rochester, said: 'Perhaps few outside the staffs and visiting committees can appreciate fully the influence which religion exercises in the lives of these small communities.' *The Times*, 18 November 1929

[3] The Home Secretary, reported in *The Times*, 24 January 1925

[4] *The Times* in a leading article, 'Fruits of the Borstal System,' 16 October 1923, stated: 'As might be expected of a former captain of the Eton Eleven, Sir Evelyn Ruggles-Brise has made the playing of cricket and other games an integral part of his system.' Under the house system, games assumed an even more prominent role.

for music or letters, an interest in flowers or animals or stamps, is to foster the growth of something good, which will occupy the stage of interest in a lad's life, and oust the idle and unclean things that formerly held possession'.[1] Middle-class values of good literature were impressed on the boys—'a lad whose attention has never been captured by anything better than the romances of Sexton Blake should be introduced to Sherlock Holmes. It is but a step from Conan Doyle to Seton Merriman, and in a little while he would bridge another little gulf and reach Stevenson. Here we can leave him securely entrenched in the field of good English literature. He will not easily return to the drivel that once enslaved him.'[2] Adventures in *Treasure Island* and *Kidnapped* were supposedly good for the mind!

### The Beginning of Classification

In 1920, a 'reception class' was opened at Feltham. The main concern of this class was to make a 'mental diagnosis' in order to separate out cases of unstable or retarded mentality; but beyond this, an attempt was also made to assess general capacity for education and training.[3]

Early in 1922 a special reception centre was opened at Wandsworth where the staff consisted of the Governor, an experienced medical officer and assistant, and a small staff of voluntary women social workers. The medical staff made a physical, temperamental and emotional study of each boy. Psychological and intelligence tests were administered in 'a thorough and tactful examination in order to find out the primary cause of wrong-doing'.[4] The permanent staff was increasingly aided by the voluntary visitors who collected information about previous careers, parents and home surroundings. These women social workers made personal contact with every boy, and with his home if he were a Londoner. Mrs Le Mesurier tells how the role of the woman social worker developed from a prison visitor into social caseworker collecting information on the boy's background and difficulties and helping in his preparation for training.[5] This information was not

[1] *Paterson on Prisons*, op. cit., p. 114     [2] ibid., p. 116
[3] *P. C. Report*, 1921–22, p. 20     [4] *P. C. Report*, 1922–23, pp. 29 and 45
[5] Mrs Le Mesurier, *Boys in Trouble* (2nd Ed.), 1939, pp. 94–5

only relevant to the allocation of boys to different institutions but also provided data which could 'set on foot and maintain a scientific study of these young offenders',[1] thus providing a 'great fund of material for research'.[2]

The centre soon became of great importance in helping to diagnose the difficulties of particular cases. But although much evidence was gathered on the boys' backgrounds, most of it probably had little influence in deciding their destination. The prime consideration was to segregate the more hardened offenders from the less criminally mature:

> Lads who have not been in prison . . . and those whose lives have hitherto been spent at home, are sent to Feltham, where also the mentally backward and unstable are received. At the other end of the scale, Portland receives those who have failed to profit by training in the industrial or Reformatory Schools and have already been for a prolonged period away from home surroundings. Those whose history does not qualify them definitely for either Feltham or Portland go to Borstal—a kind of middle class. A slight corresponding difference is noted in the tone of the institutions . . . but little difference as regards the success of their training.[3]

It can be seen that despite all the sympathetic research carried on at Wandsworth, allocation rested more on an assessment of the degree of criminality than on personal 'treatment needs'. However, the process of examination and allocation gave rise to the impression that the borstal system was aimed at 'individualization' of treatment.

While it is true that the information could have been used by the housemaster for giving advice, the regimes at the borstals at this time did not differ appreciably enough to make classification by training needs the most important consideration. Nevertheless, things were changing; the Commissioners decided to relax their rules and allow the physically and mentally handicapped to be sentenced to borstals. They were segregated and trained along with the more hopeful offenders at Feltham

---

[1] *P. C. Report*, 1923–24, pp. 23 and 26

[2] Paterson was anxious that research also should make a contribution to the improvements in training. See the Foreword to Le Mesurier, ibid., p. xiii.

[3] *P. C. Report*, 1923–24, p. 26

in a less arduous regime than that provided for the tougher offenders at Rochester and Portland. Here was the beginning of the development in training different types of offenders in different regimes, each suited to the particular needs of the group. And yet at this time, the group of physically and mentally handicapped proved a continual embarrassment to the authorities at Feltham. They tended to upset the routine of the institution and the sense of justice. It was difficult to deal with a problem group without upsetting the morale of the other inmates who wanted equal consideration. From the point of view of the backward boy himself the continual frustration at being branded as a problem or even as a 'looney' may well have made things more difficult. It was soon realized that a separate institution was needed for the proper training of these boys,[1] but at that time the general increase in the borstal population had caused overcrowding to become so acute that a new institution was more necessary for more general needs.

*Growth of the Open System*

Despite these innovations, strong and rigid discipline still had firm roots in the institutions. Although the rigid progressive grade system was somewhat modified to allow greater freedom in progress through the institutions the overcrowding militated against the developments implicit in the desire to promote the growth of self-discipline and the sense of responsibility. The interest in the appeal for a new institution lay less in the problem of easing overcrowding than in the desire for a new place in which the new philosophy of training could be put into practice. The Home Secretary said he must have a new borstal in place of an old prison, with new ideas, new ideals, new work and new hopes.[2] If the need had been only to ease the population problem or to increase possibilities for classification an old prison could have been converted.

The idea of leading a boy up to the point where he could be given a position of responsibility and increased freedom had been practised only to a very limited extent during the late years of the Ruggles-Brise era. The grade system had in-

---

[1] *P. C. Report*, 1924–25, p. 56        [2] *The Times*, 12 January 1926

corporated three rigid grades through which the inmate had to progress before he could earn his release: each grade was reached after a certain fixed period if progress was normal. The new administration was anxious to try boys in conditions of comparative freedom before they were released so that some idea could be gained of their response to a position of trust. When summer camps were started in 1922 for boys about to be released, faith was expressed in their ability to take this responsibility. A camp 'invigorated and cheered those who took part in it, and it inspired those who were left behind to earn a similar privilege'.[1] They were intended for 'boys who have proved trustworthy and shown appreciation of the spirit in which the institutions are conducted'.[2] The camps became a 'test of the reliance which can be placed on the individual's word of honour'.[3] It was the first positive proof that the new ideals of Paterson were a practicable and valuable method of training. Despite considerable prominence given to the escape of six boys from the second Feltham camp,[4] it was recognized that the object of camp was 'to train these lads to be fit for freedom'. Such training for freedom could not be 'completely done in captivity', and the camp provided a suitable 'test of the lad's progress and a taste of what lies before him'.[5] In the first few years the Commissioners did not finance these camps themselves but appealed through the columns of *The Times* for charitable donations. They appeared to consider that such 'extras' to the borstal curriculum should not be recognized as part of the financial obligation of the system. Not until camps

[1] *P. C. Report*, 1922–23, pp. 30–1

[2] *The Times*, 2 June 1923. In a comment on the camps it was noted that there had been 'happy faces . . . no bitterness, quiet friendliness with the staff . . . lessons of independence and self-reliance which . . . Borstal Institutions teach them', *The Times*, 16 August 1923.

[3] *P. C. Report*, 1924–25, commenting on Portland's first camp in 1924, p. 56. Others stressed the importance of camps. See letter from Joynson-Hicks in the *Justice of the Peace*, Vol. 89, No. 26, 27 June 1925, p. 386, in which he stated 'an essential part of Borstal training should be the development of personal initiative and of a sense of responsibility under conditions of comparative freedom'. The *Howard Journal* in a note on borstals in Vol. 1, No. 4 stated that it hoped the 'training for liberty' given by the summer camps would aid towards better success for the system, p. 208.

[4] *The Times*, 4 September 1923

[5] In an appeal for funds in *The Times*, 4 June 1924

came to be seen as a necessary and highly useful adjunct to training did they finance them out of public funds.

Since early in the twenties boys had been working outside the walls of the borstals for the best part of the day—in 1925 the Governor of Rochester could report that 75 per cent of his boys were working outside the walls[1]—but this was merely supervised work. The concept of progressive responsibility was to be extended to one of 'training for freedom'. Boys were to be placed in a situation from the beginning of their sentence where self-discipline was necessary to keep the rules of the institution— or even to keep in the institution! It was accepted that the new institution could be a completely open building.

The placing of young adult recidivists in open institutions was certainly a revolutionary move in English penological history. It was, however, undertaken both tentatively and with a number of important reservations. In the first place, only those boys who had relatively good records were to be sent to the new borstal at Lowdham; it is significant that the first party which marched from Feltham were selected cases who had done well in the early stages of training.[2] Originally, of course, the number of places available was only a very small proportion of the total in borstals and so it was natural that the Commissioners should select their most hopeful inmates for this type of training. But also the Commissioners felt that only those who had shown some ability to discipline themselves should be chosen. Paterson wrote that there was a 'prior consideration of great moment to be faced, in deciding whether the young offender will consent to stay in the freedom of the camp, and so give us a chance of training him. It is impossible to educate an absentee.'[3] Classification therefore became one stage more refined; boys had to be selected on the basis of their suitability for a particular type of training. Besides this selection, there lay another important factor, and that was the concern of the Commissioners for the goodwill of the public living in the

[1] *P. C. Report*, 1925–26, p. 52

[2] The 'march' from Feltham to Lowdham was such a matter of faith that it has become one of the most important landmarks in the official histories of borstal, in fact something of a legend. See, for example, T. L. Iremonger, *Disturbers of the Peace* (1962), pp. 80–4.

[3] In the Foreword of Le Mesurier's *Boys in Trouble*, pp. xiv–xv

neighbourhood of the institution. This concern was based on two related points. Firstly, if the system was to be extended, public anxiety had to be avoided; strong objections would be raised against open institutions if the inmates did not respect local property. Secondly, the sympathy and help of the local community was needed if the full benefits of an open institution were to be reaped. The object of the open borstal was not just to abolish external constraint and the prison atmosphere, but to establish ideal conditions in which the inmate could be properly prepared for his life in the community. One of the main new elements which the open system could introduce was a contact with the local community that would ease the feelings of social isolation which are part of the more usual institutional environment.[1]

The Commissioners were successful in their efforts to enlist local sympathy,[2] and the great success of the relations with local communities formed a valuable basis for further developments in open methods.

The new institution was built by inmate labour with the help of craftsmen, and several important lessons were learned during these first years. The pioneering spirit of the institution proved to be a great stimulus to industry and interest; a new payment scheme related to efficiency produced a more realistic attitude towards the value of doing a hard day's work; the increase in the amount of personal guidance which could be given by housemasters working alongside the boys proved to be an important influence to the good. Perhaps Governor W. W. Llewellin was right when he wrote of the 'sense of honour and loyalty inherent in every British boy'.[3] Perhaps this was a true assessment of the young adult offender of the thirties. For the great majority of those put 'on trust' did not abuse it. But there were other factors in the new institutional situation which made for success. Great stress was put upon the privilege of being sent to an open borstal; the nature of the alternative for those who would not behave was emphasized; the stimulus of

---

[1] A gift of £10,000 made by William Morris in 1927 had already made it possible for poor parents to visit their sons in the institutions.

[2] W. W. Llewellin, 'Lowdham Grange—A Borstal Experiment,' *Howard Journal*, Vol. 3, No. 4 (1933), p. 36

[3] ibid., pp. 36–8

working on a new project could be contrasted to the dull routine of the other institutions; and the exclusion of contaminating influences in the classification process made it easier for the staff to direct the values of the institution. Indeed, in a new community with no powerful inmate group traditions the housemasters were in a particularly strong position to establish their own values in the groups under their charge. Lowdham most certainly embodied many factors which would have made any new institution a success. This did not mean that the Commissioners thought Lowdham suitable for all sorts of borstal boys; they were aware of its special advantages.[1] But while recognizing the need to separate those boys needing sterner discipline, they were persuaded that for the majority of cases open institutions could *per se* yield better results.

A visit to the United States in 1931 convinced Paterson of the value of open camps[2] and led to the revival of an old scheme first considered when Ruggles-Brise was Chairman.[3] North Sea Camp was established on the edge of the Wash in 1934 and the boys were set to work on the salt-marshes in 'a determined effort to reclaim some valuable land'.[4] At this institution the belief in the value of personal contact in influencing the boys to imitate the conduct of the housemaster was put fully into practice. The camp, consisting first of tents and later of huts, had no disciplinary officers, but there was one housemaster to every fifteen boys working alongside them in their heavy work, eating with them and sharing their accommodation. The aim was to stimulate emulation among the inmates of a staff who would prove their 'devotion and their sincerity'.[5] The choice of site was not accidental; it was ideal for providing socially

---

[1] See *B. A. Minutes*, 31 July 1931. A report recognized the advantages of Lowdham due to its having the best kind of inmate, and stated that not all borstal boys could be trusted to respond to this regime.

[2] Benedict S. Alper, in Paul Tappan, *Contemporary Correction* (1951), p. 328

[3] Letter from Alexander Paterson to Sir Evelyn Ruggles-Brise, 2 February 1934. In the hands of the Borstal Division. See also *P. C. Report*, 1913–14, p. 18, and p. 31 above.

[4] See *B. A. Minutes*, 1934.

[5] W. W. Llewellin, 'The North Sea Camp—A Fresh Borstal Experiment,' *Howard Journal*, Vol. 4, No. 2 (1935), p. 252

useful work[1] of a rough labouring type for physically fit boys who would most probably have to take up labouring on their release. The process of improving work habits by forcing regular working hours on the inmates and toughening them to fit them for hard work was still at the basis of the training programme, but the new elements in training were becoming of at least equal importance. The determination to change attitudes by good example and through ethical teaching was seen to be necessary if the boys were to have the strength of character to make use of the work-training which they had received. This was the fundamental difference between the old idea of training and the new. It was at last seen that an enforced habit might not last once the boy had left the institution unless he had changed his attitude towards the value of working hard. The inculcation of an attitude to want to work hard was included in the aims of the new system.

The fact that the next two borstals opened were closed institutions shows that the principle of training in open conditions had as yet only limited applicability. Camp Hill borstal was in an old preventive detention prison and received young boys with bad records, in particular motor-car thieves and likely absconders whose activities could at least be limited to the area of the Isle of Wight. The other borstal, at the old Sherwood Prison, was to accommodate the older and more criminally mature of the population. It was particularly intended to act as an experiment to enable the Commissioners to decide whether they should recommend a rise in the age limit to 23. This institution was tough, the type of building completely militating against the kind of developments which the Commissioners were nominally committed to. The prison was in one block so that 'houses' had to consist of separate landings of cells. Despite efforts made to improve the building, the regime and atmosphere were very different from that at Lowdham and North Sea Camp.

As far as classification was concerned these four new institutions catered for two distinct sections of the borstal population. Both the best and the worst boys had been segregated into

---

[1] Paterson said the camp 'should serve to show the public that their labour can be of considerable value to the community'. Letter to Sir E. Ruggles-Brise, 2 February 1934, op. cit.

separate institutions each with a regime suited to their needs. In fact what this amounted to was that the best boys got all the benefits of the new training ideals; while the worst received a regime which was not so far different from that practised traditionally, and were likely to receive a spell in the severe corrective block at Wandsworth[1] if they were even too tough for Portland.[2] The fact that open training only existed for those boys with a good prognosis is illuminating. Had the Commissioners been convinced of the inherent superiority of the open system they would have opened other camps rather than try to convert an old and unsuitable prison. The belief in the innate trustworthiness of the British lad obviously did not extend to those with bad criminal records. One is drawn to the conclusion that those who were to be trained to be trustworthy were already so, and those who were considered untrustworthy were simply beyond being trusted.

Nevertheless, some of the important additions to the regime in the open borstals were transmitted to the closed. The inmates were allowed more freedom; outside contacts were made wherever possible (although this was more difficult with the old converted institutions because of the long-standing prejudice against them),[3] and the houses became the centre of institutional life. The staff emphasized the need to build a team spirit through which moral influences could be transmitted.[4] Needless to say, it was a different matter to try to impose dominant middle-class attitudes upon a group of the worst delinquents with their own established institutional code.

*Developments in Training Principles*

The new institutions were important too in creating an opportunity to experiment with the time factor in training. Prior to

---

[1] See p. 140 below for further discussion of the corrective block.

[2] The Governor of Portland remarked: 'There must be a small number of "toughs" who need a sterner regime than Portland can give, or who do not realize the advantages of a Borstal institution until they see it from a distance. I should be sorry to see Wandsworth removed from this institution's armoury of methods of persuasion.' *P. C. Report*, 1933, p. 41

[3] Healy and Alper, *Criminal Youth and the Borstal System* (1941), p. 153

[4] However, it seems that there were some staffing problems. In 1930 the B. A. Committee complained of the 'frequent changes of officers, and the

the opening of Lowdham almost all boys who were serving the normal three-years' sentence were not released before two years: at various times it had been stated as an axiom that this period was needed to achieve reform.[1] The new institutional experience gave an opportunity to consider the time needed to train a boy by the new methods. At Lowdham most of the boys were released in well under two years[2] and at North Sea Camp the conditions were such to persuade the Commissioners that fifteen months would be long enough. Once the whole rigid system of grades had been abandoned and the speed with which a boy could earn promotion and release had become more flexible, experimentation with the length of training became possible. Until the opening of the new borstals the Commissioners had been hampered by the need to keep uniformity in the rules and sanctions for the sake of the good morale of the institutions. It was suggested that the licensing of some boys earlier than others was apt to create a sense of unfairness, and to cause embarrassment to the institutional authorities.[3] The new institutions with their homogeneous populations made it easier to bring all the boys together

---

atmosphere of unrest and consequent lack of attention which prevails at the institutions'. See *B. A. Minutes*, 22 January 1930.

[1] A selection of such opinions:

'Less than two years is ineffective; on the other hand if the period is substantially longer, the inmate may lose in initiative and become mechanical,' *Report of the Departmental Committee on the Treatment of Young Offenders*, p. 102.

'Experience shows that the time a lad must serve was at least two years,' Mr T. P. Owens, Governor of Portland, reported in *The Times*, 12 July 1930.

Accounts such as Louis Edward's *Borstal Lives* (1939) and J. W. Gordon's *Borstalians* (1932) show that very few boys stood a chance of early release.

At a later date Mrs Le Mesurier, writing obviously about closed institutions, stated that 'it has been discovered by experiment over a long time that the average boy is not fit to be discharged before at least two years'. *Boys in Trouble*, p. 215

[2] At first it was intended that boys specially selected for Lowdham should be released after one year if they responded to training. Probably few were released this early in practice. *P. C. Report*, 1930, p. 33

[3] *Report of the Departmental Committee on the Treatment of Young Offenders*, p. 103-04

through the same stages to release in a concerted approach to training.[1] It was no longer necessary to worry about the problems of discipline and morale which arose in attempts to deal with offenders of widely differing potentials.

The tutors originally appointed under Ruggles-Brise had as their task the duty of giving elementary education to the backward boys who were then received in the institutions. It was not until 1923 that education began to be seen not only as an aim in itself but also as a means to help in a better adaptation to work and leisure. In that year, following a lead given by institutions in Italy, a small band of selected boys from Rochester had been allowed to visit the local technical college in the evenings to receive some theoretical training in the trade in which they were working at the institution. With the formation of the house groups came organized leisure activity, some of which was specifically aimed at learning trade theory, while other groups were formed to run hobbies or other spare-time activities. Libraries were formed and encouragement given to read, clubs sprang up and magazines were produced.[2] The Commissioners were able to attract men in from outside to help in the teaching and in this way a constructive use was made of the spare time after the end of the working day. The nature of some of the hobbies taught is interesting to note. Rug-making, for example, was seen as a valuable hobby because of its constructive economic value and possible use

[1] Oliver Stanley, the Under-Secretary at the Home Office, stated that by selecting lads they hoped to be able to 'put them back into the world earlier', reported in *The Times*, 18 July 1932. *Report of the Departmental Committee on the Employment of Prisoners:* Part I (Cmd. 4462, 1933), para. 95, stated that in practice early releases were rare at borstals except at Lowdham where a certain number were released after twelve months. Similar experiments followed—Healy and Alper stated that the Governor of Hollesley Bay (1939) was experimenting with a fixed fifteen-month term; see p. 87. Not all opinion, though, was in favour of shorter sentences; Healy and Alper state that Paterson believed that in roughly 20 per cent of the cases a longer period of control than three years was necessary, op. cit. pp. 229–30.

[2] See Louis Edward, *Borstal Lives*, on the place of the magazine. There was a magazine at Rochester and at Portland. Barman considered *The Phoenix*, Rochester's journal, to 'compare favourably with any ordinary average English newspaper', op. cit., p. 47. It can still be consulted in the British Museum.

during periods of unemployment.[1] This type of leisure activity is peculiar to a period when much emphasis was put on the virtue of thriftiness among the working classes. Educational activities were intended both to improve the standard of trade training and aid a boy to a new approach to his leisure time on release.

There were some considerable differences of opinion on how best to effect a change in the moral values of the delinquents. In some quarters the view that religious and ethical teaching was the only means to bring about a permanent change was still held strongly. Barman, in his review of the system in the early thirties, stated that he found it 'very encouraging that the chaplains receive a quick and favourable response from the inmates to their moral teachings'. Among the subjects he lists are: 'moral distinctions between right and wrong, motives good and bad, conflicts of conscience, need of self-control in society, sublimation of animal instincts.'[2] The Governor of North Sea Camp, among others, believed in the value of direct ethical teaching so that the boy would 'be helped to form a philosophy of life which will stand the strain of later difficulties and temptations'.[3] Ethical teaching seemed to follow logically from the assumptions about free will, self-discipline and the existence of 'good in each' on which the training scheme rested. But others, such as the Governor of Feltham, held the view that ethical teaching was useless and that boys would only change for the better through the influence of example and the 'spirit' of the housemaster. He wrote:

> Borstal lads are never impressed by moral principles. Lads have no use for virtue in the abstract, and they will love and follow virtue only when they see it exemplified in something they love and respect. The establishment of tradition depends almost entirely on example and leadership.[4]

---

[1] A list published in the *P. C. Report*, 1937, p. 52, includes stoolmaking, rug-making, basketry, upholstery, woodwork and novelties.

[2] S. Barman, op. cit., p. 47

[3] See *P. C. Report*, 1935, p. 74. The Reports of the Commissioners contain a number of similar opinions. See, for example, the statement of the Governor of Camp Hill: 'Housemasters must spend the major portion of their time in moral instruction—direct or indirect.' *P. C. Report*, 1936, p. 67

[4] *P. C. Report*, 1937, p. 61

Boys might not comprehend 'principles', but, on the other hand, be able to understand and respect the values implicit in the actions of the honest, fair, sympathetic, sporting, authoritarian housemaster, and adapt them to his own life. This latter view was based on a more sociological interpretation of delinquency than that normally accepted at the time: that the boys had come from a sub-culture which had never learned the normally accepted values of the working class and middle classes. If this were true the only means of changing their attitudes was to place them in a new environment where they could learn a new set of values. Both opinions probably held some truth: some boys shared the same standards as the staff, while to others these standards were completely foreign. At the open borstals where the best boys were it was probably more feasible to teach ethical standards. Both methods were used in practice at North Sea Camp; there was the greatest of emphasis on personal example and yet at the same time special classes were given in civics and ethics to those completing their training. The position of the housemaster embodied both guidance and authority: he set the standards for the group to emulate and provided authority for his views through his position as sole assessor of improvements in attitude.

Work still remained the most important single factor in the institutional curriculum. In a sense its importance had been obscured by the other enormous advances made in the training system. But these advances had really been embellishments to the continuing traditional function of the institutions to turn out not only competent but reliable workmen. The eight-hour day remained the lynch-pin of training. But this had not been easy to achieve. By 1923 the Commissioners had claimed that all inmates worked a full day,[1] yet in 1926 Mrs Le Mesurier reported that at Rochester there was full-time work for only 280 of the 320 boys there: this, she complained, 'cuts at the root of keenness and effort'.[2]

Behind the effort to ensure that every boy was used to working full industrial hours was the strongly-held belief that it was the idle hands which committed the crime. It was proposed to make the borstal boy into one of the nation's

[1] *P. C. Report*, 1922–23, p. 29        [2] *B. A. Minutes*, January 1926

reliable workmen, combining the virtues of restraint and sober living on which industrial authority rested. It was not only thought that the frequent job-changer was unstable and insecure and likely to commit crime whilst unemployed, but that he was also anti-social in being unreliable to employers. This was not a symptom of 'mental illness' which they wished to avert so much as the spectacle of the 'able-bodied unemployed' who were disruptive of industrial society and potentially criminal. The 'training for work' principle was founded on the simple assumption that hard work every day would convince a boy of its value. The idea that bad work-habits might be due to emotional problems which would again show themselves in the less secure environment on release appears to have had less support. The emphasis on work still lay mainly in ensuring that the youth could support himself adequately on release, even if the staff of the institution had failed to solve the emotional problems which had formerly affected his ability to settle in employment.

Work in the institutions had not been associated with any rewards other than those given for good conduct until the graded payment scheme was introduced at Lowdham. The earning of money then controlled to some extent the standard of life of the inmate—it determined his tobacco consumption and ability to partake in many of the institutional clubs to which there was a subscription. Although this can hardly be regarded as an instrument to demonstrate the association between working hard and living an honest life, it was a great incentive to harder work. As the Governor of Sherwood reported: 'There is not the slightest doubt that practically every man puts more effort into his work as a result of this [payment] scheme.'[1] The Commissioners hoped that this habit of hard work would be carried over into civilian life.

In the 1920's and 1930's when there was little prospect of social and vocational advancement for working-class boys, the

---

[1] *P. C. Report*, 1936, p. 75. Ten years earlier it had been said that there was a 'disastrous unreality . . . where all the necessities of life are provided by authority and work appears as an unrelated task, performed under threat of punishment. This will probably have to be dealt with by the introduction of some wage system.' See *Howard Journal*, Vol. 2, No. 1 (1926), pp. 64–5.

ultimate aim of the respectable workman was to learn a skilled trade. The idea of pride in one's work was closely linked with the idea of the self-respect of the working man which the borstals tried to instil into their charges. *The Times* claimed that '*many* acquire for the first time the skill and pride of craftsmanship' (my italics).[1] The judiciary firmly believed that boys would learn a trade in borstal.[2] But, in fact, the scope of trade training was very limited. In the early thirties, however, greater attempts were made to teach boys trades so that at least they stood a chance of making some advance in the status hierarchy and thereby gain in self-respect.[3] In order that trade training should be improved and more in line with the possible employment of inmates on release, experiments in Vocational Guidance were made so that a boy could be directed to the type of employment for which he had most aptitude. The results[4] showed that a far higher proportion of boys were more satisfactory at their work after being selected by means of the test. But unfortunately most of the boys were relatively poor material, for whom vocational training was useless and manual work far more suited to their requirements on release. Paterson was aware of this, for he wrote: 'It is idle to hide the fact that the great majority of men . . . have to labour all their lives on tasks so monotonous that there can be no interest in them.'[5]

The two new borstals opened in 1938 were both open institutions. At Usk, the privileges of the open system were emphasized by first placing the boys in the old prison from which they graduated to the completely open Prescoed Camp once they had proved their ability to take the responsibility. The other institution, Hollesley Bay Colony, was based on the 'small community' principle. Each house was separated from

---

[1] See article, 'Crime and Cure II, Borstal at Work—A State Economy,' *The Times*, 11 August 1928. See also *Daily Mail*, 7 May 1929.

[2] See pp. 36–7 above.

[3] Barman, op. cit., gives the impression, even so, that most boys were trained in a trade for 2–3 years and reached a reasonable proficiency, p. 40.

[4] Alec Rodger, *A Borstal Experiment on Vocational Guidance* (HMSO, 1934). For a concise summary see Alec Rodger, 'Vocational Guidance at Borstal,' *Howard Journal*, Vol. 2, No. 3 (1932), p. 51. See also *The Lancet*, 6 March 1937, p. 575.

[5] *The Principles*, p. 41

the others on a large estate so that the force of public opinion and the direction of ideals in the house could be more easily managed and have a more effective and exclusive influence upon the individual.

The fact that at both these institutions, as at North Sea Camp, the main type of work available was outdoor manual work on the land is of great interest in showing what type of work the Commissioners thought was a valuable stimulus. The pioneering spirit which was the main feature of the work at North Sea Camp remained even after the initial stimulus had gone.[1] Whether this was the main factor in making for a high success rate and low absconding rate we cannot say, but the Commissioners assumed that part of the success of the camp was due to the fact that the boys were appreciative of doing socially valuable work. While reclaiming land was not the main work at either of the two new borstals, the emphasis on farming was based on the belief that not only was this work healthy but it also provided a stimulus of interest which was a valuable reforming element in its own right.[2] Also, one of the problems of the borstals had always been what to do with those who could not, or did not wish to, return to their homes on release. Farming has often been seen as a panacea for the displaced city boy and as a means of transferring others from a disruptive environment. The large number of farm camps in the U.S.A. testifies to this, and the English farming borstals were founded on similar optimistic grounds.[3] But the experience

[1] *P. C. Report*, 1937, p. 70

[2] The Gladstone Committee had, of course, originally recommended that the penal-reformatory should be 'situated in the country with ample space for agricultural and land reclamation work', op. cit., para. 84b. In 1922 Hobhouse and Brockway had observed that 'Borstal training does not sufficiently realize the peculiar advantages presented by farm work', p. 430.

Sir J. Gilmour had observed in 1934 that 'one of the features of Borstal training is healthy outdoor work', *H. C. Debates*, Vol. 290, col. 1082, 7 June 1934; and Sir Samuel Hoare, commenting on Hollesley Bay Colony, *H. C. Debates*, Vol. 332, cols. 937–9, 1 March 1938, stated that they were finding agricultural work 'very valuable as training for Borstal boys'.

[3] An American study of the value of farming as a preparation for employment on release in a rural community has shown that it is not satisfactory. Although this study dealt with boys younger than the borstal group it showed clearly the difficulty which urban youths have in settling in an

of the Borstal Association showed that attempts at resettlement were unlikely to prove very successful.[1] Although the Commissioners hoped to settle some boys on the land,[2] they did not expect this type of work to be a realistic preparation for the release of the majority. Nevertheless, agricultural work was healthy and rewarding, and especially valuable to those who would have to accustom themselves to outdoor manual work on release.

## Developments in Classification

In 1932 the Classifying Centre was moved from Wandsworth to Wormwood Scrubs where there were better facilities for isolating the boys. During the two months the boys spent there they received much the same examination that they had received at Wandsworth.[3] The existence of such a diagnosis did not mean, as some supposed, that each boy was allocated to where he could receive training specifically suited to his needs.[4] Classification consisted of fitting a boy into a broad type,[5] in which the accent was still mainly on avoiding contamination.

---

entirely new environment. See George S. Speer, 'Social Value of Agricultural Training for Delinquent Boys,' *Social Service Review*, Vol. 12 (1934), p. 640.

[1] *B. A. Annual Report*, 1936, p. 3. See p. 179 below.

[2] In 1937 Sir John Simon stated that endeavours were made to find farm work for those trained in it. But this was before the new institutions opened. *H. C. Debates*, Vol. 322, col. 1166, 15 April 1937

[3] The information collected formed the basis of the first study of borstal inmates by Sir W. Norwood East. The work began in 1928 and was finally published as *The Adolescent Criminal* (1942).

[4] S. Barman, op. cit., states 'the whole future of the training at the institutions depends upon this diagnosis which is very carefully made by the authorities, since on it the success of the Borstal system depends', p. 164. In a review of this book, B. E. Astbury went so far as to say 'when Borstal is decided upon it is but the beginning of scientific treatment . . . It is often much more than this, it is probably the first real attempt at ascertaining the background of the young offender and coming to grips with the causes of his delinquency.' *Charity Organisation Quarterly*, Vol. 8, No. 4 (October 1934), p. 175

[5] The types sent to each institution in 1934 as listed by Barman:

'*Lowdham*—The best among young offenders are sent to it with a view to their being released on licence at a special early date if they work hard and behave well.

*Feltham*—Lads who are physically and mentally inferior and also those

By 1935 there were two institutions for the 'responsible', two for the 'intermediates', two for the worst cases, and one for the immature and less mentally efficient. For each group of offenders, roughly classified by their criminal experience, there was a choice of two institutions. Allocation could therefore be made in relation to other factors such as the type of work available, the particular qualities of the staff, the desire to segregate members of 'gangs' or to place boys in a particular physical environment. However, as far as the open borstals were concerned, one of the main differences between them lay in the environment—for example, only the physically fit who were not going to learn a trade could be sent to the North Sea Camp. In the case of the closed borstals it is difficult to see any such clear-cut divisions, and one presumes that allocation rested on a subtle division of types, on the basis of 'maturity', that is difficult to define.

The women social workers received official recognition for their services in 1932 when the chief, deputy and two others were given salaried posts. Their efforts had proved indispensable to the work of the classifying centre, but even so there were still sixteen voluntary workers, most of whom had no professional training, helping in the job of interviewing boys and visiting them in their homes. The four who received salaries were never officially civil servants and were paid by a voluntary committee which actually received funds for salaries from the Prison Commission. Healy and Alper point out that this relationship between voluntary and official services was a marked feature of the borstal system of the thirties.[1]

---

lads who are not of a very advanced type. They are lads who do not need a stiff regime and are not usually institutionalized.

*Rochester*—Lads who are of fairly high intelligence and have very few convictions but fail on probation and have a considerable inclination towards crime.

*Portland*—Older than those in other institutions, and have more experience of crime. They are physically bigger and stronger.

*Camp Hill*—The type between Rochester and Portland. Among others, motor car thieves are generally sent there as it is on an island.

*Sherwood (Nottingham)*—The oldest type of Borstal lads. Those who ought to be treated as men rather than boys. They wear trousers instead of shorts. It is a Borstal of the twenties rather than a Borstal of the teens.'

[1] *Criminal Youth and the Borstal System*, p. 79

As new institutions opened, the allocation committee broadened in its membership. Besides the members of the Commission who had always decided allocations, the committee included the Governor and housemaster of Wormwood Scrubs, the Director of the Borstal Association and the governor of an open borstal if a case was being considered for such an institution. This structure remained the same until the outbreak of the war.[1]

*Other Influences on Borstal Experiments: The Q Camps*

Although the borstal system was committed to the principle of developing responsibility and self-discipline, its methods never involved the abandonment of authoritarian discipline imposed by the staff. In contrast, a number of experiments outside the system had emphasized the need for inmate self-government and the psychological advantages of allowing free expression of choice. During the First World War, Homer Lane's legendary Little Commonwealth had (despite the unfortunate and controversial scandal which led to its closure) convinced many that inmate self-government could help young delinquents learn the necessity of obeying social norms.[2] Progressive educationalists such as A. S. Neill and W. B. Curry had also emphasized the advantages of a non-constraining environment.

One of the most influential and interesting experiments was started in 1936 by the voluntary Quaker Q Camps Committee. Relying wholly on subscriptions, and with the help of the Institute for the Study and Treatment of Delinquency, the Committee established Hawkspur Camp with David Wills as camp chief.[3] Boys were referred to the camp through the I.S.T.D. or probation officers. It differed markedly from borstal in that all the inmates went there voluntarily and not compulsorily under a court order. Hawkspur had no authoritarian discipline and relied entirely on the force of opinion and good sense and upon the decisions taken by democratically organized Camp Councils. Furthermore, it made use of the borstal

[1] L. Fox, *The Modern English Prison* (1934), p. 179
[2] See E. T. Bazeley, *Homer Lane and the Little Commonwealth* (1928) and David Wills, *Homer Lane* (1964).
[3] David Wills, *The Hawkspur Experiment* (1941)

experience with pioneering conditions and relied on these to give the boys a sense of purpose in their work. Although the Hawkspur experiment was not designed to deal with boys of the same criminal maturity of those in borstals, its leader stressed that the principle of instilling discipline by allowing complete freedom of decision (the boys did not have to work if they so chose) combined with the guidance of a non-authoritarian father figure should ideally be used with all delinquents.

The group dealt with was small; there were never more than twenty at the camp at the time; the age range was dispersed between 16½ and 25 or over; most had psychological troubles already diagnosed and about 40 per cent had secondary education as compared with the 2·6 per cent found in borstal by Mannheim in his *Social Aspects*.[1] The harmonious working of the Treatment Committee in dealing with the psychological troubles of inmates was one of the most important contributions of the camp. It showed that experts could combine from outside the institution to plan a realistic treatment policy for the delinquent. Previously, as Mannheim has pointed out, the experts were either incorporated into the institution, in which case various difficulties arose, or were so remote from the institution that they precipitated divided loyalties between the staff and the psychologists.[2] As far as the borstal system was concerned, the Hawkspur Camp proved a useful model for showing that intensive personal relationships could achieve remarkable transferences; that inmate councils could work and prove useful in shaping and controlling institutional behaviour even with neurotics; that more emphasis could be placed on self-discipline to ensure that the inmate properly understood the value of work and education; and that psychological treatment could be successfully integrated into an institutional regime. In particular it emphasized the value of working with small groups.

Wills frequently compared borstal methods unfavourably with those adopted at Hawkspur and evidently made an attempt to get the camp recognized at least as a probation

[1] H. Mannheim, *Social Aspects of Crime Between the Wars* (1940), p. 255
[2] H. Mannheim, *Group Problems in Crime and Punishment* (1955), p. 33

hostel or home. He recalls that the official reason for refusal was 'some obscure piece of red tape' but that the real reason was 'that we should have to have much more "discipline" before we could ever be recognized by them'.[1] There was clearly little hope that his methods could be officially recognized as being appropriate to borstal detention. When war came the camp was disbanded, being chronically short of funds.

While the dominant disciplinary element in the borstal system was in theory a reliance on self-discipline, in practice the principle was only extended to a basic trust in the inmate's ability to honour his place in an open institution or outside the walls of the closed borstal. There were, admittedly, some relaxations of smaller details—for instance, boys were no longer paraded for work but expected to assemble by themselves. The Governor of Rochester remarked: 'There is food for thought in the recollection that for years we have tried to teach lads punctuality without making it possible for them to be late!'[2] Yet at no time was it suggested that boys should be allowed to be late, or to make up their own minds whether they worked or attended evening classes or even religious services. The borstals did acknowledge the value of small groups, but despite the early hopes raised by Sir Maurice Waller in 1922 self-government had been very limited. The houses were supposed to give possibilities for community decisions 'in matters of general organization and discipline',[3] but the inmates had no say in the general running of the institution. It was not until after the war that there was a limited and apparently short-lived experiment allowing the freedom of inmate councils or the possibility of collective decision-making.[4]

---

[1] op. cit., p. 187

[2] *P. C. Report*, 1935, p. 62

[3] See S. Barman, op. cit., p. 35. He recognized the importance of group decisions but saw the 'gradual development of self-government' in the future of the system.

[4] H. Kenyon, 'The Concept of Shared Responsibility in Borstal Training,' *Howard Journal*, Vol. 8, No. 3 (1952), p. 189. See also the note on the extension of this principle at Pollington borstal in the late fifties, p. 146 below.

# V

# Training Since the War

## The War Years

By 1939 the system embraced five closed institutions (Rochester, Portland, Feltham, Camp Hill and Sherwood) and four open institutions (Lowdham, North Sea Camp, Usk and Hollesley Bay Colony). Out of the daily average population of 2,020 in 1938, 1,567 were in the closed borstals, 351 in the three open borstals (Usk was not operating until 1939, and there are no figures for that year) and 102 in the disciplinary block at Wandsworth. Thus, the open system only catered for 17 per cent of the total borstal population.

The war changed borstal training radically, mainly through administrative pressures[1] but partly also through changes of policy. The mass discharge of boys in 1939 and the loss of experienced staff to the forces meant that house traditions were destroyed. The institutions were forced to run on limited lines. A number of borstals were closed and training became as brief as possible due to the shortage of accommodation and the Commissioners' policy of releasing boys early to aid in the war effort.

The basic principles of training did not change; it simply became impossible to put them into practice. On the work side, training ceased entirely, as the workshops made production their main aim. Since most of the boys were to be released into the forces, military discipline would take over from borstal discipline, and the considerable problem of planning for release consequently vanished.[2]

[1] One interesting change brought about through administrative pressures was the system of allocating boys to leave the institutions and work on local farms. This system was particularly highly developed at Usk and proved very successful. It was suspended after the war when agricultural labour was no longer scarce.

[2] Article, 'Impact of War on the Young Offender,' *The Times*, 24 March 1943

At the same time the Commissioners were convinced that they were getting a more difficult type of boy in the institutions. The accepted view was that the conditions of evacuation, fathers away from home, general unrest and violence were producing a more disturbed and difficult type of boy than borstals had hitherto had to deal with.[1] But it was thought that the condition was only temporary—that after the war the boys would again present the normal lazy criminal symptoms which had been tackled by the methods of the thirties. The new type of borstal boy posed several problems for training. He appeared to take less note of appeals to his sense of responsibility and absconded far more frequently than boys had done formerly. The problem of absconding was to cause much concern to the administration in the expansion of the system after the war.

*Post-War Expansion*

As already pointed out,[2] the attempt to open Dartmoor as a borstal at the end of the war met with so much criticism that the Commissioners were forced to look for other sites. The only alternatives to old prisons were disused army camps and converted country houses. In 1946 four new open institutions were established—Gaynes Hall, Huntercombe, Hewell Grange and Gringley Camp, a satellite of Sherwood—as well as a new classifying centre at Latchmere House. In 1948 there was a total daily average population of 2,885 of whom 1,441 were in closed borstals, 1,004 in open, 313 in the reception centres and the remainder in the recall centre and punitive establishment. What had before the war been an experiment carefully applied to specially selected boys became quite suddenly a substantial part of the system. As the population of the borstals increased, so did the proportion in open institutions. Before the war the open borstals had proved a marked success and no one saw any reason why they should not continue to be so after the war once the boys had become more settled and the staff had found its feet.

The rate of absconding soon became so high that it caused considerable concern. There was a tremendous rise from 542 escapes in 1946 to 1,071 in 1947 and a continued figure of over

---

[1] *P. C. Report*, 1942–44, p. 56          [2] See pp. 66–7 above.

1,000 in the following years, reaching a peak of over 1,200 in 1950 and 1951.[1] Although less than half had escaped from the open borstals (bearing in mind that it is impossible to guess what proportion of the 374 listed under the corrective wing at Wandsworth had come from open borstals) it was assumed that the increase in abscondings was due mainly to the increase in the number of open institutions. Questions were asked in the Commons about escapes from various open borstals,[2] which particularly drew attention to their good record before the war. But the Commissioners were sufficiently optimistic to hope that when the immediate effect of the war had passed the boys would once more settle down and respond to the appeal to their sense of responsibility.

The new institutions changed two aspects of the training system. Open training was no longer a privilege to be kept only for those who could be trusted, and finer classification became possible. Because there was no alternative, boys now had to be sent to the open borstals who, before the war, would have been considered too bad a risk. While this was probably the cause of some of the increase in absconding, it did on the other hand lead to more experimentation. Work and educational factors became more important in the allocation decision as the criterion for 'fitness for open training' no longer rested on a simple division into the 'responsible' and the 'irresponsible'.

*Improvements in Classification*

When the first completely detached allocation centre was opened at Latchmere House in 1946, the Commissioners enlarged the staff to include experts who could help with the more complicated task of classification in the larger and more diverse system. Besides the medical men there were now an

[1] Details are available in Table 6, Appendix 1, of the author's unpublished University of Cambridge PH.D. dissertation.

[2] Between 1948 and 1951 a number of questions were asked in the Commons about escapes from Hollesley Bay Colony, Gaynes Hall, Camp Hill and Rochester. The members for the constituencies in which the borstals were situated expressed concern for local property and even for personal safety. See *H. C. Debates*, Vol. 48, cols. 215–16, 14 December 1950, in which Mr Granville states that local residents near Hollesley Bay 'many of whom are elderly people, are at present living in a state of fear and anxiety, and are afraid to go out alone at night'.

educationalist, a psychologist, a vocational guidance officer, a visiting psychiatrist and professional social workers. Certain members of the staff were largely concerned with making enquiries; others helped to prepare the boy for the training he was going to receive: the psychologist, educationalist and social workers spent most of their time in diagnosing the problems of the cases, while the housemasters and governor prepared the boy for training. All these people took their place on the allocating board along with members of the Prison Commission. Everyone had a part in trying to map out a training programme; but in practice all the peculiarities of the individual case could probably not have been catered for in allocation.

The boy has to be 'fitted in' to one of several different institutional regimes, and this in turn involves selecting priorities. It is difficult to know whether it is the work programme, the character of the staff, the educational system, the dominant group spirit, the desire to segregate members of a gang, or simply an administrative decision based on the availability of accommodation that is most important when allocation is finally decided.[1] Probably all members of the team cannot be of equal importance in affecting allocation; for instance the report of the vocational guidance officer on suitability for trade training 'in practice rarely provides information which affects allocation'. Apparently 'it can only be a fortunate coincidence if a boy specially suited to one of the less common trades finds himself at one of the very few (or the only) borstals where this is taught'.[2] However, all members of the team make known to the institutional staffs the boy's problems and suggest ways in which he can be helped. All this material is also of great value to the after-care plans which are made at an early stage by the Borstal Association (now Division).[3]

[1] R. L. Morrison, 'Borstal Allocation,' *British Journal of Delinquency* Vol. 8, No. 2 (October 1957), p. 95. Also, H. Mannheim and J. C. Spencer *Problems of Classification in the English Penal and Reformatory System* (ISTD) (1949), pp. 13 et seq.

[2] 'Work and Vocational Training in Borstals (England and Wales),' *Report of the Advisory Council on the Employment of Prisoners* (1962), pp. 12 and 14

[3] Some recent set-backs for classification are discussed below on pp. 159–60.

Wormwood Scrubs continued as the other centre. Here was a great division between the type of environment to which boys were subject early in their sentence. Some boys had the disadvantage of starting their sentence still in the prison environment of London's largest prison. The opening of Latchmere House was a further attempt by the Commissioners to separate the borstal system entirely from its old prison connexions.

## New Problems for Open Training

The new situation forced the borstal system into a position which was more consistent with the Patersonian doctrine of training for freedom through the development of self-control. As already shown, only those who were not in any way a risk were given the benefit of the doubt in the thirties, while those who most obviously needed to be taught responsibility were not, because of the security risk and the fear of contamination. The increase in the number of open institutions enabled the Commissioners to separate the 'mature' from the 'immature' and so minimize the possibilities of contamination. Furthermore, they were forced to allocate a number of boys to open institutions who were obviously more difficult to deal with by these methods and to whom the appeal for self-control and to their sense of honour meant little. It was obvious that if the system was to expand in the direction of open training this problem had to be tackled realistically.

Not only was there an increasing absconding rate, but there were also reports of indiscipline.[1] This, together with the fact that published results showed that for the first time the system had 'successes' (boys not reconvicted) in less than 50 per cent of the cases, led to the appointment of a Departmental Committee to examine punishments and discipline. In the section dealing with borstals[2] it concluded that: bearing in mind that

[1] Mr G. E. Lawrie declared in his presidential address to the Annual Conference of the Prison Officers' Association that discipline in borstal establishments had seriously deteriorated. Reported in *The Times*, 31 May 1951

[2] *Report of the Committee to Review Punishments in Prisons, Borstal Institutions, Approved Schools and Remand Homes: Part II, Borstal Institutions* (Cmd. 8256), 1950–51

'(a) many officers—not all of them of subordinate rank, feel that discipline has deteriorated; (b) the "success" rate has decreased; (c) absconding has increased and is increasing; we are of the opinion that discipline in general requires tightening, even at the cost of an increase in punishments, and that the policy of leniency, appeasement, or soft treatment as at present interpreted is not having the success expected or desired'.[1] Although the Commissioners repudiated the notion that indiscipline was common[2] they did admit that the results were disappointing and that consequently there was a constant need to review their policy.[3]

The 'Patersonian ideal' had received a severe blow. The progressive methods which had been so well received in the thirties were now being characterized as 'soft' and 'lenient'. The Departmental Committee, however, did have basically the same conception of discipline as the Commissioners. They defined it as 'a right attitude in the individual and in the community to society, to work, to authority, to decency and order, to life'.[4] This was exactly the kind of attitude which the borstals were aiming at producing. But the Committee went on to say that good discipline embraces 'diligence, conduct, cleanliness and deportment' and to point out that in their view the Commissioners had swung too far in the opposite direction in their attempt to abandon the military type of discipline. They believed that the Commissioners had disregarded basic character training by not emphasizing the value of tidiness, deportment and respect for those in authority. In fact the Commissioners did believe these elements were important, but their method of emphasizing these virtues without using direct disciplinary methods as sanctions was not endorsed by the Committee. As *The Lancet* pointed out, unless the change in bearing was an outward sign of an inward change it could only have a convenience value at the most.[5]

The Committee also noted that there were certain boys who would not respond at all to the methods used, but who abused

[1] Para. 33
[2] Para. 29
[3] *P. C. Report*, 1949, p. 56
[4] Para. 27
[5] Leading article, 'The Borstal Puzzle,' *The Lancet*, 30 June 1951, p. 1399

the privileges given by the system.[1] The Commissioners were already aware of this and had decided to separate the trouble-makers[2] who were described by the Committee as 'of a type so vicious and obdurate as to be incapable of influence by the good example and quality of the staff or by admonition and advice however wise or wholesome' and for whom 'the sanctions of misconduct now available are to this type of man no deterrent at all'.[3] Although this group was supposed to be only about 2 or 3 per cent[4] of the total, the Commissioners decided to open Hull Prison as a separate institution. Here, both boys who were receiving their second sentences and those who were 'seriously subversive of the morale of their houses' were to be dealt with under a strict routine in which amenities would be earned by hard work and good conduct.[5] The Departmental Committee had seen the new borstal primarily as a relief to the others and only as 'possibly salutary'[6] to the inmates. The Commissioners were anxious to make some progress on the treatment side through careful consideration of individual problems, but the house system was scrapped and 'training for freedom' through the learning of progressive responsibility left out. In principle the new borstal was more like one from the Ruggles-Brise regime than the other progressive institutions. It was no longer believed simply that there was a 'basic good' in the British lad which could be reached through an appeal to his innate sense of 'decency' and social sense. Only *The Lancet* pointed out that if the group were so vicious and obdurate as the Committee believed, they 'were surely not fit for any kind

[1] The borstal system had come up against the problem of those who would not conform to normal discipline before. Nottingham Prison (Sherwood), reopened in 1932, took the worst elements from Portland and Camp Hill and subjected them to a more strict discipline. But this had been an experiment, on which was based the decision to raise the age limit in 1936, and not a permanent feature of the borstal system based on a despair of the ability of some boys to react to the 'progressive methods'.

[2] *P. C. Report*, 1950, p. 64

[3] Para. 54. Whether homosexuals were included in this category is not known. This problem has been noted by writers such as Benny, Gordon and by Healy and Alper, but never officially mentioned by the Commissioners.

[4] Para. 61

[5] *P. C. Report*, 1950, p. 64

[6] Para. 61—although it stressed that the purpose was to 'train and not to punish' (para. 63)

of Borstal training', and that they were certainly not going to pick up better habits in unrelieved society of others like themselves.[1]

There had of course always been disciplinary sanctions for those who would not behave. Those who persistently caused trouble or absconded frequently had been sent to a special corrective block. This block had first been opened in 1911 at Canterbury Prison but was later transferred, first to a wing of Wormwood Scrubs and then to Wandsworth before finally being established as an independent centre at Reading Prison in 1951.

The regime at Wandsworth had been tough, and mainly aimed at deterring the boy from misbehaving by giving him onerous tasks and severely limiting his privileges.[2] Louis Edward wrote of its effects in the thirties on boys in his institution; Sir Lionel Fox spoke just after the war of boys being 'put through it . . . with a severity that will surpass anything he could experience in prison'[3]; and, although there may be now more personal attention given, the Commissioners' report for 1952 does not make any brighter reading: 'Routine is strict, discipline tight. Boys do not like Reading, nor are they meant to.'[4] These methods have always been kept in the background because they have not been an essential part of the training, but their use has nevertheless shown that the borstal system has never given up the idea that one must coerce those who do not respond to its particular type of appeal. Hull borstal was different from the corrective centre in that it dealt with a difficult group for a major part of their training, and was not just a disciplinary adjunct to normal borstal life. The Centre at Reading continued to operate for those who were not so bad that they needed to be permanently deprived of the normal training regime.

Not long after the committee on punishments had reported,

[1] *The Lancet*, op. cit.

[2] 'Inmates are put through a course of hard and monotonous labour, such as wood chopping, pouch-making and stone-breaking with a greatly restricted rubric of free association, in the hope that where smoother measures failed the sterner discipline may have an effect.' *P. C. Report*, 1932, p. 53

[3] L. W. Fox, 'Borstal since the War'. *The Magistrate*, Vol. VIII, No. 6 (November–December 1947), p. 82          [4] p. 79

a report of the Select Committee on Estimates[1] was published in which Sir Lionel Fox, Chairman of the Commissioners, made the frank admission that he actually had at his disposal 'less closed Borstal accommodation than we really need which is partly responsible for the very large increase in absconding from the very large number of open Borstals which we have been forced to open'.[2] It was obvious that the great experiment of open training begun so enthusiastically and hopefully by Paterson had reached its limit. Even though open training had been limited in the thirties to the most trustworthy, it had been felt that in principle this method of training should be applicable to all delinquent youth. Now it was realized that only a limited number could benefit from such training. Why was this?

The boys received after the war were tougher and more undisciplined than those who had been to borstal in the thirties. Symptomatic of the change in attitudes towards these boys was the fact that they were allowed to wear long trousers whereas in the thirties they had worn shorts like boy scouts. Moreover, boys in open institutions no longer felt that they were there as a very special privilege; neither were the pioneering conditions so novel. It may be that boys did consider that they were being leniently treated and abused their privileges, but it is more likely that at the root of the trouble there were some more fundamental changes in the problems and personalities of post-war youth, and in their reaction to a middle-class moralizing system.[3]

The Commissioners had been led to the conclusion, albeit unhappily, that it was in the best interests of both the public and the boys that a definite proportion of boys should be kept in secure or semi-secure institutions. Their plans for new institutions were therefore aimed at providing small secure establishments.[4]

---

[1] *Report of the Select Committee on Estimates: Session 1951–2, 7th Report*
[2] Question 2322
[3] This point is developed more fully on pp. 153–5 below.
[4] *Session 1952–53, Second Report of the Select Committee on Estimates—Departmental Reply to the 7th Report 51–52*, p. 10. 'The Prison Commissioners' plans provide for . . . two secure borstal institutions each for 150 boys . . . to start in 1955.' A logical conclusion about the doubt 'whether the large closed

*Post-War Training Ideas*

(*a*) *Principles and methods.* Sir Lionel Fox's authoritative statement of borstal training principles made in 1952 reads very
much like the pre-war writings of Paterson.[1] Since 1952 there
have been no revolutionary changes in the system. But there
has been an increasing awareness on the part of the Commissioners of the need to challenge the relevance of ideas
and methods developed in the thirties. The reports of the
Commissioners in the early sixties show a complete lack of
dogmatism about the nature of the problem and its solution.
Nevertheless, despite the appearance of group counselling, and
some important shifts of emphasis, the basic structure of the
system has remained much as it was when Sir Lionel wrote.

The introduction of group counselling at Pollington borstal
late in 1957 established the place of modern sociological and
psychological theory in the reformatory system. It is now no
longer believed that the personal example of a devoted staff is
all that is needed to achieve reform. Some attention is being
paid to the concept of the institution as a therapeutic community in which the group values can best be influenced by the
group working together. The basis of this idea can be found in
small-group and reference-group theory in sociology and its
application stems from advances in the development of techniques of group work in psychology. Broadly speaking, the
sociological theories state that values are acquired by identifica-
tion or reference to a group and that the desire to be accepted
by the reference group is the force which determines the
tenacity with which the values are retained.[2] The methods of

---

borstals give the best opportunities for training the difficult, wayward and
feckless population which they serve'—see *P. C. Report*, 1950, p. 64. All the
new post-war open borstals had been for 150 boys, but it is interesting to
note that in 1963 plans were being made for a secure borstal for 300 boys
at Onley (Northants).

[1] L. W. Fox, *The English Prison and Borstal Systems* (1952), Chapters 21
and 22. See also the account in Winifred A. Elkin, *The English Penal
System* (1957), pp. 250ff.

[2] Rose has called the conflict between self-interest and group loyalty and
the gradual adaptation of the individual to the 'equilibrium' of the group
the 'core of training'. See 'The Sociological Analysis of Borstal Training' in
*British Journal of Delinquency*, Vol. 6, No. 3 (January 1956), p. 202ff.

using the strength of the group to influence attitude change are those associated with group therapy and group counselling. Group therapy is a method of helping emotionally disturbed persons; group counselling, on the other hand, is a method of enabling the individual to work out his difficulties with the help of his peers and to use the group as a means of changing attitudes. 'The essential object of group counselling,' the Commissioners state, 'is to help correct, in some degree, the distorted view which many inmates have of themselves and of society, and which is often responsible for the behaviour which has brought them into conflict with the law.'[1] The methods used at Pollington were based on the experience of Californian institutions and the writings of Dr Norman Fenton.[2]

Boys were selected for Pollington from among those with the best prognosis and the training was intended to last little more than a year. Pollington was intended as an experiment, but so many different variables—counselling, the best boys, the short period, and some limited forms of self-government—were introduced at once that it will not be possible to disentangle the influence of all the elements in the final results. Since 1961 the population has been changed so as to deal, as an experiment, with a group 'with an average probability of success'. The scheme has also been gradually extended to a number of other borstals including Rochester and the recall centre at Portsmouth, but at these institutions it is apparently practised more on a simple group discussion basis and not as a central element in the regime.

What has been written about the success of counselling programmes has so far been confined to statements about the effect on training—on its influence on staff-boy relationships, on the level of tension in the institution—and not on results as judged by reconvictions on release. From all accounts[3] the

[1] 'Group Counselling: An Instruction by the Prison Commissioners,' *Howard Journal*, Vol. 11, No. 1 (1962), pp. 37–40

[2] Norman Fenton: *What Will be Your Life?* (1957); *An Introduction to Group Counselling in State Correctional Service* (1958); *Group Counselling: A Preface to Its Use in Correctional and Welfare Agencies* (1961).

[3] R. L. Morrison, 'Group Counselling in Penal Institutions,' *Howard Journal*, Vol. 10, No. 4 (1961), p. 279; and critical notice of Fenton's 'Group Counselling' in *Prison Service Journal*, Vol. 1, No. 3 (July 1961), p. 49; Norman Bishop, 'Group Work at Pollington Borstal'; *Howard*

group counselling situation is one which has particularly relieved many of the institutional tensions normally (and previously) found between staff and boys. It has aided the staff to understand more about a boy's background and particular worries; of his opinions about his sentence and of his view of life in general. The all-important question is whether group counselling (as presently perceived) can do anything to convince the boy that he should not commit crime but instead live a normal law-abiding life. One of the main tenets of the social worker (and group worker in this context) is that the client should be helped towards a realistic view of his problems and towards a satisfactory solution. In the context of delinquency it assumes that the delinquent will think of his offences as 'problems', and that if he does he will want a solution. Group counselling may help the boy to air his views; but does it help him to see his delinquency as a problem which needs a solution, or help him discover ways in which to deal with it effectively?

Within the institutional setting there are clearly a number of drawbacks to a fully-effective use of counselling methods. The discipline-staff are used as counsellors, partly because there are no professional counsellors to undertake the work and partly as a matter of policy, in order to give them the opportunity to learn more about their charges. This involves the counsellor-staff member in a role-conflict situation. He has to act within the group as a confidant and as a guide to discussion, and in other situations outside the group as an authority figure who is

---

*Journal*, Vol. 10, No. 3 (1960), p. 185; Michael Bird, 'Group Counselling at Pollington', *Prison Service Journal*, Vol. 1, No. 2 (January 1961), p. 33

See also, A. W. Peterson, 'Modern Developments in the Prison System,' *Howard Journal*, Vol. 10, No. 3 (1960), p. 167

The Commissioners report that counselling had spread to other institutions with a 'considerable measure of success'. 'The spread of group counselling and other forms of group work has deepened staff interest in the problems and attitudes of the individual.' One Governor wrote: 'Incidents and situations which in another setting would be seen as harmful, irritating or hindering, were seen more as learning or treatment situations and as opportunities for personal and social development.' *P. C. Report*, 1961 p. 36. The Governor of another borstal to which counselling has been extended said, 'I believe the staff/lad relationship is improving. Lads are more prepared to approach staff with problems.' ibid., p. 90

bound by his job to put the question of security and discipline as the first priority. In order that these two roles may conflict as little as possible it appears to be customary that groups do not discuss staff-boy grievances, or problems which might lead the boy into trouble with the institutional authorities. At the same time, officers are anxious to avoid any threatening situation which might undermine their status, and so do not allow themselves to be interrogated to any extent or their own personal life to be discussed. All these problems appear to be clearly recognized by the institution's Governor and by the Commissioners,[1] but they must limit the therapeutic value which free discussion and exchange within the group might eventually be able to achieve. Although there are no adequate methods of measuring the value of this innovation, there can be little doubt that it is a step in the right direction.

The change-over at Pollington to boys with a lower probability of success apparently had little effect on the institution and 'the response of boys to group counselling continued to be good'.[2] However, the Commissioners have expressed doubt as to whether all boys can benefit from counselling. They suggest that those with low I.Q.s, the socially inadequate or those with considerable institutional experience may 'become bewildered or unhappy by a lack of a clear framework and a clear definition of relationship'.[3] But as they point out, traditional training is also of little success with these cases, apart from making them contented. Yet, on the other hand, counselling has been the main element in training at Portsmouth where many of the cases are of the type the Commissioners think unlikely to respond to this form of training. The relationship between staff

---

[1] The Commissioners clearly state: 'The proceedings of the group are normally treated as confidential to the group; but at the same time it must be understood that the staff member taking part in the group retains complete discretion to use information as he thinks fit, either in the interests of security and good order of the institution or in the interests of a particular individual . . . It is, of course, clearly understood by the group that sessions are not used as a means of redressing grievances or obtaining material benefits of any kind.' 'Group Counselling: An Instruction by the Prison Commissioners,' op. cit.          [2] *P. C. Report*, 1961, p. 36

[3] *P. C. Report*, 1961, p. 37, and 1962, p. 30, although the remarks in the latter report appear to be largely about the suitability of boys for the casework approach.

and boys (described as 'poorly-equipped inadequates') at Portsmouth has apparently been put 'on a sounder and more understanding basis: advice is more readily sought and more readily given: boys appear to be less bitter and to have a more realistic appreciation of their problems: more boys work outside the establishment than ever before: discipline is more easily maintained'.[1] These boys are not bewildered, but time alone can tell whether what they have learned in counselling sessions will aid them outside.

At Pollington, counselling has been carried on in conjunction with inmate self-government on a limited scale. This is an innovation which has been pressed for over many years, particularly by the critics of borstal. Although little progress has been made towards real self-government on the pattern of the Q camps, there is now a willingness to agree that inmates should be able to decide for themselves on questions such as entertainment and the organization of such facilities as libraries and films. This, at least, is some remove from the dogmatism which laid down the types of entertainment which alone were suitable for improving the borstal boy's mind. With limited exceptions, such as the existence of an inmate disciplinary committee at one open camp,[2] the principle of self-government has not spread to borstals in general.

Even though methods of group counselling are now being used, psychotherapy proper is still almost unknown in borstal. The role of the housemaster has been described as analogous to that of the psychotherapist[3] but few have received any formal training in psychology or in casework techniques. With the

---

[1] *P. C. Report*, 1961, p. 43

[2] *P. C. Report*, 1962, pp. 32–3. Also reported is a scheme at a semi-secure borstal whereby boys in the last stage of their training move into a hostel where they are responsible for going to bed, getting up, writing off to employers for jobs, etc. The scheme is considered to be making a good start—p. 31.

[3] W. Healy and B. S. Alper, op. cit., pp. 123, 228; also Gordon Rose in *Penal Practice in a Changing Society: A Critical Examination of White Paper Policy* (1960), p. 14. See also Negley Teeters, *World Penal Systems* (1944), who criticizes the lack of formal psychiatric treatment in borstal, p. 21ff. See also K. R. H. Wardrop, 'Treatment of the Adolescent Offender,' *British Journal of Delinquency*, Vol. 8, No. 2 (October 1957), p. 106ff., which discusses treatment in a Scottish borstal.

exception of Pollington only one other borstal is committed to involving its housemasters and other staff in a casework-orientated programme.[1] The value of this method in the institutional setting is clearly open to some doubt, particularly because it assumes the willingness of the inmate to co-operate with, and share, the aims of the social worker. But the Governor and his staff have reported that casework 'offers a lot to certain types of boys and this would tend to be borne out by some successes with boys with low prediction scoring who would be seen in normal borstal terms as having little prospect of success'.[2] As with counselling, the Commissioners doubt whether this method will be appropriate to the dull inadequate institutionalized offender. In some senses, the casework approach places on a more formal footing one of the long-accepted roles of the housemaster as 'confessor' and helper.[3] In general, however, most housemasters continue to play the traditional role of attempting to influence their charges by personal example and quiet persuasiveness rather than any more direct casework technique.[4] From all available evidence, the authorities still select their staff on the assumption that qualities of leadership combined with a fine upstanding example of decency are those needed if the boy is to benefit from the contact. The idea of the thirties that boys would be influenced by the example of

[1] See Alan Roberton, 'Casework in Borstal,' *Prison Service Journal*, Vol. 1, No. 2 (January 1961), p. 15.      [2] *P. C. Report*, 1962, p. 30
[3] See Alexander Leitch, 'A Survey of Reformatory Influences in Borstal Training'—A Socio-Psychological Study, *British Journal of Medical Psychology*, Vol. 20, No. 1 (1944), p. 77. This study was based on interviews with 176 boys at Camp Hill borstal. It suffers from being neither straightforward reporting of the results nor all interpretation. For example, he is willing to accept the fact that the boys put the housemasters at the top of the list of good reformatory influences, but unwilling to accept the low place given by the boys to religion—stating that it is really more important than they think.
[4] Winifred A. Elkin, *The English Penal System*, p. 252. See also Borstal Rules, S.R. & O., 1949 (No. 1283) I, p. 25—'the purpose of Borstal training requires that every inmate, while conforming to the rules necessary for well-ordered community life, shall be able to develop his individuality on right lines with a proper sense of personal responsibility. Officers shall therefore, while firmly maintaining discipline and order, seek to do so by influencing the inmates through their own example and leadership and by enlisting their willing co-operation.'

gentlemanly conduct is still very much reflected in the writings of the fifties. However, the Advisory Council on the Treatment of Offenders' report *The Organisation of After-Care*, published in 1963, stressed that housemasters should be expected to undertake the functions of a social worker in borstals. This would obviously require a reappraisal of the present basis of recruitment and the provision of more adequate training than the present six-month course provided by the prison service at Wakefield.[1]

Religion appears to be slightly less stressed than formerly, but by many it is still thought to be a most important influence.[2] At all borstals there is a chaplain, and religious services are attended by all. Few in the service would pretend, however, that many boys make a lasting contact with religious organizations.

(*b*) *Work, education and leisure*. The work programmes of the borstals have changed considerably over the last thirty years,

---

[1] *The Organisation of After-Care*, pp. 26–7. See also, John P. Conrad, 'The Assistant Governor in the English Prison,' *British Journal of Delinquency*, Vol. 10, No. 4 (April 1960), pp. 245ff. This interesting article reviews the task of the assistant governor, particularly in relation to borstal work, and comments on recruitment and training. Conrad notes that the Commissioners have had little success at getting suitable candidates from the ranks of prison officers and states that the intake 'range is extraordinarily wide extending from men with rich experience of life and affairs to others whose opportunities for growth have been restricted'. In relation to the training course at Wakefield he concludes: 'The assistant governor who takes full advantage of the potentialities of his position will have to function as a caseworker, a group worker, an administrator, a trainer of staff, and as a criminologist. Six months is not nearly long enough to produce an assistant governor fully proficient in all these fields.' In particular he criticizes the lack of formal training in casework methods and counselling.

[2] See comments on housemasters and on the influence of religion by a borstal chaplain in Winifred A. Elkin and Rev. D. B. Kittermaster, *Borstal: A Critical Survey* (The Howard League), 1950.

A borstal governor referred to contact with the church as '. . . at the centre of our excellent and most happy relationship with our neighbours and is, I am sure, directly responsible for a complete change in the social attitude and outlook of many lads. Its contribution to the training of the lads can hardly be assessed if one can believe, as I do, that a true change can only come about with at least a recognition, if not an acceptance of the spiritual values of the Christian standard of life . . .' *P. C. Report*, 1950, p. 105. See also the sections on religion and the reports of the chaplains in *P. C. Report*, 1961, pp. 38–9 and 95–6; 1962, pp. 37–8 and 84–5.

although the principles on which the idea of regular work are based have remained the same. In their report for 1962, the Commissioners state: 'When there is so much of general interest to discuss in matters of borstal training, the importance of the working day may appear to be displaced by other more exciting activities. In practice this is not so . . .'[1]

After the war, vocational training was expanded considerably when Ministry of Labour and National Service courses became available at all borstals. Although it was not easy to find enough boys with the suitable 'mental equipment' to pass the stiff courses,[2] at least a higher proportion of boys had more constructive work to do. It was certainly considered that the sense of purpose which these courses gave was a powerful influence in gaining the confidence of the boys. One borstal governor stated that it was his 'firm conviction that the introduction of trade training in its present form has done more to convince the boy of our intentions than any other piece of training'.[3] In the years following the war, trade training of some sort has in fact been offered to more boys than previously. The Advisory Council on the Employment of Prisoners, reporting on *Work and Vocational Guidance in Borstal* in 1962, noted that about 30 per cent of boys underwent six months' trade training courses, and of these about 85 per cent passed.[4] The expansion of trade training was based upon the old assumption that skilled work would give security, higher wages and a sense of achievement. The boy would be both shielded from unemployment and be stronger in 'character'. The Advisory Council agreed that trade training was an important developer of character, but had to conclude that its practical value was rather limited by the fact that only about 30 per cent of those who passed followed the trade on discharge.[5] In fact, the position after the war was not at all analogous to that of the twenties when trade training had been thought of as potentially

---

[1] *P. C. Report*, 1962, p. 33    [2] *P. C. Report*, 1946, p. 72
[3] *P. C. Report*, 1949, p. 115    [4] op. cit., p. 8
[5] This figure is for those working on discharge in their trade. It does not show what proportion *remain* in their trade. A study of homeless cases showed that 17 per cent of those who had received vocational training followed their trade for as long as four months. See the author's PH.D. dissertation, op. cit.

B.R.—11

the most valuable element in training. The working-class boy released into an environment of full employment is faced no longer with a struggle for economic survival. What is perhaps more important is that in terms of earning power, skilled work means (for a time at least) less, not more, money. The Council stated that 'the commonest reason' why boys did not follow their trade 'was the attraction of higher immediate wages in other occupations'.[1] Borstal boys are usually over 19 years of age on discharge, and yet if they wish to take up the trade they have learned, they must accept work at an 'improver's grade' at wages far below what they could get in labouring work. The Council found that because of their age it was 'difficult to reach any formal general agreement on their admission to apprenticeship schemes'. They did, however, suggest that the boys' chances might be improved if they spent all their time in borstal working in their chosen trade, instead of spending some of it on domestic chores and other sorts of work, and if arrangements could be made to continue their training after discharge.[2]

But the majority of boys receive no training in a trade, and a considerable proportion work on simple labouring and farm jobs. The Council concluded that 'too sharp a distinction seems to be made between boys who are considered capable of benefiting from vocational training in a skilled trade and boys who are not', and advocated that much more attention should be given to providing training in semi-skilled work and in manufacturing.[3] Work in its own right, they stressed, was of little value; it must be purposeful and constructive. If it were, it would not only prepare boys for getting a job on discharge, but would also develop their skills, make them appreciate communication, teach them to accept the disciplines of production, and 'enable them to see what contribution they can make to society'. 'Clearly [the Council thought] they need

[1] ibid., p. 12. It has often been noted that delinquents (as do many others) prefer immediate high wages to long training at a low wage. See *The Adolescent Delinquent Boy:* A report of the Joint Committee on Psychiatry and the Law, appointed by the British Medical Association and the Magistrates' Association (1951), para. 36.

[2] ibid., pp. 15 and 29. They also suggest that fewer courses should be offered so that training can be better organized and more intensive—p. 15.

[3] ibid., pp. 18 and 24

to be taught the moral need for contributing as a condition of receiving benefits.'[1] The borstal boy is expected to master the problems which might easily lead him to throw up his job— 'getting on with workmates, respecting the "boss", and mastering boredom on a monotonous job'.[2]

In recent years a good deal more emphasis has been placed on educational training. In the thirties, education was largely a matter of providing further theoretical training for those learning trades and of teaching useful hobbies to the remainder. But, after the war, with the shortening of working hours and the dramatic rise in incomes for unskilled and semi-skilled labour, the problem changed. It was recognized that 'the direct teaching to those adolescents of civics and citizenship or an academic subject has limited value. But the proper use of their free time when they return as members of society needs to be tackled thoroughly as a vital part of borstal training.' The aim was to make borstal training 'an integral period of social re-education in its widest and fullest sense'. What this exactly means it is difficult to say, for it is reported that the first emphasis is on the use of English and an appreciation of literature, and then upon hobbies—drama and music and other activities—in which a satisfactory performance is 'seen as a valuable aspect of training'.[3] The hope, presumably, is that 'good taste' will encourage 'decency' and that boys will find some interest in their activities in borstal which they will pursue on their release and which will keep them off the streets and out of trouble.[4]

There are undoubtedly great problems in trying to overcome 'anti-school' hostility in the borstal situation, and recent reports show an awareness of this problem which was entirely absent from pre-war descriptions. At least one governor is now of the opinion that the content of the education is of little importance when compared to the attitudes and relationships which the classroom can engender.[5] It is this wider definition

[1] ibid., pp. 6 and 7      [2] *P. C. Report*, 1961, p. 39
[3] *P. C. Report*, 1951, p. 72
[4] Paterson, it will be remembered, had for probably similar reasons encouraged the reading of Stevenson in preference to Sexton Blake. See p. 112 above.
[5] *P. C. Report*, 1962, p. 77

of education which may be more important in future developments.

Related to the ideas held in the educational field are those
which are at the base of other developments, particularly the
emphasis now being placed on physical education and activities
which require endurance. According to the Commissioners
'physical education continues to form an integral part of
training in borstals'. Its value is believed to be in 'stressing the
importance of quick response to instructions' and in making
the boy 'fit, strong, and *mentally alert*' (my italics).[1] The recent
annual reports note canoeing expeditions, mountain climbing
and camping treks and similar events organized from the
institutions as well as by outside agencies such as the Outward
Bound organization. All these activities are clearly regarded as
a most valuable feature of training.[2] These ventures are all
designed to harden the boy and to develop his sense of responsibility towards others in the expedition, as well as to provide
tests of courage and leadership. It is thought that the experience
of such activities will enable the boy to widen his interests on
his return home as well as to develop his 'character'. The
assumption behind these measures is that the way to teach boys
responsibility for others is to put them in a situation where they
are forced to work as a team and recognize their duties to the
other members. It is important, however, to establish whether
the boy will be able to transfer his recognition of the need to
take notice of other persons on the rope on a mountain side, to a
need to respect the property of others in the every-day life
situation with which he will be confronted when he leaves
borstal. The idea that team games teach one to become a more
responsible citizen is certainly questionable. Although these
expeditions provide a good deal of interest during training and
do widen the range of experience of borstal boys there may be
very little chance for them to take them up on release. What is
even more important is that a concentration on a healthy
outdoor life may not reduce the temptation to steal, unless the
only cause of crime is boredom. As Lady Wootton comments:

See *P. C. Report*, 1961, p. 41; and 1962, p. 35.
[2] See 'Canoes, Canals and Calories,' *Prison Service Journal*, Vol. 1, No. 3
(January 1961), p. 49; and *P. C. Report*, 1960, pp. 43-4 and 95; 1961,
pp. 41-2 and 91-4; 1962, pp. 35-6 and 79-80.

'We must give attention, above everything, to the relevance of the ways in which we try to educate those who will not keep the rules.' She suggests that training should be related to 'the actual lives which people are going to live and the actual temptations which they are going to experience'.[1] But there are those who clearly believe in the value of a more authoritarian approach. Lord Dilhorne, speaking as Lord Chancellor on this subject, said:

> If you start from smartness and proceed from smartness to combine it with fitness and endurance, and if you teach at the same time the ability to take orders without resentment, and often with pride, then you come not only to hope and expectation of efficiency in yourself but to a mastery of yourself which I cannot but believe is helpful on a return to the outside world.[2]

There can be no doubt that the problem for the Commissioners is acute. No longer is there the same steady working-class *persona* which they apparently found in the youth of the twenties and thirties:

> Lads now coming in Borstal do not speak the same kind of language as the staff. They are now so often coming from a background that has a different type of mental outlook. When we discuss matters of ethics, dishonesty, deceit, lying and such like and show we consider them to have wrong standards, we are looked upon as not being part of this world. So often these warped ways have become the accepted standards of whole areas and places from which our population comes. The only idea is . . . 'Well, I was one of the unlucky ones, I got caught. But it won't happen again.' Not meaning as we would hope, that they will not again commit crime, but that next time they will be too clever for the police.[3]

Not only are borstal boys reported as 'initially hostile to authority and adults generally' but to 'lack character' and have a 'shameful lack of awareness of moral, social and religious standards'.[4] Over a third of the boys received into borstal in 1961 had previous institutional experience in approved schools, detention centres or prison. In 1952 under one boy in eight had six previous convictions or more, in 1962 the proportion was

[1] *H. L. Debates*, Vol. 230, col. 1154, 1 May 1961
[2] ibid., cols. 1157–8
[3] *P. C. Report*, 1957, p. 117      [4] *P. C. Report*, 1962, p. 27

almost one in every two.[1] Not only is the borstal population more conditioned to institutional life, but it is also probable that an authority based upon social prestige and religious principles is less meaningful to a generation brought up in an era of greater social awareness which is antagonistic to the traditional class system.[2] The appeal to 'hobbies', and 'decent' standards of leisure competes against 'sophisticated entertainment'. Nor is there any pattern of the proper use of free time which can be pointed to as an example: the non-delinquents have also failed conspicuously in many areas to tackle the problem of how to spend their leisure.[3] Furthermore, the problem of unravelling the elements involved in the cause of crime does not appear as simple as it did before the war, when it could blandly be attributed to unemployment or poverty. The system has no adequate theories of crime causation on which to base its training programme. It is surely far from easy to establish a clear-cut philosophy of training when it is not known what factors have to be dealt with.

Of course the system still has to deal with the mentally retarded, the institutionalized homeless and those who have been genuinely led astray, but these groups may all need special attention. The number of physically and mentally handicapped has increased, and the present organization of training has not been designed to cope with the problems posed by these boys. In 1955, the Director of the Borstal Division stated, 'I have drawn attention in previous reports to the change in the type of boy being committed to Borstal and have said that the Borstal system is being asked to solve problems, physical and emotional, that were certainly not in the minds of its founders and indeed to accept boys who, because of physical disabilities, would not in the early years of the Borstal system

[1] *C.A.C.A. Report*, 1962, p. 17
[2] For a novelist's impression see Alan Sillitoe, *The Loneliness of the Long-distance Runner* (1959).
[3] See 'Rising Eighteen in a London Suburb' by R. F. L. Logan and E. M. Goldsberg in *British Journal of Sociology*, Vol. 4, No. 4 (December 1953), p. 323. The interesting conclusion of their study of the leisure time activities of non-delinquents is that 'there were few signs of awakening interest in civil or communal activities. The lack of creative and constructive leisure pursuits is surprising . . .' See also T. R. Fyvel, *The Insecure Offenders* (1962), for a description of working-class 'teddy-boy' life.

have been eligible for Borstal training at all.'[1] The institutionalized clearly also present a peculiar training problem: for these are offenders with whom normal methods of institutional training have already conspicuously failed.[2] The genuinely 'led-astray', on the other hand, should clearly be protected from more contaminating influences once in an institution. But still, it is the 'normal' but 'difficult' borstal boy who presents the greatest challenge. The problems of training him to take his place in society and not to steal have changed immensely since the thirties when the basic principles were laid down. The system can no longer make a convincing appeal to 'play the game' or to 'stand by the flag' or to obey authority or respect the 'better class'. Its appeal must be based on a realistic appraisal of the type of life which the boy will live on release so that he will be well equipped to deal with the kind of problem which will face him. There are signs that this is being recognized. In the 1962 report the Commissioners state their belief that traditional methods of training are still appropriate for many borstals, but go on to question whether the borstal boy will respond to formal teaching as his counterpart did thirty years ago: 'Much thought has been taken to break through the barrier between staff and lad which is created by the authoritarian and paternalistic pattern of borstal training.' They are aware that lack of communication is an obstacle which must be overcome before training can begin. Attempts are apparently being made in at least one borstal to involve boys more fully in the running of the houses so that a community spirit can be built up on a 'foundation of intelligence and understanding which has not always been present in the old-fashioned, unthinking *esprit de corps*'.[3] But if the system is to develop along new lines, appropriate to the times, there is a greater need for experiment and research than has hitherto taken place.

[1] *C.A.C.A. Report*, 1955, p. 20

[2] In a study of two samples of homeless boys released in 1953 and 1957 the author found that 75 per cent were reconvicted, and 45 per cent more than once, in a follow-up period of two years. Of those with over four-and-a-half years institutional experience prior to borstal, 73 per cent were reconvicted twice or more. See the author's PH.D. dissertation, op. cit. See also Derek Miller's *Growth to Freedom* (1964) which discusses the problems and a new method of treatment for these cases.

[3] *P. C. Report*, 1962, pp. 28–30

(c) *Experiment and research*. The main feature of post-war research has clearly been the Mannheim-Wilkins prediction study which by classifying boys in terms of their potential future delinquency has enabled the Commissioners to sort out the best risk from the worst.[1] Three important by-products of this study were:

1. to show that shorter training (under two years) did not increase the chances of failure;
2. that the open borstals had a higher success rate than the closed; and
3. in providing a tool to aid in the process of classification.

The disclosure that shorter training was as effective as longer sentences made it possible for the Commissioners to consider reducing the amount of the sentence to be spent in the institutions, a suggestion which was incorporated into the Criminal Justice Act 1961. The study certainly did not solve the problem of fixing the right time for release, but it did destroy the notion that long training was needed *per se* to correct the borstal boy.[2] In particular, the Commissioners have stated that a long indeterminate sentence does not get the best out of the boy and that they are anxious that the training regime should be far brisker and more demanding with a foreseeable date of release for those who respond well.[3] The prediction study and recent developments in training have led to a number of interesting speculations about the time factor in training[4] as well as to the

[1] There had been an earlier attempt at prediction in which a psychological 'typology' of offenders had been established. This showed, for example, that four years following release from Camp Hill borstal, 89 per cent of the 'egocentric' type had been reconvicted, and 43 per cent of the 'emotionally unstable'. Interesting as this technique is for developing hypotheses about possible treatments, it could not compete in terms of reliability and power with the statistical techniques used by Mannheim and Wilkins. See D. G. Ogden, 'A Borstal Typological Survey', *British Journal of Delinquency*, Vol. 5, No. 2 (October 1954), p. 99.

[2] Mannheim and Wilkins, op. cit., p. 120. See also Healy and Alper, op. cit., pp. 229–30—'The Commissioner who has been the leading spirit of the Borstal movement believes that in roughly 20 per cent of the cases a longer period of control is highly desirable.'

[3] *P. C. Report*, 1958, pp. 75–6; 1960, p. 36. Considerations of overcrowding and cost may also have been of some importance in this decision.

[4] A. Gould, 'Time and Training,' *Howard Journal*, Vol. 10, No. 1 (1958), p. 50

experiment at Pollington. Other studies, especially the High-fields experiment in which results from a short-term intensive, group-orientated programme were at least as good as those from a long-term institution, have also had a similar influence.[1] On the basis of a study of the attitudes and personalities of sixty boys in one house of an open institution, and of its inmate culture and social structure, Little has observed that attitudes towards the staff and the system deteriorate with time. He suggests that this is due to a discharge policy through which 'good influences' earn early discharge and the 'failures' become the senior 'tone-setting' members of the group. The inmates he says are in 'a state of anomie, there are defined goals, early discharge, but limited means of achieving them', and those who do not achieve early discharge react by rejecting the values of the system.[2] Clearly the results of this study, if validated by a larger research programme, pose a problem for classification and for a need to reconsider the principle of the indeterminate, or indefinite, sentence.

The second conclusion (that open borstals were more successful than closed ones) had already been accepted as a 'principle' many years before, but in effect it highlighted a problem which the Commissioners still had to face. The study showed that the gross difference of 22 per cent in the success rates of open and closed borstals dropped to 8 per cent when the rates were adjusted to allow for the types of boys being sent to each.[3] This 8 per cent difference could be said to be due to treatment, whilst the 14 per cent was due to allocation. Wilkins attributed the greater success of the open borstals to what he called the 'normative effect',[4] or, as Martin has put it, the open borstals may succeed more frequently through the effect of the composition of the social groups to be found there rather than as a direct result of the type of training given.[5] It must not be

---

[1] H. Ashley Weeks, *Youthful Offenders at Highfields* (1958); also Lloyd W. McCorkle, A. Elias and F. L. Bixby, *The Highfields Story* (1958)

[2] A. Little, *Borstal: A Study of Inmates' Attitudes to the Staff and the System* (unpublished University of London PH.D. dissertation, 1961)

[3] op. cit., p. 135

[4] L. T. Wilkins, *Classification and Contamination*, (unpublished memorandum)

[5] J. P. Martin, *Case Conference*, Vol. 2, No. 7 (November 1955), p. 27

forgotten of course that the converse could account for the lower success rate of the closed borstals. Perhaps the continued insistence on avoiding contamination has led to isolating the problem boys into an environment where they cannot hope to improve. Consequently the aims of positive training cannot be realized. As in the thirties, it is the 'good boys' who get the advantages of innovations. Those who are most in need of learning self-discipline and who might benefit most from group counselling cannot receive this kind of training in institutions dominated by the need for caution and discipline. The existence of inmate groups with strong anti-social attitudes necessitates disciplinary methods on the part of the staff: these conditions are the very antithesis of those required if borstal training as perceived by the administrators is going to succeed.[1]

Now that the number of institutions has increased,[2] it should be possible to experiment more freely with allocation procedures. Of the total daily population in 1962, 1,962 were in closed training borstals and 1,652 in the open. At least some of the most difficult cases in closed borstals might benefit from mixing with a better type of inmate in the freer environment of the open borstals. Basic premises about the influence of bad boys upon good, as well as anxiety about public relations, have by and large kept the most difficult cases out of the open borstals. In fact the Commissioners have decided to train all the worst elements together. Hindley borstal now takes those boys who are 'resistant to training by reason of their experience of other forms of institutional treatment, and who were also

---

[1] See *P. C. Report*, 1961, p. 37; and 1962, p. 32: 'in closed borstals . . . the pressures on a lad from the inmates themselves can be damaging to his relations to the staff and to his training generally.' See also for an interesting comparison with American experience, Howard W. Polsky, *Cottage Six— The Social System of Delinquent Boys in Residential Treatment* (1962). He has shown, by participant observation, that in a cottage-system reformatory the inmate social structure dominates the behaviour and attitudes of the boys. This, he suggests, is reinforced by the cottage parents who, being isolated from professional therapeutic staff, 're-inforced the delinquent subculture by manipulating the boys' social hierarchy, wooing the leadership and dominating weak members . . .', all in the interests of good order, p. 85.

[2] In the 1962 Report, twenty training borstals (including satellite camps) of which eight were closed establishments are listed.

security risks'. Apparently these boys have in practice proved 'an embarrassment to other training establishments'. The Commissioners hope that 'by isolating the problem we shall be able to devote special attention to it'.[1] It remains to be seen what measures will be introduced for their special training.

The Mannheim-Wilkins study also made it possible for the allocation centres to consider the prognosis of the boy during classification. In fact the allocation of boys to Pollington has been based almost entirely on the prediction scores. However, this technical advance in the allocation process has been followed by a decrease in the time and effort devoted to classification. The need to get the increasing number of committals out of local prisons and into training institutions has led to a cut in the time formerly devoted to classifying.[2] In addition, the centres have been hampered by the lack of suitably trained staff, particularly psychologists. The chief psychologist remarked in 1961, 'we have fallen back seriously in borstal allocation work'.[3] Distressing as it must be to the Commissioners that they have, so far, only managed to open one remand centre, it is of great interest that the allocation process should have been sacrificed. Only the most obviously difficult cases are fully examined and documented: not only is there a loss of material which, if properly collected, would have benefited future research,[4] but allocation has to be made on superficial information. If it is really of the utmost importance that a boy should go to the *right* borstal haphazard allocation must result in many misfits and so upset the training of the boy

---

[1] *P. C. Report*, 1962, p. 28

[2] The question of borstal boys waiting for long periods in prison on remand has been raised on a number of occasions in the last few years. See for example, *H. C. Debates*, Vol. 592, cols. 549–50, 24 July 1958; Vol. 614, col. 139, 2 December 1959; Vol. 633, col. 153, 2 February 1961. Also, *P. C. Report*, 1961, p. 34.

[3] *P. C. Report*, 1961, p. 67

[4] This also affects the amount of information that can be passed on to the Borstal Division to aid them during after-care. It is also of some note that at least enough information is collected at the centres to allow the computation of the prediction score. An emphasis on collecting this data might well in the long run prove to have diminished the range of data collected for diagnostic and treatment purposes, as well as future prediction studies.

himself and the institution in general.[1] But perhaps it is an indication of the similarity of many of the institutions that allocation can be so quickly expedited. In a widely variegated system, with many different types of institutions, allocation would be one of the principal processes which it would be impossible to sacrifice.

Despite the venture at Pollington, little real experimentation has been carried out. Gordon Rose has asked, 'where is the family group borstal, the forestry camp borstal, the therapeutic community borstal? Indeed what about the hostel borstal where everyone works in industry, and the self-governing borstal where nobody is forced to work at all?'[2] Perhaps the main factor making such developments 'impracticable'[3] is the fact that the Commissioners are aware that borstals are viewed as penal establishments, and that public opinion would not tolerate institutions which lacked what is traditionally thought of as 'discipline'. In a public statement made at an enquiry on the opening of an open institution in 1959, the Commissioner found it necessary to assert that 'an open borstal is not a progressive school. The standards of discipline are as high as anywhere else. There is no sort of long-haired business about open borstal training.'[4] While reformatory treatment for young offenders retains its penal connexions there is probably little hope that it will make the strides which Dr Rose suggests. The recent Act of Parliament has emphasized discipline and closed institutions; has insisted that borstals and young persons' prisons should be thought of as properly belonging to the same

---

[1] In an attempt to try to overcome the problem of deciding which boys to trust in open conditions, the Commissioners started an experiment at Northallerton borstal in 1958. Boys who it was thought might possibly respond to open conditions were sent there for an initial trial and observation period before re-allocation. This interesting experiment in two-stage classification was abandoned, however, because it both lengthened training time, and broke up relationships which boys had established at Northallerton; furthermore, it was felt that more boys were sent to closed institutions from Northallerton than was perhaps necessary. See *P. C. Report*, 1960, p. 36.

[2] A. G. Rose, op. cit. (1960), p. 14

[3] See Rose's comments on his own suggestions, ibid., p. 14.

[4] Mr Taylor, the Commissioner responsible for borstal institutions, reported in *The Times*, 13 November 1959.

system. This surely has made it even less likely that borstal can dissociate itself completely from its prison past and experiment freely with many different methods of training and treatment. If, as Sir Lionel Fox said, the punishment is in the deprivation of liberty, there should be no real need to emphasize these elements within the system itself.

# VI

# After-Care

*The Beginning* [1]

The Gladstone Committee in its recommendations for a juvenile-adult reformatory added that 'special arrangements ought to be made for receiving and helping the inmates on discharge',[2] in much the same way as help was given to boys leaving ordinary reformatories. Any boys who failed after receiving such help would, the Committee assumed, have obviously relapsed into crime of 'their own deliberate choice' and so be rightly exposed to the 'far sterner penalties of prison life'.

When the first experimental class was started at Bedford there was no provision for after-care. But in his second report, the Governor strongly urged that action should be taken to discharge the cases on 'ticket of leave' which could be revoked if the boy was found in bad company. He thought that the Church Army or Salvation Army could be persuaded to supervise the cases and so 'follow up in an unbroken chain the amount of training they gain in prison'. This, he concluded, would be 'the most vital and important part of the whole scheme'.[3] Early in 1901, Sir Evelyn Ruggles-Brise decided to organize on a voluntary basis the after-care for the new scheme.[4] The new organization was called the London

[1] For a detailed history of the *administration* of after-care, see W. R. Burkhardt, *A Study of the Borstal After-Care System*, unpublished M.A. thesis, University of London, 1956.

[2] *Departmental Committee*, para. 846, p. 31

[3] Second report of the Governor of Bedford in *P. C. Report*, 1899–1900, p. 20

[4] The scheme was started through invitations to a dinner party followed by an appeal for help from Sir Evelyn. See Sir Haldane Porter, 'Memories,' in Shane Leslie, *Sir Evelyn Ruggles-Brise: A Memoir of the Founder of Borstal* (1938), p. 141.

Prison Visitors' Association. Its secretary was Haldane Porter, a young barrister. Members of the Association visited Penton-ville, Wandsworth and Wormwood Scrubs and after consulta-tion with the chaplain and other staff selected cases that seemed 'suitable'. There was no intention of trying to help all cases. Haldane Porter said in a letter to *The Times* asking for financial support and the sympathy of employers and voluntary workers, that only a 'limited and promising number' would be aided.[1] The Association was also charged with giving special attention to the boys at Bedford who would be discharged to the London district,[2] and later when Borstal was opened, dealt with all the cases receiving the new treatment, irrespective of their diffi-culty. In 1904, the name of the organization was changed to The Borstal Association. But it was not only the name that was changed; the new body undertook its work in much greater earnest. As Haldane Porter has remarked: 'The London Prison Visitors' Association . . . was in truth a somewhat amateurish effort, run without any sort of staff from my chambers in Lincoln's Inn . . . The Borstal Association was a much more serious affair, and soon developed into a real organization for helping and keeping in human touch with the discharged Borstalites.'[3] The secretary of the new Association was Wemyss Grant-Wilson, a young barrister who was to devote himself to the work of Honorary Director for over thirty years. The B.A. received a Treasury grant of £100 but otherwise had to rely on the collection of annual subscriptions from personal friends—an appeal to the public through the columns of *The Times* having produced 'only a disappointing result'.[4] The Association was formed under a 'powerful patronage', consisting of the Home Secretary, the Lord Chief Justice, the Archbishop of Canter-bury, Mr Asquith and other important parliamentarians, and designed to give 'a permanent form and name to a change in the prison system, tentatively begun, and slowly realized'.[5]

The Commissioners believed that it was upon after-care that the 'success of the system must depend', and if it were not successful the after-care would have at least provided knowledge

---

[1] *The Times*, 18 October 1901
[2] *London Prison Visitors' Association*, First Report, 1901–02
[3] Sir Haldane Porter, 'Memories,' in Shane Leslie, op. cit., pp. 141–3
[4] *The English Prison System*, p. 92      [5] *P. C. Report*, 1903–04, pp. 18–19

about the causes of failure.[1] Besides its value in giving support
to boys released into the open community, the Commissioners
saw clearly that information could be gleaned about the
success of the system which could be presented as hard facts to
the public. They would then be able to judge for themselves
whether the new system had led to an improvement. There can
be little doubt that the publication of good results enormously
enhanced the reputation of borstals and particularly of the
B.A.[2] Commentators were convinced that everything necessary
to help the boy was done effectively by the B.A., and that 'it is
only the lad's fault if he does not do well then'.[3]

In these early years those who judged the system placed far
more stress upon the importance of after-care than upon the
training carried out in the institutions. The Commissioners
were certainly most impressed by the work of the B.A. They
wrote, 'We are not aware that at any previous period in the
history of the prison system of this country, has so determined
an effort been made by a body of voluntary workers',[4] and later
that 'we fully recognize that without the after-care of the
Borstal Association, the Borstal Scheme during imprisonment
would have little or no effect'.[5] In the discussion on the
Prevention of Crime Bill in 1908, Mr Gladstone remarked that
'the most essential part of the Borstal system was what was
known as the "after-care system" '.[6] In the House of Lords, the
Lord Steward went even further and described the clauses
relating to after-care as 'really the essence of the Bill'.[7] On the
completion of the Prevention of Crime Act, *The Times* commented: 'It is only right to say that the action of Parliament
would have been *futile* but for the formation of the Central
Borstal Association [my italics].'[8] After-care was seen as more
than a useful adjunct to training; the work of resettling boys in
the community was an integral part of the total training process.

---

[1] *P. C. Report*, 1900–07, p. 13
[2] For a discussion of results see pp. 203–4 below.
[3] Russell and Rigby, op. cit., p. 86
[4] *P. C. Report*, 1905–06, p. 18          [5] *P. C. Report*, 1906–07, p. 24
[6] *H. C. Debates*, Vol. 197, col. 233, 24 November 1908
[7] *H. L. Debates*, Vol. 198, cols. 681–82, 10 December 1908
[8] Leading article, 'The Results of the Borstal System,' *The Times*,
4 August 1909

## Statutory Recognition

After-care was made a statutory part of the borstal sentence under section 5 of the Prevention of Crime Act 1908. But in this section no society was specifically authorized to carry out the work.[1] Yet this did not matter, for the Treasury recognized the Borstal Association by increasing its grant to £1,000 and providing £3 for every one that the society collected from voluntary funds, thus putting a premium on encouraging voluntary support. It is certainly interesting that the B.A. should remain without full support from statutory funds for forty years until the passing of the Criminal Justice Act 1948, while adult convicts on the other hand had been aided by the publicly supported Central Association for the Aid of Discharged Convicts since 1911. The Director of the B.A. stated that he believed that 'in co-operation with the resources of the State and the enthusiasm and freedom of action possessed by a voluntary association lies the solution of the problem of the diminution of crime'.[2] But important as the voluntary effort was, probably the main reason why the Association did not receive full support was that the Government preferred to rely on voluntary efforts and provide subsidies whenever money could be saved in this way. In the nature of the case, ex-borstal boys could elicit charity where ex-convicts could not: borstal was seen as an exciting new venture in the reclamation of youth. Besides this, there was the idea that an independent body could provide the boy with a kind of enthusiastic support and guidance that a public body could not match. This independence made it more possible to experiment and to enlist the support of voluntary workers and philanthropists who would not so readily come to the aid of a state organization. It was considered important that the boys should think of their after-care as being given by 'friends' and not by a branch of the penal system. Only after it had become apparent that the probation service was the best-equipped body to give both practical and casework aid did it become essential that the Association should be part of an organized public social service.

[1] Roman Catholics were supervised by the St Vincent de Paul Society.
[2] *Borstal in Nineteen Hundred and Nineteen*, p. 11

B.R.—12

The 1908 Act, by giving the Commissioners power to release an offender on a licence that could be revoked, strengthened the hand of the B.A., and in consequence added to after-care the function of supervision. Without sanctions the B.A. had been powerless to order a boy to conform to any particular form of conduct. In the face of misconduct 'moral suasion' was all the Association had at its command.[1] 'The boys want', said the author of an article in *The Times*, 'taking, metaphorically, if not literally, by the scruff of the neck, with the threat that their licence will be revoked and their liberty again curtailed.'[2] On the other hand, it is particularly illuminating that the Association managed to build up such a strong reputation, based on good results[3] without the sanction of recall. Yet the B.A. was concerned about 'much unfruitful expenditure of time and money, and a sad waste of young lives'.[4] It was thought that the licence would particularly help 'offenders of the coster and newspaper-selling class, from which the failures are chiefly drawn'.[5]

Under the 1908 Act supervision was to last until six months after the expiration of the sentence, with a period of recall of up to three months. The amending act of 1914 increased this licence period to one year and enabled recall to be ordered for six months. The Association had been dissatisfied with the short time boys were under supervision (seldom more than a few months), and had suggested that 'if the licence lasted in every case for two or three years the great majority would settle into regular work, and the minority would have shown themselves unfit for a life of freedom'.[6] It is of interest to note that Ruggles-Brise had criticized Elmira for having 'a period of surveillance' of only one year, and yet he apparently did not press for a longer period for borstal boys.[7] The licence was, in fact, the stimulus 'to the formation of regular habits'.[8] It

[1] *B. A. Annual Report*, 1905, p. 8
[2] Article, 'The Borstal Scheme', *The Times*, 1 December 1904
[3] For a comment on results in the years prior to 1908 see p. 203 below.
[4] *B. A. Annual Report*, 1908, p. 7. See also *Annual Report*, 1907, p. 8.
[5] Russell and Rigby, op. cit., p. 130
[6] *Borstal in Nineteen Hundred and Eleevn*, p. 10
[7] See p. 12 above.
[8] *B. A. Annual Report*, 1914, p. 8

provided a deterrent to those who would make little effort—'an invaluable spur and control in the first weeks of freedom, and sometimes later; when first good resolutions need reviving'.[1] Revocation of the licence appears to have been fairly readily used for boys who refused to work or who absconded from the place to which they had been sent.[2]

## Supervision under the Ruggles-Brise Regime

The Borstal Association was a philanthropic body imbued with much of the spirit of the Charity Organization Society:

> It has been objected [stated the B.A.] that the young offender has more money and care lavished on him than is spent on an honest boy. So it is with the case in hospital . . . Our object is, of course, not simply to make things easy for our charges, but to set them on their own feet as soon as possible, and *our help is conditioned by an earnest response on their part*[3] [my italics].

Its officers were the *bourgeois*, its patrons the church and the law. Much emphasis was placed on the importance of confining help to the 'deserving' and on the need for strict discipline. Ruggles-Brise openly referred to the B.A. as a system of 'patronage' or charity. Its officers continued in the role of the governors, tutors and chaplains in the institutions, dispensing advice and help willingly yet never forgetting discipline. In the early days, the 'Associate', as the voluntary helper was called, was the definite social superior of the delinquent—while giving practical assistance and advice, he could supposedly both command the authority necessary for the militaristic idea of discipline and provide the example of gentlemanly conduct to which the boy should aspire. Respect for the gentleman's way of life, combined with a feeling of gratitude that someone so important was bothering to help, was thus intended to provide a positive stimulus to the youth.

[1] *B. A. Annual Report*, 1918, p. 5

[2] In the comments in *Borstal in Nineteen Hundred and Eleven* it is noted that in 21 cases out of 212 in the past year, licences had been revoked for infringements of the licence other than committing offences—a higher proportion than in recent years. Of 100 homeless boys released in 1957, none were recalled for unsatisfactory behaviour, although 75 per cent were reconvicted within two years. See the author's PH.D. dissertation, op. cit.

[3] *B. A. Annual Report*, 1908, p. 9

Appeals for funds and help were made to the philanthropic and patriotic feelings of the middle classes. They were also reminded, in an indirect way, that to contribute to the Association was in the interests of social stability. In their report for 1920, the B.A. wrote:

> This Report is addressed to the educated and intelligent. They can appreciate both the value to them of our present stage of civilization, and the dangers and difficulties which the same civilization allots as their portion to boys and girls of spirit whose lives are poor and dull and street bound. Great is the value to our impoverished state of the young and strong and alert: this is an appeal to help some of those who, born under a happier star, might have been amongst the best.[1]

Appeals had been made by Ruggles-Brise 'not only in the name of charity but in the name of patriotism',[2] and employers had been told that giving jobs to boys was 'a form of service to the State'.[3]

The Association did, however, manage to enlist the support of men who were genuinely interested in helping the boys to lead a more settled life and in general did their work, according to Hobhouse and Brockway, 'kindly, tactfully and in the spirit contemplated when the Borstal Association was formed'.[4] Hobhouse and Brockway apparently had no criticisms to make of this 'spirit'.

From 1911 onwards, the number of Associates throughout the country continued to increase. Help was enlisted from the members of such organizations as the Church of England Temperance Society, the Society of Friends, and the Missions to Seamen in the ports. An arrangement was also made with the police so that boys could go to them for help if they were in a strange part of the country and without resources.

In 1905 the B.A. sent a circular to over 2,000 employers in London asking for their help in employing boys, but although a 'nucleus' of helpers was formed the response was not encouraging.[5] In fact, for many years the Association had great difficulty in finding work for boys, for there was a continuously

---

[1] *B. A. Annual Report*, 1920, p. 5
[2] Letter in *The Times*, 16 March 1907
[3] *The Borstal System for the Reformation of Young Prisoners*, 1908, p. 6
[4] *English Prisons Today*, p. 443      [5] *B. A. Annual Report*, 1905, p. 9

high level of unemployment. When the 'honest' were unemployed, those 'without character' stood little chance. As the
1907 report states: 'In one period of ten days alone nearly
forty firms expressed to our Visitors their sympathy, but
exhibited long lists of former employees awaiting re-engage-
ment.'[1] The Association's agent reported in 1910 that 'there is
little or no demand for our class of lad; the openings that are
found are generally given out of sympathy'. Where work was
given, boys may not even have been given the rate for the job.[2]
No wonder the aspirations of the boys were greater than the
openings, particularly if they believed the bench that they
would be taught a trade and given a new start in life.[3] Even
the B.A. advertised asking employers to give jobs to boys
'trained as carpenters . . . smiths, gardeners . . .'[4] In the early
years the exceptionally promising were helped to emigrate but
this was considered an unusual form of expenditure. In these
circumstances, a large number of boys were sent to sea, special
homes being opened at Cardiff and Bermondsey.[5] The Association approved of this occupation: 'Seafaring is an occupation
which is wisely chosen by those of high spirit who are bored
by the somewhat clockbound character of honest life ashore.'[6]
If the official accounts of after-care are correct (and unfortunately there are no others) a great deal was done to help
the boys on discharge. 'Work is found for him, necessary tools
or special outfits are provided, and if his wages are not sufficient
at first to maintain him, they are supplemented.'[7] The local
Associate was also charged with befriending the boy and trying
to connect him with 'a club or some other means of spending
his spare time honestly'.[8] Although the after-care relationship
may have been based on patronage with a strong emphasis on
helping the 'deserving' while deterring the 'undeserving'
through means of the licence, it seems that the Association had
laid firm the foundations for a successful system of after-care.

---

[1] B. A. Annual Report, 1907, p. 6    [2] B. A. Minutes, 9 November 1910
[3] B. A. Annual Report, 1908, p. 4    [4] In The Times, 13 January 1910
[5] The Lord Chancellor drew the Lords' attention particularly to the fact
that boys were assisted to go to sea. H. L. Debates, Vol. 17, col. 245, 29 July
1914
[6] B. A. Annual Report, 1914, p. 16
[7] B. A. Annual Report, 1912, p. 11    [8] B. A. Annual Report, 1915, p. 12

The Departmental Committee on Reformatories and Industrial Schools, reporting in 1913, stated: 'The careful arrangements for after-care made by the Borstal Association . . . might be taken as a model for this work.'[1] Members of the borstal service testified to the good work—for example, the Chaplain of Feltham:

> I desire to bear my testimony to the great work of the Borstal Association. I have had fair experience of after-care work and I consider that the thorough and practical manner in which every lad is provided with a really solid chance in life on discharge at the capable hands of the Association is nothing short of wonderful.[2]

To some extent the Borstal Association became involved in the confusion created by the use of the term 'modified borstal'.[3] A Borstal Committee was set up at each local prison, consisting of magistrates and members of the local Discharged Prisoners' Aid Society. This committee was charged with organizing the supervision of young prisoners aged 16 to 21. Members of the committees became honorary members of the Borstal Association so that the central body could keep an overall watch on, and interest in, the after-care of all young persons.[4] The reports of the local committees were published in the B. A. Report for 1907, and given equal weight to the work of the B.A. with borstal boys.[5] However, this was the only year in which the reports appeared. It had soon become apparent that just as modified borstal was a pale imitation of full borstal training, so the after-care provided by the committees could not be compared with the work done by the B.A. The Association was anxious to clearly separate the two classes of offenders, for it remarked: 'Of necessity it cannot be urged, in approaching employers, that the reformation of character has been effected which is possible only as the result of the training afforded by

[1] Quoted in B. A. Annual Report, 1913, p. 9
[2] P. C. Report, 1913–14, Part II, pp. 112–13
[3] See pp. 17–18 and 25–7 above.
[4] 'He [Sir Evelyn] hoped that the B.A. would become a sort of central body which, with the aid of affiliated societies in different parts of the country, would become responsible for the care on discharge of all young prisoners.' Reported in Justice of the Peace, Vol. 69, 26 August 1905, p. 354
[5] B. A. Annual Report, 1907, pp. 3 and 4, and 22–58

the longer sentences.'[1] The Association did not seem to think that the young prisoners might have been better in the first place.

The Borstal Association through its visits to the institutions to see the boys, as well as through contact with them when released, was in an excellent position to criticize the work of the institutions. There is no doubt that after World War I it became an important vocal pressure group, repeatedly expressing dissatisfaction with the slowness of developments. In all respects the B. A. Annual Reports were much more 'progressive' in tone than those of the Commissioners. Sir Wemyss Grant-Wilson and his visitors were much more in sympathy with the ideas of their colleague Alexander Paterson than with those of Ruggles-Brise. In fact, the Minutes of the Borstal Association indicate that Paterson frequently wrote articles on its behalf. But when Sir Evelyn retired, the B.A. paid tribute to him. The Report for 1921 states that Ruggles-Brise and his colleagues 'may justly claim that they have made a revolution within the prison system and in the attitude of the judiciary and the public to the treatment of the young offender'. Among the qualities asked of his successor was a similar 'undaunted belief in progress which has inspired and directed his development of the Borstal system'.[2] In fact, for a number of years, relations between the B.A. and Ruggles-Brise had been strained. The Executive Committee sent a letter to Sir Evelyn sometime in 1917 which caused a *furor*. They wrote:

> The Committee regret to feel it their duty to bring to your notice the fact that the system of training and education at present carried out in Borstal Institutions differs essentially and radically from the principles laid down by Mr McKenna the Home Secretary . . . in 1914[3] . . . the Committee have hitherto refrained from formal representations in the hope of increased activity in development, but they fear that for some time past there has been a relative decrease in the rate of such activity and an actual introduction of certain retrograde practices.

Ruggles-Brise seemed astounded at the letter. He firmly repudiated the allegations, stating that he could not see the

---

[1] *The Borstal System for the Reformation of Young Prisoners*, 1908, p. 7
[2] *B. A. Annual Report*, 1921, pp. 2–3
[3] This statement is reproduced on pp. 23–4 above.

criticisms as 'friendly co-operation towards the common end'. Furthermore, he pointed out that the Association had been founded for the purposes of after-care and that, strictly speaking, questions of internal administration would not, in the ordinary course, come within the scope of their duties! He rightly reminded the Committee that its opinions conflicted with those normally presented in Annual Reports,[1] and that the information in the Report did, of course, have an important influence upon the courts. In other words, if the B.A. was dissatisfied why had it not said so publicly? Feelings ran so high that Haldane Porter, at that time a lawyer in the Home Office, felt obliged to resign from the Executive Committee.[2] The matter did not end there. In 1921 Paterson proposed a resolution to the Executive Committee (of which he was a member) deploring 'the inadequacy of the present system of training' and calling for the appointment of 'a special Borstal Commissioner'—the job he was to get the following year.[3] On the retirement of Ruggles-Brise, Grant-Wilson sent a memorandum to Maurice Waller, the new Chairman of the Commission, stating that 'under their late Chairman, the Commissioners have not taken a sufficiently serious view of their responsibilities. They have not provided in Borstal Institutions something sufficiently different from prisons to render justifiable the long sentences to Borstal Treatment which are given as an alternative to short sentences of imprisonment.'[4] It was only with the new regime of Waller and Paterson that Grant-Wilson and the B.A. felt confident that progress was really being made.[5]

The difficulties associated with the opening of Portland had serious repercussions on the B.A., just as they had affected the prestige of the system in general.[6] In the memorandum to

[1] This seems to place some doubt on the reliability of the accounts of after-care noted in this section.

[2] B. A. Minutes, 1917. Ruggles-Brise's letter in reply is dated 21 December 1917.

[3] B. A. Minutes, 8 April 1921

[4] B. A. Minutes. Memorandum dated 21 November 1921. There was, however, a slight intimation of this in the report, Borstal in Nineteen Hundred and Twenty-two, p. 7.

[5] See the letter from Grant-Wilson in Justice of the Peace, Vol. 87, 2 June 1923, p. 435.      [6] See pp. 34–5 above

Waller, Grant-Wilson stated plainly, 'We are going to have a good deal of trouble over this newspaper talk because some of our best Associates are getting restless and magistrates are getting doubtful. I hope that a plain statement of the case admitting defects and promising more resolute progress will be issued soon.'[1] Eighteen months later one prominent member of the Executive Committee 'reported several rebuffs from persons whom he had asked for subscriptions', and the Committee in general considered that the 'delirious articles' published in the popular press 'denouncing the unsympathetic treatment meted out by the Borstal Association' seriously prejudiced its financial position.[2] So serious was the situation that the Home Secretary made a statement to the press praising the B.A., and in its annual report the Association, rather than 'admitting the defects', completely denied the substance of all the criticisms made of Portland.[3] In all events, it was not until 1926 that the criticisms were finally ended by the publication of Moseley's *The Truth about Borstal*, which fully exonerated thé Association.

*An Expansion of Activity*

The increased use of the borstals in the late twenties meant more work for the Association and a consequent expansion in its organization. To cater for the care of those who lived outside London new 'friends' had to be found. Helpers were found, presumably from among professional people, charitable organizations and such bodies as the Church of England Men's Society, but gradually the proportion of probation officers undertaking this work in a voluntary capacity increased. The probation officers began to form wide and useful contacts in their areas, which were particularly helpful in finding work for borstal boys.[4] Within London the staff of the Association was responsible for all the after-care arrangements, but in the provinces voluntary Associates were recruited to help the

---

[1] *B. A. Minutes*, 21 November 1921

[2] *B. A. Minutes*, April and May 1923

[3] *B. A. Annual Report*, 1922, pp. 8 and 11–13. It is impossible to tell whether this report was published before or after the meeting of the B.A. Executive Committee in April 1923, referred to above.

[4] Especially after the Criminal Justice Act 1925 which established probation officers in *all* courts

official Associates with their work. These 'unofficial Associates' were enlisted to provide the kind of help which it was felt the official responsible for supervision could not give because of his relationship to authority. They were, in other words, expected to help as friends and in particular to provide suitable leisure activities and social contacts. The number of these voluntary Associates expanded rapidly until in 1925 it was estimated that there were about 1,000 of them, 'of every class', helping in various parts of the country.[1] The Association was trying to combine the supervisory and friendly aspects of after-care by splitting the work between officials and more casual helpers.

With the changes in the institutional regime in the mid-twenties the boys benefited from a new type of personal contact with the housemasters which was not entirely based on 'authority'. In the field of after-care an important change was brought by the increasing amount of work being performed by probation officers. They gained their prestige with the boys not through social superiority or humanitarianism, but through specific skills which could be valuable to the boy in solving not only his problems of finding employment but his personal difficulties as well. However, it was not until the thirties that the probation officers finally established themselves as the chief after-care officers. It was apparent, also, that it was invaluable to have a permanent staff to deal with after-care, but there were few areas where there were enough boys to warrant a specialized staff. Only in Liverpool were there sufficient, and here a small office was opened in 1929. Professional after-care workers were probably better than Associates who had other activities during the day, or even probation officers who had other heavy commitments or who were not fresh to the case; yet no other attempts were made to establish them elsewhere. In any case, the Association had no funds to open offices to serve the other great conurbations with an organized and comprehensive service.

*The Departmental Committee on the Treatment of Young Offenders* made two suggestions which had some effect on the development of the after-care system. Firstly it recommended that local

---

[1] See B.A. appeal for funds on its twenty-first birthday. *The Times*, and all leading papers, 7 May 1925.

committees should be set up in the principal discharge areas[1] to organize and co-ordinate the work of after-care and secondly that the Home Office Probation Advisory Committee should also consider after-care.[2]

Although the Association had been trying to find friends who could act without official sanctions to mar the relationship, they still felt that the official associate was in a good position to help find work and arrange suitable leisure-time activity. Nevertheless, in this task he needed the support of the community. It was thought that a local committee made up of influential citizens could possibly persuade others to take an interest in the work and leisure of borstal boys and so make a positive contribution to their rehabilitation. However, it was not until 1936 that the first of these Voluntary Committees was set up to help associates find employment and make other contacts in relation to accommodation and leisure activities.

As the probation service was taking an increasing amount of work from the Association, it was considered that after-care should be recognized officially as one of its functions so that advice could be given by the central authority. In 1928 the Home Office Advisory Committee was reconstituted as the Advisory Committee on Probation and After-Care. While this step indicated an essential similarity between both kinds of work, it was still doubted whether probation officers would be willing to take on after-care as part of their official duty instead of it being part-time social work which they could accept or reject as they pleased.[3] In January 1931, the Advisory Committee sent a letter to the National Association of Probation

---

[1] *Departmental Committee*, p. 112. 'We consider that it would be a great advantage if, in the principal centres to which lads and girls are sent from Home Office Schools and Borstal Institutions, local committees (which we suggest might be called guidance committees) could be set up to organise and co-ordinate the work of after-care. It should be the business of such a committee to find local friends on request, to confer with them and discuss difficulties, and to help and advise generally as to the condition of labour and avenues of employment in the neighbourhood.' They suggested that it should be the duty of the Home Office to establish these locally where needed, and that the Local Education Authority should take the initiative locally. [2] ibid., p. 112

[3] In March 1928, the Clerk to the Justices at Birmingham wrote to the B.A. asking whether probation officers could help with after-care. In their

Officers stating that they wanted their views on whether they should accept an obligation to carry out after-care. At the Twentieth Annual Conference in May 1932, the probation officers accepted the principle that they should be officially responsible for the after-care of ex-Home Office schoolboys, borstal boys and discharged prisoners.[1] A circular to justices of 21 October 1932 made it clear that the Home Office was in favour of appointing probation officers as after-care Associates.[2] But here the discussion did not end: as will be shown later, the question of the suitability of probation officers for after-care work reappeared at the end of the thirties.

## The Main Problems of After-Care in the Thirties

Three main problems troubled the Association during the twenties and thirties: how to find work during a period of mass unemployment; how to deal with those with no homes and who were a constant disciplinary problem; and how best to bridge the gap between the institution and sudden freedom.

(a) *Preparing for employment.* In periods of mass unemployment the ex-criminal is especially at a disadvantage. The problem of the B.A. in finding employment for the boys was particularly difficult before World War I and again throughout the twenties and thirties. In 1925, when the Associate in Hull wrote to the B.A. about the problems of finding work for boys at sea, he concluded: 'We have something like 11,000 men and boys on the Labour Exchange books and sufficient men hanging around the shipping offices to carry the ships ashore!'[3] In order to try to overcome some of the difficulties of boys who found them-selves unemployed on release a scheme was started in 1922 whereby some boys were paroled before being licensed so that they could look for work. If work could not be found, they

---

reply the B.A. said that at present the work was satisfactorily done by the local discharged prisoners' aid society and individual Associates 'some of whom have probation experience'. The letter concluded by saying, 'we should welcome an organization which would secure for the help of our lads . . . the experience of Probation Officers and the system of supervision which they work'. *B. A. Minutes*, 22 March 1928

[1] Mrs Le Mesurier, *Handbook of Probation*, p. 151

[2] Reprinted in *Handbook of Probation*, p. 343. It was stated that at this time about 25 per cent of the work was being done by probation officers.

[3] *B. A. Minutes*, 16 June 1925

returned to the institution 'without the discredit of a revoked licence'.[1] But they had to be released sooner or later, and then the problem was the same.

Boys had to be fitted into whatever jobs were available. Those who had acquired a smattering of skill in the trade shops had to revert to labouring or to work in the catering trade. The position was realized by the Commissioners who made sure that each boy was fit to do labouring work on release. At Portland, for instance, a discharge class was formed to which a boy was sent two months before his release. This class was put to work on the hardest possible manual work available because, as it was stated, 'so many lads from the three principal trade shops find on discharge that the "technical" market is hopeless and therefore have to accept any labouring job going. We can and should at least ensure that such lads are fit for labouring work.'[2] Even so, the B.A. stated that 'we are not at present helped by the material sent out by the institutions. A great many lads come out without any serious intention to work. We gather that it is considered bad form to discuss a lad's past history with him, which may account for this state of affairs.'[3]

The Association could find work for almost all those who did not find it themselves or through their relatives, but not the type of work for which they had been trained.[4] The advances in trade training were rendered useless by outside circumstances.

From the reports of ex-borstal boys[5] one gets the impression that most of the boys were put on work which was either

[1] *P. C. Report*, 1922–23, p. 31
[2] Governor of Portland: see *P. C. Report*, 1934, p. 68.
[3] *B. A. Minutes*, 22 January 1930
[4] In *P. C. Report*, 1935, p. 25. The Commissioners state that, although the Borstal Association was successful in finding work for all but a small proportion of cases, it was often difficult to find work of a similar kind to that in which lads had been trained in the institutions'. According to the Governor of Oxford Prison the position was no better in 1939. He referred to 'slender chances'. See *The Times*, 8 May 1939. Mannheim showed that of the boys in his study 23 per cent found work within a month after discharge (but he had no information for over half his sample), and 20 per cent found work in the same or similar trade, etc. (interpreted in the 'widest sense') as learnt in borstal. op. cit., p. 257
[5] J. W. Gordon, *Borstalians* (1932), pp. 211–13 and 215. He states that in the seven years prior to 1932 he had come into contact with dozens of ex-borstal boys who were generally embittered and disgusted by the

temporary (as some labouring contracts) or which was completely 'dead-end' such as in cafés and as hotel porters. Paterson
believed that it was dead-end jobs and transitional work that
led to unemployment and that this in turn led to delinquency.
The whole idea of trade training had been to train boys so that
they could compete for better and more stable work. It is clear
now that penal reform cannot work in a vacuum: the logical
condition of Paterson's proposition precluded the existence of
involuntary unemployment. If in fact unemployment was one
of the prime causes of delinquency as he believed, then institutional training was not the answer to it when the boy was faced
with almost certain unemployment through no fault of his own
on release.

(b) *The problem cases.* It is possible to trace a transition in attitude
which is reflected in the way that the Association have tackled
the problem of dealing with the most difficult cases released
from the institutions. Broadly speaking, this change is from one
which emphasized help for those who would help themselves to
one emphasizing the need for intense casework with those who
either cannot or will not make the effort on their own. This
change has been paralleled in many other branches of social
work in the last few decades, particularly in the abandonment
of the distinction between the 'deserving' and 'undeserving'
poor.

---

'lodgings, employment and support given them on discharge'. This book
was in fact ghosted by a journalist, and was criticized as being completely
untrue by a member of the B.A. at the time (information through personal
contact): see also the review in *The Magistrate*, Vol. II, No. 40 (June-July
1932), p. 608. According to a Memorandum written by Grant-Wilson
(undated and in the hands of the Borstal Division), Gordon (alias Wright)
had first written articles favourable to the B.A. in the magazine *Answers*.
He had subsequently been given permission to visit institutions and the
B.A., had somehow 'felt himself affronted' and changed his tone. He had,
in fact, the B.A. claimed, received much help and had written after
supervision 'in friendly and grateful terms to us'. Grant-Wilson stated,
'Wright has apologised for these lies which appear to be the product of a
disordered mind'. The Association considered taking legal action against
the publishers. However, the evidence of Mark Benney in his *Low Company*
(1937), pp. 247 and 252, supports Gordon's contention that once a job of
some sort had been found other help and supervision were negligible. At
that time the Association found work for about half the boys; the other half
finding work themselves or through relatives.

The main problem of after-care has always been what to do with those boys who are either homeless, come from unsatisfactory homes, do not want to return to their homes or are in danger of contamination from their old companions. As early as 1925, the B.A. had evolved a scheme for classifying boys on their committal into three groups:

(a) those who having no home or an undesirable one must be self-supporting from the moment of their discharge, (b) those who would be likely to return to previous occupations such as mining, farming and sea, (c) those who would be unlikely to benefit by workshop training. As a result of this classification, the B.A. suggested that the workshops should be reserved for class (a).[1]

In an attempt to better the environment of some boys on release 'the most ready remedy . . . was . . . to transplant them to a new environment, and find them a new home and satisfactory work away from bad influences'.[2] The paradox for training is that boys will only settle in those areas which they consider their home and where they are once more open to the environmental influences that the borstals have tried to counteract. The Association gradually realized from experience that most boys will not stay in a town where they are strangers, and where they have for friendship only an official who holds over their head the sanction of recall. Until 1936 a fair proportion of boys were transplanted—in 1927, for example, of 538 discharges 175 were sent to surroundings which were considered better than their home area—but in that year a study showed that about 50 per cent of the transplanted boys returned to their original environment. From then on it was decided only to send boys to a new area if it appeared extremely necessary.[3] Some attempt was made to use the farm training for resettlement, particularly once the farming borstals were opened in the

[1] *B. A. Minutes*, October 1925

[2] In the Commons it was suggested that 'if a scheme can be found by which a boy, having come from an institution of a reforming nature, was then sent to a situation in a different part of the country amid an entirely different environment, these boys would have the opportunity to lead a straight career as they often wished to do'. *H. C. Debates*, Vol. 265, col. 883, 28 April 1932. See also F. Brockway, *A New Way with Crime* (1928), p. 107, who suggests special hostels for the homeless seeking work.

[3] *B. A. Annual Report*, 1936, p. 3

late thirties; but it is impossible to calculate how many boys trained in agricultural work actually settled on the land.[1]

The most unreliable boys presented the Association with their biggest dilemma: those who were homeless and unstable, the work-shy and the reconvicted. These were the boys who needed the most help and encouragement, but they were also an embarrassment to the Association. It must have been fairly widely known that about 40 per cent of borstal boys were likely to commit crimes again, and very difficult to get employers to take on such odds when there was a plentiful supply of 'honest labour'. The B.A. reported: 'At no time within living memory has the task of finding work for lads . . . without character been a more desperate undertaking.'[2] In these circumstances the Associates were extremely cautious and refused to recommend boys for work if they looked unreliable, on the grounds that they could not afford to have their contacts lose faith in their integrity and good sense.[3] They also did very little to help those released from the recall centre because they felt that first releases should be given preference over those who already had squandered a chance. This meant that the Association was refusing to help those who probably were in most need of help; presumably the more stable and reliable elements would have needed less incentive to go straight. It was not until the economic situation began to improve towards the end of the thirties that help was extended to all types of offenders.[4]

[1] The Home Secretary stated that efforts would be made to find farm work for those trained in it. *H. C. Debates*, Vol. 322, col. 1166, 15 April 1937

[2] *B. A. Annual Report*, 1926, p. 7. In the report for 1927 it was stated '[there were] long queues of unemployed . . . men of skill and good character with a first claim to employment . . .', p. 1.

[3] 'They (the Associates) do not indeed recommend for work those who have shown no disposition to do well at the institutions', in *Borstal in Nineteen Hundred and Twenty Five*, p. 6. Also in the *B. A. Annual Report*, 1935, there is a copy of the notice introducing boys to the Association which includes the following: 'The help given by the B.A. on your discharge will depend on your conduct. We cannot afford to recommend to employers any lad who is likely to let them down, as by doing so we should injure the prospects of other lads.' (p. 1)

[4] In the *B. A. Annual Report*, 1936, it is stated 'Hitherto, owing to the large numbers dealt with and the expense involved, it has not been possible to do much for lads discharged after revocation of licence; but during this year

(c) *Preparing for discharge.* The increasing emphasis in the thirties on the importance of close relationships between house-masters and boys posed the problem of how to avoid any ill-effects due to this relationship being suddenly broken at the end of training. In theory the Associate was to replace the housemaster, but it was clear that in practice this could not occur immediately on release when the boy was most in need of a close and sympathetic relationship. There were two possible remedies; and both were tried. On the one hand the boy could be weaned away from the housemaster and forced to become more independent; or alternatively an attempt could be made to build up a relationship between the boy and the future Associate during training so that a relationship based on trust and confidence would exist from the moment of release. As an experiment at Camp Hill Borstal in 1934, a discharge class was opened where boys were placed two or three months before release and where they were not supervised by a house-master. The Governor reported:

> The discharge house has been continued and in our opinion the experiment is worth continuing still further. The lads miss the housemaster when first removed, but the weaning serves to make them fitter on the whole for the complete severence when discharge arrives.[1]

But this experiment was not extended (presumably because it was not, in fact, entirely successful), and it appears that the Association concentrated on the second alternative.[2]

The main experiment in preparing a boy for discharge and introducing him to his future Associate was 'home leave'. Originally leave was granted as a special favour for a few exceptional boys at Feltham at Christmas 1933, but was later

---

labour conditions have become much easier and numbers have fallen, and it was found possible to take licence revoked cases and give them a fresh start. The natural result is that lads who are anxious to redeem their past have another opportunity to do so . . .', p. 2.

[1] *P. C. Report*, 1934, p. 61

[2] 'Discharge classes' to help prepare the youths for the problems they meet had been a feature of borstals since Llewellin started them at North Sea Camp. However, they did not involve any 'weaning', nor did they exist at all institutions.

extended to Camp Hill and Rochester and finally to the institutions for the toughest offenders.[1] This leave had to be earned by good conduct and was not generally regarded as part of the training process. The Commissioners were at first wary of abuse, just as they had been with open borstals and summer camps, but it soon became apparent that most boys could be trusted. Never more than 5 per cent of the boys failed to return or returned late. This leave was also regarded as a valuable part of training in the exercise of trust and was said to do much in increasing self-respect. By the end of the thirties the four-day leave was being enjoyed by an increasing number of boys who were able to make some tentative plans for their future and make contact with their Associates, who were in their turn able to assess the home situation and plan for release. But this leave period was naturally insufficient to deal with anything but the most immediate problems. Associates were therefore encouraged to visit their charges during training if at all possible, or to write regularly to them. It appears that visiting was not a constant feature of the preparation for release, and that even correspondence was probably very limited and usually only carried out with the most difficult cases.

Although some progress was made before the war in establishing well-planned after-care for those who most needed support on release, the Association was still more concerned with aid on discharge than with providing intensive casework. It had not been until 1936 that those who were the biggest risk received any help at all.

*Administrative Arrangements*

During the twenties and thirties the administrative arrangements were not very different from what they are today. An officer of the Association interviewed the boys at the reception centre and made them aware of the aims and practice of after-care. Each boy was told that every month a member of the Association would visit the institution, and that he could be

---

[1] *P. C. Report*, 1934, p. 31. Home leave was still regarded as an 'experiment' three years later. *The Times* reported on 23 December 1937 that 'as an experiment 15 youths at the B.I. at Camp Hill I.O.W. will be allowed to go home for five days Christmas leave. It is understood that similar leave will be given to the B.I's at Feltham and Rochester.'

seen to discuss any problems relating to his home or his future on which he wanted advice or immediate help. When it became known when the boy was due to be released he was again interviewed by the official and plans were made for his resettlement. Probably there was less intensive long-term planning for resettlement than there is now, but the basic pattern of work was the same as that used today. One of the changes introduced by Paterson which has persisted as an integral element of after-care was the development of close relationships between the staff in the institutions and those planning after-care. In 1923 housemasters were seconded for a period to the B.A. so that they could learn at first hand the organization of after-care and study the after conduct of boys who had already passed through their hands.[1]

However, there is some evidence that before 1935 the visits made by B.A. officials to the institutions had both failed to establish good relations with the boys or to build up a close liaison with the housemasters. The boys had been paraded for formal interviews in the Board Room, and because of shortage of time the visitor had not seen them in their houses, at work or recreation.

> Nor was time available for an intimate discussion of each lad's case with the Housemaster and Governor. The consequence of this was that the relationship of the Borstal Association to the lad was rather formal and official and coming after the lad's two years' experience of the close friendly contact of Housemaster and officer, produced a stiff atmosphere not conducive to that regard which it is felt should exist between the lad and those responsible for his care on discharge.

The practice was therefore changed so that the visitor saw the boy in the evening and at work during the day. As a result there was 'a very great improvement in the attitude of the lads to the Borstal Association'.[2]

It is impossible to say whether the Borstal Association was more or less successful than it is today. We know that it managed to find work for most boys, but we do not know how long boys kept in their jobs, how many were found satisfactory

[1] See *B. A. Minutes*, November 1923
[2] In the draft annual report for 1935. See *B. A. Minutes*, 1935

homes or how many even got on well with their supervisors. The most notable thing about after-care in the thirties was the final acceptance of trained social workers as the proper persons to undertake after-care work, but even so, if the published success rates are anything to go by, not even this produced better results for the borstal system.[1]

## The Role of Probation Officers

The arguments for and against probation officers being accepted as after-care Associates were fully discussed by the *Departmental Committee on the Employment of Prisoners, Part II*, in 1935. The following points were made:

> For the appointment of a probation officer it has been presented to us that:
>
> He usually knows the lad already.
>
> He has experience in obtaining employment.
>
> He has an office in which the lad can report.
>
> He is in touch with all the social and religious bodies of the district.
>
> He is far less liable than a voluntary worker to be absent at a critical time.
>
> He is in a semi-official position which facilitates him taking the necessary steps if the lad fails to fulfil the conditions of his licence.
>
> Against the appointment of probation officers it has been represented to us that:
>
> The lad has probably already 'let him down' in the past, and he is less likely than a new helper to take a hopeful view of the case. He is likely to treat a discharged lad—now really a man—rather too much as a boy.
>
> It is discouraging for a lad to go back to the same round of reporting in the same office under the same control as before he was sent away.
>
> The relationship tends to be rather an official one. The probation officer is often an elderly person—a younger man would understand the lad's difficulties better, and be more helpful in suggesting a right use of leisure.
>
> There is a danger in reporting to an office. Discharged Borstal lads meet one another (instances are quoted) in the probation officer's office and undesirable associations are reformed.

---

[1] See pp. 208–11 below.

Almost all probation officers are overworked and the Borstal lad comes off 'second best' in comparison with probationers, nor have they time to visit the institutions as often as is desirable.

It would probably be unwise to lay down a fixed rule in this matter, but where the probation officers continue to act as Associates the suggestion made to us by one of the Borstal Governors that their work might well be supplemented by the appointment for each lad of an unofficial friend and adviser seems worthy of a trial.[1]

The Committee itself did not decide where they stood on this issue. Some of the reasons given against the appointment of probation officers appear particularly naïve today. They arose from the belief that the real sphere of influence of the probation officer was with young delinquents, and that he was not so competent to deal with adults (an attitude which is still reflected in the sentencing practices of many magistrates' courts).[2] Why on the one hand he should be thought too old to deal with the problems of ex-borstal boys, and yet on the other considered most suitable to deal with the children and younger adolescents is a paradox difficult to understand.

The question of the influence of any former probation relationship does pose serious problems, yet it has never been estimated how many boys have previously come into contact with the same officer. The dangers inherent in reporting to an office were discussed by the *Departmental Committee on the Social Services in Courts of Summary Jurisdiction*, which was particularly concerned that young probationers might be contaminated by ex-borstalians.[3] This is a difficulty which can of course be overcome by a well-planned timetable, but the Departmental Committee claimed further that the probation officers had not enough time to deal with the kind of after-care programme which was generally envisaged. However, they did not repeat the claim that officers would naturally put after-care low on their list of priorities.

Those who were sceptical of the probation officers' ability

[1] *Report of the Departmental Committee on the Employment of Prisoners*: Part II, 1935 (Cmd. 4897), para. 51
[2] See Roger Hood, *Sentencing in Magistrates' Courts* (1962), pp. 86–96.
[3] *Report of the Departmental Committee on the Social Services in Courts of Summary Jurisdiction*, 1936 (Cmd. 5122), p. 88

to tackle the task of after-care competently seemed unable to view the alternative in its proper perspective. Admittedly the officers had other claims on their time, but so had other Associates. At least the probation officers' work was always connected with the supervision of delinquents and was likely to provide useful contacts. The real doubt about the probation officers lay basically in the fact that they were officials. The Association had grown up as a charitable body relying on a number of people of 'good will' to provide the spiritual guidance which they imagined the boy needed most. It was feared that the acceptance of official social workers in place of 'friends' would mean the breakdown of the type of sympathetic and friendly relationship which the B.A. had always tried to foster. Implicit in the evidence heard by the Committee on Employment of Prisoners was the assumption that boys needed this friendship and guidance as much as contact with employers and clubs.[1] It seems to have been overlooked that the probation officers could bring to bear the experience and training of social work. But it is doubtful whether the probation officers' claim to the work could have been seriously challenged even if the Committee had decided definitely that they were un-suitable. The Director of the Association had informed the Committee on Social Services that he attached great impor-tance to the work of the officers and that he doubted whether he could have replaced them. The Committee therefore had to conclude that they were 'reluctant' to suggest that officers should not be allowed to continue with their after-care work.

With the increase in the numbers discharged the Association would have had great difficulty in finding sufficient voluntary workers. In 1925 to 1926, 576 boys were discharged, and there were a further 500 from previous years still on licence; in 1937, 1,001 boys were discharged. The permanent staff of the London office, and later of the Liverpool office, dealt with a decreasing proportion of boys as the number released rose. In 1930, the first year of the Liverpool office's work, the officers of the Association dealt with 44 per cent of the licensees, but by 1934 the Association reported that of the 1,600 lads on licence 'over 400 of these have been under the direct care of the staffs

[1] ibid., pp. 38–9

of our offices': a decrease of nearly 20 per cent in the work handled by officials.[1] The probation service was conveniently at hand to take on this increasing volume of work.

By the outbreak of the war the probation officers were aided by forty-four Voluntary Committees set up in the major urban areas to help find friends for the boys and to add their prestige to applications for work so as to reduce the immediate effects of the borstal stigma.[2] The Voluntary Committee scheme was 'received with intense enthusiasm to begin with', but, as the B.A. expected, there was a falling away until a working nucleus was left. The Association said it found 'much encouragement in the real and sound assistance we are receiving from all committees'.[3] In particular, the committees were supposed to offset the official interest of the probation officer-associate. But in practice the scheme did not last. By 1945 there were only ten committees left,[4] and when the Borstal Division was formed in 1948 they were all disbanded. Apparently they had contributed little to the solution of after-care problems.

*The Reorganization of After-Care*

During the war, with 75 per cent of the boys going into the army, there was little after-care in the peace-time sense. But during these years the future of the B.A. was hotly debated. The Director, Henry Scott, was in favour of a national statutory organization for all juvenile after-care and wanted an early statement on the future position of borstal after-care.[5] Paterson suggested that the Executive Committee of the B.A. should formally tell the Commissioners that they could no longer get voluntary subscriptions and so force the issue.[6] But when in 1946 no decision had yet been reached on the future position and status of the B.A., Scott resigned in protest.[7] It was a

[1] These figures are taken from the publications *Borstal in 1925*, etc., issued annually as a supplement to the B. A. Report.
[2] H. Mannheim, *The Dilemma of Penal Reform* (1939), p. 148
[3] *B. A. Minutes*, 1938
[4] H. Scott, 'Borstal Voluntary Committees Past, Present and Future,' Church Army Press, February 1945
[5] *B. A. Minutes*, 25 September 1944
[6] At a special conference on the future of the Association. See *B. A. Minutes*, 30 October 1942.
[7] *B. A. Minutes*, 7 November 1946

further two years before the after-care of borstal boys was made a statutory responsibility.

Under the Criminal Justice Act 1948 the after-care of borstal boys was to be handed over to a 'specified' society or persons. This society was the newly formed Central After-Care Association, a body designed to co-ordinate all the work of statutory after-care. This body was to ensure 'that what is in essence one problem should be treated on common principles' and that 'the actual working in the field . . . should equally be co-ordinated and treated on common principles by a competent body of qualified social workers'.[1] The Borstal Division was a separate part of this body, responsible to the Council of the Association.[2] The full co-operation of qualified workers was brought about by specifying in the Act that it should be the duty of probation officers to 'advise, assist and befriend, in such cases and such manner as may be prescribed, persons who have been released from custody . . .'[3] This was the final recognition that efficient after-care could not be provided by a partly charitable organization, but only by a well-organized body of professional social workers.

Excellent accounts of the administrative arrangements and work of Borstal After-Care are available elsewhere and it serves no purpose to reproduce the material here.[4] What is most important is to note the way in which the work with borstal boys has become a model for improvements.[5] The question of providing adequate after-care for adult offenders has become particularly prominent in the last few years, especially in view of the obvious inadequacies of simple aid-on-discharge.[6] More intensive after-care on the lines of the work with borstal boys has commended itself, the main elements of which are the planning from the beginning of the sentence, the home visiting

[1] L. W. Fox, *The English Prison and Borstal Systems*, p. 266
[2] Normally officially referred to as Borstal After-Care
[3] Fifth Schedule, para. 3 (5)
[4] F. C. Foster, 'Borstal After-Care in England and Wales,' *International Review of Criminal Policy*, No. 2 (July 1952), p. 27; also in the *Howard Journal*, Vol. 9, No. 2 (1955), p. 136. See also W. R. Burkhardt, *A Study of the Borstal After-Care System* (unpublished M.A. thesis, University of London, 1956).
[5] See leading article, *The Times*, 8 October 1958.
[6] See *Committee on Discharged Prisoners' Aid Societies*, 1952–53.

and contact kept during the sentence, and the lengthy period of supervision which includes not only help in finding a home and a job but also more personal casework.

The 1961 Criminal Justice Act made one major change in the provision of after-care. It imposed a standard two-year period of supervision from the day of a boy's discharge from the institution. Under the old system the statutory length of after-care had been one year from the end of the three-year sentence. But because most boys were released in well under two years, the period of supervision had become longer than the period of training. Also, those who remained longest in the institutions, either because of their slow response to training or due to definite misbehaviour, received a shorter period of supervision than those who had earned an early release. In many cases it was the former boys who most needed an adequate length of after-care, while many of the better boys did not need nearly three years under supervision. The Act, by imposing a standard period, recognized the inconsistency of the old formula. For those who do not need two years' care, Borstal After-Care retain their power to cancel the supervision order if the boy's response is very good.

The recommendations of the recent report of the Advisory Council on the Treatment of Offenders on *The Organization of After-Care* were fully accepted and will bring to an end the Borstal Division. The Council (with the dissent of Professor Radzinowicz, Lady Inskip and Mr Price) support the setting-up of a joint probation and after-care service with a Central Council for Probation and After-Care at the Home Office. The work of arranging the individual after-care will be carried out by staff in the institutions in conjunction with the local probation and after-care officers. The only function at present carried out by Borstal After-Care which will remain a central responsibility will be the power of recalling those in breach of their supervision order. This function will be entrusted to the new Central Council. Apparently this central organization will be 'advisory, rather than executive' and will aim to stimulate the work of the new decentralized service. The report expresses the hope that the experience of the present staff of Borstal After-Care will be made use of by the Central Council. 'The functions now exercised centrally by the Central After-Care

Association will be devolved as the other services [are] built up'—this presumably will take a long time.[1]

More attention has been paid in recent years both to the theoretical and to the realistic practical problems of providing care and supervision for the ex-borstal boy. This is probably mostly due to the increased professionalization of the after-care service. It is clearly realized by Borstal After-Care that the often 'idealized picture of the discharged offender as a poor fellow whose one ardent desire in life is to find work and keep it . . . is not always true to life. Sometimes his one real desire is to avoid hard and regular work and to evade the pressure we put on him to work.'[2] The emphasis on providing care in a casework setting during the supervision period poses a number of problems, some of which are discussed below.

*The Role of After-Care*

In theory, at least, after-care has always been regarded as an integral part of the borstal sentence. Paterson insisted that the supervision period was equally as significant as institutional training in the final outcome of the sentence. He wrote, 'The *second part* of training is in some respects even more difficult than the first part, for it is not always easy to control a lad who is tasting again the wine of a free life'[3] (my italics). And again, later, 'this leap from control to liberty would overbalance him were it not for the training continued after he left the institution'.[4] But it is doubtful whether, in practice, after-care has ever played such an important *training* role. Boys have always been discharged from the institutions when it was considered that they had reformed (or at least made progress), and never before. Historically, after-care has always had a strong supervisory element for the purpose of making sure that the boy obeys the conditions of his early discharge. On top of this, the care on discharge has been intended to supply material and personal help as a safeguard against bad environmental and moral influences. After-care has, therefore, been more strongly

---

[1] See, in particular, paras. 156–62 and 173 and the memorandum of dissent.                                        [2] *C.A.C.A. Report*, 1959, p. 18

[3] See article, 'Borstal Lads III, From Control to Liberty,' *The Times*, 6 August 1925.                                        [4] *The Principles*, p. 16

concerned with prevention than with training. Nevertheless, it is still true that training and after-care 'constitute a total process'.[1] There has always existed a working partnership between the institutional staff and those planning for the boys' resettlement, and much of the work during training would undoubtedly be undone if there were no help on discharge. It is the nature of this help which particularly distinguishes borstal after-care. As the length of training became shorter, what was originally planned in 1908 as a short period of supervision, gradually became as long, or longer than the time spent in the institution. The Criminal Justice Act 1961 ensured that nearly all boys would receive a longer period of after-care than institutional training. But with the exception of recent years there has been remarkably little reappraising of the role that long-term supervision and care is supposed to play in the total borstal sentence. In this respect the service has made a noticeable advance, being more introspective, open to criticism and ready to try new ideas than at any previous period.

Borstal After-Care consists of three elements: aid-on-discharge and physical aid throughout the period; continuous guiding social casework; and supervision. Although the amount of physical aid that is given to a boy is far more inclusive and better planned than that given by voluntary prisoners' aid societies, it is the elements of casework and supervision that most distinguish this type of after-care. The existence of these two facets of the work side-by-side, carried out by the same person, involves the service in its greatest conflict.

(a) *Aid-on-discharge*. Characteristic of borstal aid-on-discharge is the great care taken to prepare for the boy's release. From early in his sentence contacts with his home are made, and with the officer who is to be his Associate on release. By the time the boy is discharged he will have somewhere to go and in many cases a job waiting for him. The Associate is charged at all times to make sure that the boy is in steady work and that he has a home in which to live. In fact, few boys go short of physical help of this sort. It is this initial work, and continuing help which can form the basis of casework. Without it little

[1] *C.A.C.A. Report*, 1962, p. 20

would be achieved. As the Director of After-Care pointed out:

> The offender's attitude towards his supervisor usually stops well this side of idolatory . . . It falls to the supervisor therefore to *demonstrate* that authority is understanding and willing and able to help, and this must be demonstrated to the satisfaction of the offender. In the simplest terms it is useless to try to develop a casework situation until the basic needs of food, clothes, work and a roof have been met. Man is an unresponsive animal on an empty belly.[1]

He goes on to point out that casework skills are of little use if the offender does not believe that the worker is genuinely concerned with his well-being.

(*b*) *Casework and supervision.* Genuine concern and understanding are the basis of casework. But the Associate has also another role—that of the supervisor. In this role he is called upon to act as an authority figure who both directs the ways in which the boy leads his life and acts as an informant of the Prison Commission. The idea of supervision is connected with the attempt to continue training in the community after release. In practice this may be extremely difficult. At the same time it invests the Associate with the cloak of officialdom which may make it impossible for him to build up a good casework relationship. The Associate has to gain the confidence of the youth while sumultaneously impressing on him that he is still subject to the conditions of his supervision order.[2] This can be no easy

---

[1] *C.A.C.A. Report*, 1959, p. 17

[2] The conditions of the supervision order are reproduced below:

Prison Act, 1952: '*Notice to Person Released from a Borstal:* . . . From the date of your release until . . . you will be under the supervision of the Central After-Care Association, unless the Prison Commissioners decide that you shall cease to be under supervision, or order your recall to a borstal.

So long as you are under supervision you must comply with the requirements set out below, unless they are altered or cancelled by the Prison Commissioners.

If you do not comply with these requirements you will be liable to be recalled to a borstal.

Requirements—1. On your release you must go to the place agreed with the Central After-Care Association (Borstal After-Care) or to which they have directed you. 2. You must keep in touch with your supervisor in accordance with his instructions; you must be truthful in your dealings

task.[1] It is probably even more difficult to get the boy to consider this period of liberty as properly part of his sentence. Lord Moynihan has put the problem well in stating:

> If we believe that the Borstal idea is right . . . then the fault can only be in after-care . . . when they come out these boys do not seem to remember that they have done anything wrong. They do not seem to realise that they have not finished their sentences and that they should prove their worth before being accepted as normal citizens again.[2]

It is only too easy for the boy to think that he has 'done his time' and regard supervision as unnecessary interference.

In one sense supervision acts as a sort of trial period during which the Associate attempts to keep the youth up to the standards learned during institutional training: in another it can continue the process of training by directing the boy and helping him to adapt to the problems of living a well-ordered life. In practice, however, it is less easy to ensure that the youth leads the type of life which is approved, or to build close relationships, and least of all is it easy to decide *what* standards should be applied.

The Associate has a difficult task if he wishes to enforce a certain pattern of life upon the boy during supervision. If the youth naturally seeks the advice of the officer, it may be possible for the Associate to know what sort of life he is living; but if he does not confide, the Associate may have little idea

---

with him. 3. You must tell your supervisor immediately of any change of address or place of employment and any such change must be approved by the Borstal After-Care. 4. You must lead an honest, sober and industrious life and you must be punctual and regular at your work. 5. You must not break the law or keep company with persons of bad character. 6. If you need help or advice urgently and you are unable to get in touch with your supervisor you should write or telephone to the Borstal After-Care in London.'

[1] The Borstal Division in *C.A.C.A. Report*, 1955, notes the statement of the *Report of the Working Party on Supervision and After-Care*, 1955, that after-care is 'concerned with the whole personality of the individual in the context of his environment' and refers to the 'establishment of friendly relationships of confidence and goodwill'. The Division comment that 'it would be satisfying to know that [these phrases] are invariably translated into action', p. 17.

[2] *H. L. Debates*, Vol. 192, col. 775, 4 May 1955

what the boy is doing outside of working hours. There is always the sanction of recall which can be used to threaten those who do not obey advice, but this cannot be used against those who commit only minor breaches of their licence. In fact, recall is only ordered when the boy's behaviour has become acutely bad. The Associates are well aware that threats of recall are likely to breed mistrust, and are contrary to the principle of building up close relationships. It is clearly most difficult to build any relationship which is not built on either authority or patronage. As Borstal After-Care have pointed out:

> Although the threat of recall clearly cannot produce any fundamental effect in the outlook of the offender there is evidence that in many cases a timely reminder to a boy that his present course of conduct is likely to lead to his losing his freedom for a time may have a salutary effect.

But they go on to say that

> 'no conscientious social worker can be happy about this externally imposed change of conduct unless it is accompanied by an improvement in the relationship between him and the boy concerned.[1]

Only in so far as the Associate can use his personal influence can supervision control the total conduct of the licensee.

There is possibly some difference of opinion on what standards the Associate should set for the conduct of his licensee. It is the policy of Borstal After-Care that boys should be steady in their work and live a settled life, but beyond this there are no rules. The boy is supposed to stay clear of bad company and spend his leisure time engaged in approved hobbies, but it is most difficult to enforce a rigid standard over choice of friends or over what can be considered reasonable ways of spending leisure. Some officers may consider that the boy should be allowed to live whatever sort of life he likes provided that he

---

[1] In the *C.A.C.A. Report*, 1955, p. 16. In the *Annual Report*, 1956, commenting on the need for a sympathetic relationship, Borstal After-Care state, 'too frequently when interviewing boys recalled to Portsmouth Recall Centre, it is apparent that if they only had sufficient confidence in and a sufficient sympathetic rapport with their Associates at the time of the crisis, their failure and recall might have been avoided', p. 17.

shows an ability to keep out of trouble. And yet others may take a strong moral line and condemn certain types of behaviour outright. For example, the attitude of the officer to pre-marital sexual relationships may be either permissive or condemnatory. There appear to be two schools of thought here: one which considers that supervision should be confined to helping the boy only when it becomes apparent that his mode of life is leading him into problems which he cannot face alone, and that advice should be made on an estimate of the capacity of the boy to withstand the stresses which his way of life involves; and the other which considers that boys should live only a prescribed 'decent and socially approved' pattern. The first view is based on 'mental health' criteria, the second on absolute moral values. The content of supervision will thus vary according to which point of view the officer takes. In relation to the recent moves to extend this supervisory type of after-care to other offenders, there is clearly a need to examine more closely what officers should be doing when they are trying to 'develop and educate any talents and capacities in those under their care, to fit them to take their place as useful citizens'.[1]

Probably in practice, then, the element of training in the after-care process is at a minimum for most boys. They do accept aid in terms of job finding and occasionally may seek advice on personal problems, but the extent to which the Associate can really affect the attitudes of the boy will depend on the type of relationship which he has managed to build up, which in turn will depend on a positive attitude in the boy towards accepting supervision. Probably, the relationship between officer and boy will be most successful where the case-work role is paramount, and the supervisory role relatively ignored. For those who are anti-supervision there is only the threat of recall.

Only with one group of boys does after-care in any positive sense continue the training started in the institution. The

[1] Pakenham/Thompson Committee: *Problems of the Ex-Prisoner*; National Council of Social Service, 1961, pp. 26–7. Also, Report of Advisory Council on the Treatment of Offenders (Home Office, 1958). *The After-Care and Supervision of Discharged Prisoners.* Also, Pauline Morris, *Prison After-Care: charity or public responsibility?* (Fabian Research Series 218, 1960)

homeless and institutionalized boys in fact *need* to be trained in the open community, for their problem is social inadequacy which is aggravated rather than helped by institutional life. Supervision for these boys is most definitely part of the training process. It involves a long and continuous effort to help the boy to settle down in an environment where he has usually no friends, and with which he is unable to deal on his own. The socially inadequate cannot be trained in institutions; they must be taught how to handle their problems in the community, and helped to overcome them there. With this group a close supervision over all aspects of their life is essential if they are to be helped to stay clear of trouble. Borstal After-Care, therefore, has recently made special provision for them. Homeless boys are identified at the beginning of their training and are from then onwards dealt with by a special pre-discharge planning unit, which was set up in 1953. The unit's object is to make every attempt to establish contact with parents or relatives and, failing this, to make adequate preparations for the boy's reintroduction into the community. Special efforts are made to find suitable lodgings and jobs and to establish good relations between the boy and his after-care Associate. The author has compared the after-conduct and after-care of boys released before the unit was set up with those who had received the benefit of the unit's work. He found that after-conduct in terms of reconvictions, work habits, settlement in accommodation and relationships with Associates was no better for the latter group than for the former.

On examining the background of the boys it was apparent that there were two rather distinct types of boy classified under the general heading of 'homeless'. One group had lost contact with their homes in the recent past due to death or disagreements; the other group had been for many years without a home and consequently had a great deal of institutional experience prior to being committed to borstal. It is among this group that most of the socially inadequate failures of borstal occur. Clearly their problem is much more deep-seated than one of needing good lodgings, a job and friendly supervisor. They have through lengthy institutional experience become unable to make personal relationships, plan for the future or manage their lives. Their delinquencies are frequently trivial and in many cases they appear to welcome a return to the shelter of institutions. The problem is to help them mature sufficiently so that they no longer need institutional care.[1] In order to deal more effectively with these boys, Borstal After-Care set up a home in London in January 1961, with the support of a charitable organization. Derek Miller has described in detail the principles behind the therapeutic methods used at 'Northways' and shown that as compared with a control group, over a short period, the home is proving extremely effective with these institutionalized boys.[2]

In theory after-care should be a much more inclusive and more controlling service than is in fact possible. Inadequacies are due to the sheer mechanics of providing substantial control over youths in the open community, and not due to lack of effort in meeting the problems associated with work, homes and leisure. Even if increased efforts were made to provide better jobs and more congenial homes there is no guarantee that supervision could be more intensive. What is most difficult is to gain the willing co-operation of the boy under circumstances in which constraint is at a minimum.

With such varied views on the theoretical aims of after-care and with no definitive consensus about the solutions to practical problems posed by the work, it is not surprising that there are great difficulties inherent in attempting to assess the success of a period of supervision. Not only is it virtually impossible to disentangle the institutional from the post-institutional influences, but it is also difficult to decide upon adequate criteria with which to measure the 'success' of both after-care and institutional training. Some of the problems involved are discussed below.

*Problems of Assessing the Success of Training and After-Care*

The figures which the Prison Commissioners give in their reports of the number of boys reconvicted once or more frequently since release really tell very little about after-conduct. Even to base an assessment of success in terms of reconviction on these raw figures is somewhat misleading. They

---

[1] See the author's PH.D. dissertation, op. cit.
[2] See Derek Miller, op. cit.

B.R.—14

tell nothing of the type of offence, or the circumstances in which it was committed, or of the time during after-care at which it occurred.[1] There is a great deal of difference between petty larceny and robbery with violence; between an offence committed under circumstances of exceptional deprivation and one carried out systematically as a 'professional activity'; between offences committed in the first few difficult weeks and those carried out at the very end of the supervision period.

The main distinction is between those boys who have been found guilty of an offence and those who have at least achieved the basic purpose of training and after-care and kept completely crime-free (or have not been caught!). Yet this division is not necessarily one which commends itself as a criterion of success. In fact it is in some way at variance with the policy and ideas of the Commissioners who, until very recently, always drew attention to the last column of their tables showing the numbers reconvicted twice or more, and preferred to count only these as failures. Some of those only reconvicted once have clearly been convicted of a relatively minor offence, or have committed crime in exceptional circumstances. Others have gone straight after their first offence and completely settled. Two reconvictions or more at least distinguishes those who have gone further than a first, possibly pardonable, lapse. But even this more austere criterion has its limitations. Possibly a boy may be reconvicted twice in the early part of the supervision period and still have ceased criminal activity well before the end. It also may be that all the convictions are for more or less trivial offences not to be compared even with one very serious offence.[2] There is also the difficulty of deciding how to classify crime committed after the licence has expired. Is the boy who has remained crime-free throughout supervision but who later takes to crime to be regarded as an after-care success? It might be said that training judged in the long run was here a failure

---

[1] Borstal After-Care publish figures showing whether those reconvicted failed during supervision or afterwards. Useful as this information is, it could still be made more valuable. The supervision period does, after all, cover two years.

[2] See Peter Scott's interesting attempt to measure the seriousness of reconvictions using the device developed by Sellin and Wolfgang; 'Approved School Success Rates,' *British Journal of Criminology*, Vol. 4, No. 6 (October 1964), p. 525.

but that supervision appeared to have been a success. Again, it has been argued that the Commissioners were misjudging the success of borstal by taking two or more convictions as the criterion of failure because the fact that a boy has stayed clear of trouble after his first conviction might be due to the sentence he received for that offence and not because of borstal training or after-care.[1] However, a fair proportion of offenders are not imprisoned for their first offence but recalled for up to six months' further training or get off more lightly with a fine or discharge. To view the process of recall as independent of the whole system of training and after-care would be incorrect. The recall centre exists as an after-care sanction in the same way that the correction centre at Reading exists as an addition to normal institutional training. Because a boy spends some time in the correctional centre he is not automatically classified as a failure. Similarly, boys who are recalled ought not to be so readily regarded as failures. On the other hand, if a boy is sent to prison for his first or subsequent post-borstal offences, it is impossible to disentangle the effects of institutional training, imprisonment and supervision.

From this it is clear that figures showing reconvictions should also include not only the number of offences but also details of the time after release that the offences took place, the seriousness of the offences and the way in which they were dealt with by the courts. From these figures a number of different criteria involving reconviction could be formulated. There is a strong case, for example, for making reconvictions in the last six months of supervision a criterion of failure as this isolates a group who are still unsettled after all efforts by the Associate. What happens under the present system of assessing success is that after-care is completely ignored. It seems reasonable to assert that after-care should only be judged after it has run its full course. At the moment the effect of supervision is not being taken into account in the assessment of success simply because difficulties which occur under this form of conditional liberty entail public, not institutional, law enforcement. This is no reason for pre-judging the whole supervision process at an early stage. As the result of a review of his cases

---

[1] Howard Jones, *Crime and the Penal System* (1956 ed.), p. 194

the Director of After-Care sheds some light on this issue. He reported:

> Of the 1953 discharges (since reconvicted), up to the end of 1957, 35 per cent could be said, as far as human assessment can go, to have stabilised and to have been leading normal lives. 14 per cent are hopeful prospects, 31 per cent can for one reason or another be regarded as doubtful prospects, and 20 per cent seem to be following the road to recidivism. This analysis throws a rather different light on our statistical tables and reminds us that one reconviction, or even more, after discharge from borstal by no means pre-supposes failure.[1]

Reconviction tells nothing about the way in which the institutions have changed the pattern of the boys' lives through all the elements incorporated in the training regime, unless of course reconviction and other criteria are inter-correlated.[2]

Training is aimed at improving the boys' work records, at preparing many of them for work in a trade, at building up a respect for authority and good personal relationships with those who help them, as well as preparing them to spend their leisure in pursuit of constructive pastimes. If the borstal system is to be judged it must be assessed in terms of the vocational, personal and educational effects it has had on the boy. Similarly, after-care should be judged on the success it has achieved in finding work, in ironing out difficulties in the home or providing good homes for the homeless, in directing leisure-time activity, and in particular in establishing a satisfactory personal relationship between the Associate and the boy.[3] Above all, supervision should not be judged before it has run its full course. Many boys make a bad start and later mend their ways; some who are never reconvicted are still completely work-shy and socially inadequate two years after their discharge from borstal.

Although it is possible to widen the criteria used for assessing

[1] C.A.C.A. Report, 1957, p. 20
[2] In the author's study of homeless borstal boys it was found that there was a high inter-correlation between all criteria of 'success' and, e.g., reconvictions, job stability, reporting behaviour, settlement in accommodation. See PH.D. dissertation, op. cit.
[3] See W. A. Elkin and D. B. Kittermaster, op. cit. Miss Elkin states, 'It is by its success or failure on . . . more personal lines [than reconviction] that Borstal after-care work must be judged,' p. 25.

the success of borstal so as to take into account all the elements in training and the total period of after-care, it is not possible to disentangle the effects of all these elements. For example, if a boy settles well one does not know whether this is due to the influence of the institution, to the influence of the after-care Associate, or simply to the process of maturation,[1] or to a combination of all of these. Alternatively, if a boy makes no attempt to settle during his supervision period, should one blame inadequate after-care? All attempts made to help him may simply have been refused. With such a great emphasis on the need to provide more adequate after-care for an increasing proportion of offenders it is important to know something about the system of supervision. There is obviously a need for much research in this field. In the first instance this research should be directed at fact-finding. Its main purpose should be to fill in the large gap of knowledge about what actually happens to boys on their release from institutions.[2] Such research may provide some pointers to the way in which more

---

[1] Dr Young, the Director of Medical Services, stated that 'inmates of the Borstal age group who are liable to disturbances of mental and physical inbalance would naturally tend to develop a more mature attitude with the passage of time alone', *P. C. Report*, 1950, p. 83. Sir Norwood East has made the same observation—see *Society and the Criminal*, H.M.S.O. (1949), p. 175.

[2] Past studies have made little progress in this direction. In 1940, Healy and Alper pointed out that 'it appears that no thoroughgoing, scientifically oriented study of the after-results of Borstal treatment has been carried out', op. cit., p. 213. Dr Mannheim's study of boys released between 1922 and 1929 was mainly concerned with aetiology, but besides giving some reconviction figures, he did present some limited data on the length of time boys had to wait after discharge before they found jobs, and the number who found work in the same job as they had done in borstal. Mannheim pointed to the deficiencies in the records which did not make possible a more thorough study of the supervision period. See *Social Aspects of Crime in England Between the Wars*, pp. 25ff. The two main post-war studies have presented much data on after-conduct. Rose unfortunately deals with the rather atypical experience of boys trained during the war but he does show the important relationship between regular work habits and remaining clear of reconvictions. See *Five Hundred Borstal Boys*, p. 100. For a detailed study of the records of 200 homeless borstal cases see the author's PH.D. dissertation, op. cit. However, as this study shows, records are a comparatively poor source of data for studying this problem, and future studies should concentrate on getting their data direct from the boys themselves.

detailed studies of the problems of assessing the effect of after-care might be carried out.

In the absence of any such studies it is necessary, for the purposes of assessing changes in the effectiveness of the system, to rely on the published reconviction figures.

# VII

# Results

## Early Results and Their Effect

The Gladstone Committee had not expected the new penal-reformatory to achieve spectacular results.[1] It was convinced that '*even a moderate percentage of success* would justify much effort and expense devoted to an improvement of the system'[2] (my italics). Only after 'the experiment [proved] more successful than its authors anticipated', with a 'degree of success which promises to reduce greatly ten or twenty years hence our prison population',[3] did a high rate of success come to be expected from the system.

In their first report, the London Prison Visitors'Association reviewed the progress of twenty-three boys released from Bedford. Six had been only recently discharged; of the remaining seventeen, two had been reconvicted but only seven were reported as 'doing well'. The Association stated that they were 'the most difficult material imaginable' on which to produce a good effect.[4] The Prison Commissioners, in their report for 1903 to 1904, published figures relating to the after-conduct of all the 122 boys released from Borstal since the scheme started. They reported '54 are now known to be in employment, 24 are known to have been reconvicted, 30 have been lost sight of. Of the remaining 14 it is hoped that at least 6 do well.' Considering that 'the lads represented the worst products of the London Streets', the Commissioners considered the 'satis-factory results in about 50 per cent of cases very praiseworthy,

---

[1] Even though a success rate of 95 per cent had been claimed for Red Hill Reformatory, and one of 80 per cent for Elmira.

[2] Gladstone Committee, para. 84, p. 30

[3] See leading article, 'The Results of the Borstal System,' *The Times*, 4 August 1909.

[4] *London Prison Visitor's Association*, First Report, 1901–02, pp. 2–3

and constitutes a sufficient justification, not only for the existence of such an association [the B.A.] *but also for its development on broad and comprehensive lines*[1] (my italics). The B.A. and the Commissioners were, however, concerned that the concentration of effort should 'produce results *proportionate to the time, and effort and expenditure of money it must entail*'[2] (my italics). Time alone would tell. But at least there were signs which could be regarded as hopeful. Between 1906 and 1907, the number of 16 to 21 year olds convicted dropped by nearly 15 per cent. The Commissioners saw this as possible evidence of the efficacy of their new methods:

> Time may perhaps prove this to be only a casual diminution; but we are sanguine enough to believe that the concentration of individual attention on young prisoners of this age, from the application of the Borstal system in its full sense at Borstal and Lincoln, and in its modified sense at all other local prisons in the country has already begun to bear good fruit.[3]

On the other hand, they had ignored the fact that the number of convictions had been about 13 per cent lower in 1900 than in 1907, and that was before the system had started!

In their Annual Report for 1908, the B.A. revealed that of the 189 boys released in that year only twenty-seven had been reconvicted and twenty-three were 'unsatisfactory'. It considered that these figures were a 'remarkable justification for the experiment' and predicted 'that they will be passed when the system is further developed'.[4] In particular they had in mind that these results were achieved without the aid of any after-care sanctions. With the aid of the licence granted by the 1908 Act, a Government spokesman confidently asserted that 'in future years the system would be an even greater success'.[5] In fact, expectations were aroused which far exceeded those of the Gladstone Committee.

---

[1] *P. C. Report*, 1903–04, p. 19. See also *Justice of the Peace*, Vol. 69, 26 August 1905, p. 354.        [2] *P. C. Report*, 1905–06, p. 19

[3] *P. C. Report*, 1906–07, pp. 15–16. Also *P. C. Report*, 1910–11, p. 27. Modified borstal claimed a percentage reconvicted of only 8 per cent, with 9 per cent doing indifferently. But, of course, there was no system of after-care to check on results.

[4] *B. A. Annual Report*, 1908, pp. 5–6

[5] Mr Renton in *H. C. Debates*, Vol. 197, col. 222, 24 November 1908

By 1911 Sir Evelyn Ruggles-Brise was claiming that the 'success of the last 12 months has been 82 per cent',[1] and it was believed that within ten years the number of prisons could be reduced by half.[2] Speaking in the Commons in 1914, Mr McKenna asserted that 'by far and away the majority . . . have . . . begun to do well in life . . . we have been able to say that the number of failures is very small'. When pressed for more exact figures he claimed he 'could not give them with any certainty, because there is a number which we are not certain about, and we cannot say what has become of them. There is a considerable number who have gone to sea, and we could not give with any certainty a percentage as to the number who have come through satisfactorily.' The best figures he could supply were: 40 per cent satisfactory, 25 per cent unsatisfactory, the rest unknown.[3] Less than a month later, Mr McKenna produced more figures, this time for boys released in the year ending 31 March 1914. He claimed that satisfactory reports were received for 82 per cent of the boys, and that of 411 released only twenty-five had actually been reconvicted. 'These results', he said with justification, 'were most remarkable.'[4]

These results were, however, based on very short follow-up periods. The earliest attempt at a long-term follow-up study was made by the B.A. in 1915. They studied the records of the 1,454 boys released between 1909 and 1914, some of whom had been at liberty for one year and others for up to four and a half years. The source of information was the local Associate and the 'criminal records of all Great Britain'.[5] The study showed that 65 per cent had not been reconvicted and were satisfactory when last heard of; 8 per cent were unsatisfactory but had not been reconvicted; and 27 per cent had been reconvicted. Of those released in 1910, however, 35 per cent had been reconvicted. It was probably this study which provided the

---

[1] Reported in *The Times*, 13 May 1911
[2] Mr Thomas Holmes, speech to the National Free Church Council Conference on the borstal system, *The Times*, 13 May 1911
[3] *H. C. Debates*, Vol. 61, cols. 198–9, 214, 15 April 1914
[4] In Standing Committee Debate. Reported in *The Times*, 6 May 1914
[5] Healy and Alper, op. cit., p. 221

Commissioners with the data on which they made their assessment of results in their report for 1922–23. In this report they claimed that 60 per cent of the boys who had been released in 1912 had not again come into conflict with the law. These 'relatively poor results' were believed to be due to the turmoil of war and uncertain industrial conditions. Commenting on these figures, a special article in *The Times* stated: 'There appears to be some basis for the opinion expressed by those engaged in this work that in *normal times* the Borstal system will establish in an honest and honourable method of life *all who have passed through its gates*, unless they are hampered by mental or physical defects'[1] (my italics). Sir Evelyn Ruggles-Brise made an even more favourable assessment in 1921, claiming that since 1908 only 27 per cent had been reconvicted.[2] These figures were quoted in *The Times* as proving that '73 per cent of the young fellows sentenced to detention . . . are permanently reformed'.[3] There is no clue why Ruggles-Brise's figures should differ so substantially from those in the Commissioner's report. It is doubtful, in any case, whether these claims for long-term results can strictly be compared with later figures which refer to a shorter, more specific follow-up period. Not only was there no systematic reporting of offences to the Association by the police, but there had also been the disruption caused by four years of war. It is still likely, however, that the Associates managed to report quite a high proportion of the boys' offences, at least during the supervision period when they were probably most likely to occur.[4] After supervision had ended it is probable that information would mainly have been gathered for those who again entered prison. In fact, it later became something of a practice to represent results in terms of

[1] See article, 'Borstal—Record of 21 Years' Work,' *The Times*, 16 October 1923. In the *B. A. Annual Report*, 1920, it was stated: 'When mental deficients have been eliminated, Borstal Institutions should be able to give a good account of all but a very few of their young charges,' p. 5. Later, in 1932 when it was proposed to open Bagthorpe Prison as a special recall centre, it was 'hoped to reduce the failure rate to 5 per cent'. See *B. A. Minutes* for a press report from the *Nottingham Evening News*, 17 October 1932.

[2] *The English Prison System*, p. 95

[3] *The Times*, 18 March 1921. See also leading article, 9 August 1921.

[4] Mannheim and Wilkins, op. cit., p. 127, among others, have shown that reconviction is most likely to occur in the early part of supervision.

the proportion of ex-borstal boys in the prison population.[1] The system had, after all, been initially intended to cut recidivism off at the source. The fall in the number of prisoners serving penal servitude from 4,029 in 1899 to 1,378 in 1921 which led to the close of Portland as a convict prison was attributed largely to the effects of the borstal system—there was no mention of changes in sentencing practices.[2]

Good results in the early years, combined with the rapid improvements made to the system from 1922 onwards, convinced many that borstal could achieve an enormously high success rate. It was against this optimism that the level of success came to be measured. Forgotten was the initial statement that even a moderate success would be considered satisfactory.

## Success Rates since 1922

(a) *An evaluation of the evidence.* Apart from some figures given by the B.A. during the twenties of the cases which were 'unsatisfactory', it is necessary to rely on reconviction data for a comparative analysis over a number of years.

One of the main difficulties in comparing the figures for reconvictions at different times is the variation in the length of the follow-up period. In each year that the Commissioners gave figures for the numbers reconvicted of those released in a number of previous years, the more recent years had a shorter follow-up period than the other years. No attempt was made to standardize the follow-up period, although with the exception of the war years it is possible to do this.

In the early years the Commissioners did not give details of reconvictions in all of their reports; but in some years (under the section describing the work of the B.A.) figures were given

[*text continues on p. 210*

---

[1] The *P. C. Report*, 1936, p. 28, states 'on February 1st 1936 in a total male prison population of 8,462, there were only 8.1% ex-Borstal lads serving sentences of imprisonment, penal servitude or preventive detention. At that time, 13,298 had graduated from Borstal training.'

[2] See article, 'Fewer Convicts: Effects of Borstal Reform,' *The Times*, 18 March 1921; also a speech by Paterson in which he said: 'the effect of the Borstal Institutions was seen in the halving of the prison population at Dartmoor, and the closing of Portland Convict Prison,' *The Times*, 27 April 1923.

## TABLE 1

### Reconviction rates since 1932 with a standard two- and three-year follow-up period

*(Where only figures for longer periods are available these are shown in brackets)*[1]

| Year | Number released | follow-up two years | | | follow-up three years (longer periods in brackets) | | |
|---|---|---|---|---|---|---|---|
| | | Per cent not reconvicted | Per cent reconvicted once only | Per cent reconvicted twice or more | Per cent not reconvicted | Per cent reconvicted once only | Per cent reconvicted twice or more |
| 1932 | 769 | | | | 49·9 | 24·6 | 25·5 (4 yrs.) |
| 1933 | 883 | | | | 56·2 | 22·9 | 20·9 |
| 1934 | 900 | 66·4 | 19·8 | 13·8 | 61·0 | 20·8 | 18·2 |
| 1935 | 808 | 67·7 | 21·8 | 10·5 | 62·5 | 22·3 | 15·2 |
| 1936 | 818 | 70·2 | 18·2 | 11·6 | | | |
| 1937 | 822 | | | | 56·2 | 20·4 | 23·4 (6 yrs.) |
| 1938 | 919 | | | | 64·1 | 18·2 | 17·7 (5 yrs.) |
| 1939 Jan.–Aug. | 812 | | | | 60·7 | 18·4 | 20·9 (4 yrs.) |
| Sept.–Dec. | 2,005 | | | | 57·5 | 20·6 | 21·9 |
| 1940 | 843 | | | | 53·7 | 21·6 | 24·7 |
| 1941 | 1,014 | 61·9 | 22·3 | 15·8 | 57·8 | 20·4 | 21·8 |
| 1942 | 1,381 | 64·7 | 20·7 | 14·6 | 60·8 | 18·7 | 20·5 |
| 1943 | 1,414 | 60·3 | 21·6 | 18·1 | 55·7 | 20·1 | 24·2 |
| 1944 | 1,236 | 60·1 | 23·5 | 16·4 | 55·2 | 22·3 | 22·5 |
| 1945 | 1,279 | 59·7 | 21·4 | 18·9 | 53·5 | 21·6 | 24·9 |
| 1946 | 1,858 | 55·4 | 24·9 | 19·7 | 46·2 | 24·3 | 29·5 |
| 1947 | 1,856 | 53·6 | 26·6 | 19·6 | 48·4 | 26·2 | 25·4 |
| 1948 | 1,655 | 54·1 | 26·5 | 19·4 | 47·9 | 25·5 | 26·6 |
| 1949 | 1,871 | 52·9 | 29·4 | 17·7 | 46·2 | 29·7 | 24·1 |
| 1950 | 1,790 | 51·0 | 28·4 | 20·6 | | | |
| 1951 | 1,697 | | | | | | |
| 1952 | 1,753 | 56·8 | 26·6 | 16·6 | 49·5 | 26·5 | 24·0 |
| 1953 | 1,784 | 54·1 | 26·8 | 19·1 | 47·6 | 28·8 | 23·6 |
| 1954 | 1,741 | 51·8 | 25·8 | 22·8 | 47·4 | 24·3 | 28·3 |
| 1955 | 1,667 | 53·5 | 24·8 | 21·7 | 47·7 | 27·7 | 24·6 |
| 1956 | 1,484 | 45·1 | 26·6 | 28·3 | 40·0 | 25·9 | 34·1 |
| 1957 | 1,703 | 40·5 | 27·0 | 32·5 | 34·6 | | |
| 1958 | 2,178 | 39·8 | | | 35·1 | | |
| 1959 | 3,115 | 38·5 | | | 32·2 | 24·0 | 43·7 |
| 1960 | 3,126 | 35·8 | 25·0 | 39·1 | | | |

[1] It has not proved possible to standardize the length of the follow-up for all the years since 1932 (the year for which figures were first given). When the figures were first published in the 1935 report they referred to the position at the end of 1936 (the 1935 report being published in 1937): so

Table 2 shows the reconviction rates as published in December 1959, showing follow-up periods of four years and up to twenty years.

## TABLE 2

**Reconvictions of boys released 1937 to 1955: showing reconvictions with a follow-up of four years or more**

| Year | Not reconvicted | Reconvicted once | Reconvicted twice plus |
|------|-----------------|------------------|------------------------|
| 1937–38 | 59·5 | 19·5 | 21·0 |
| 1940–42 | 50·7 | 21·3 | 28·0 |
| 1943–45 | 41·9 | 23·3 | 34·8 |
| 1946–48 | 38·8 | 25·9 | 35·5 |
| 1949 | 38·7 | 29·3 | 32·0 |
| 1950 | 37·5 | 26·8 | 35·7 |
| 1951 | 40·6 | 27·0 | 32·4 |
| 1952 | 43·5 | 25·1 | 31·4 |
| 1953 | 41·5 | 28·9 | 29·6 |
| 1954 | 42·7 | 25·8 | 31·5 |
| 1955 | 43·7 | 28·8 | 28·0 |

that for 1932 and 1933 there was a four- and three-year follow-up respectively. The 1938 report gave the figures for the 1936 discharges; but the intervention of the war prevented the normal sequence of reports. The next published figures refer to the position at the end of 1943, so that for the years 1937, 1938, 1939 and 1940 there was longer than a two-year follow-up period. Since then, except for one break, it has been possible to standardize the figures so that for each year the proportions reconvicted after two or three years can be given. The one break in this sequence is the absence of comparable figures for 1951 discharges. The 1953 report did not give figures for the 1951 discharges because it grouped them with the 1949 and 1950 discharges. The 1954 report again began to give figures for 1952, but gave no separate three-year follow-up figures for 1951. Later reports which give figures for 1951 with a much longer follow-up than three years show that this year was not atypical. Since 1959 it has been impossible to standardize the follow-up period in terms of the number of subsequent convictions. Since 1960 the Commissioners' reports have only given statistics for the number not reconvicted and the proportions of the convicted who have been recommitted to prison and borstal. Since 1962 no figures have been given. The Borstal Division statistics make a distinction between those reconvicted during supervision and those convicted after. In 1962, they reverted to former practice and gave figures for those reconvicted more than once.

for the number reconvicted at least once among those released two years earlier. It was not until the report for 1935 that separate figures were given for the numbers reconvicted only once and those reconvicted twice or more. It was in this year that the B.A. reached an agreement with Scotland Yard to report all reconvictions up to five years after discharge starting from 1931. The figures for the years prior to 1935 are not then strictly comparable with those after this date. The figures in the former years did not tell how many boys had been reconvicted twice or more, nor were they based on such accurate information. Table 1 shows such a standardization for both pre- and post-war years with a two-year and three-year follow-up.

(b) *The results.* The Commissioners' report for 1923–24 stated that among those released two years earlier 75 per cent were still clear of trouble: in 1924 the figure was 67 per cent, in 1925 66 per cent. There is no obvious reason to suppose that efficiency in reporting reconvictions could have varied between these years, so the figures most probably reflect a true decrease in success. One important factor was that these years were ones characterized by an increase in the number of boys sent to borstals. The institutions were overcrowded and boys were waiting long periods in prison before transfer to borstal. At this time the Commissioners were also happy to call those who had stayed out of trouble for two years 'successes', 'considering the difficulties and temptations to which lads of the labouring class have been exposed by the abnormal state of industry'.[1] Such variations in the conditions prevailing on release pose a problem for the interpretation of results. If conditions in the labour market are far worse at one period than another this is likely to affect the chances of boys keeping out of trouble. It is therefore impossible to assert that it was the overcrowding in the institutions which produced the less favourable results of the later twenties. Possibly it was a combination of both factors: changing conditions on discharge must certainly be taken into account in comparing the success of the system in different periods.

[1] *P. C. Report*, 1927, p. 27. Also, the *P. C. Report*, 1921–22, had thought the results 'remarkable considering the condition of industry', p. 7.

Statistics of reconvictions were (for some unaccountable reason) not given in the reports for 1930 to 1934, but since 1935 they have regularly included figures for both boys reconvicted once only, and more than once. By 1932 the proportion of boys not reconvicted had dropped as low as 50 per cent: a drop of a third in the success rate in ten years. This may have been a continuation of the effect of overcrowding, for the success rate rose again to around 60 per cent in the years 1934 to 1938[1] when the new institutions had been provided and the inmate population fell. A study made by the Borstal Association in 1939 of the records of boys released from the five institutions which had been in full operation since 1932 showed similar general results but also that Lowdham Grange had the highest success rate of 77 per cent, and Portland the lowest, of 50 per cent.[2] Although these figures were based upon a variable follow-up period they did show that the new institution was producing better results than the old. The classification of the most trustworthy boys in an open environment was producing better results for at least some of the borstal population. There does seem to be strong evidence that the expansion in training, combined with a decrease in the inmate population and better employment conditions on discharge, brought about a definite improvement in the general results at the end of the thirties. Not only did the number reconvicted only once decrease, but also the number who became recidivists. However, it should still be remembered that these results, although an improvement on those of the early thirties, are not as good as those claimed for the strict and limited regime of the early twenties. How much of this difference is due to better record-keeping at the later date it is impossible to say.

The 1939 figures are most interesting. Separate statistics were given for the January to August discharges who had

[1] Similar figures were given by Dr Radzinowicz in 'After Conduct of Convicted Offenders' in L. Radzinowicz and J. C. Turner, *The Modern Approach to Criminal Law* (1945), pp. 153, 157–8. He notes that this figure omits those who have reverted to crime but have not been detected, but states that these are 'very favourable results'. The *B. A. Annual Report*, 1938, stated that there were 15,000 ex-borstal men in England, 'most of them married and in their own homes'. The figures in the text above refer to a three-year follow-up period.

[2] See Healy and Alper, op. cit., pp. 216ff., for a discussion of this study.

served their full period in borstal, and for September to December discharges who had their training cut short by the mass discharge. The proportions of boys avoiding reconvictions and reconvicted more than once were similar for both periods. These figures appear to show that the length of training, or the completion of a full training course, did not appreciably affect the chances of going straight on release. The mass-discharged boys also received less well-planned after-care (although both groups did not receive the care of pre-war years). These boys were released before training was complete, and due to the war did not have full after-care, and yet results compare very favourably with pre-war years. It may be, however, that the proportion of reconvictions was under-recorded because of the war-time conditions. And, of course, the Services may have provided an environment which compensated for the lack of complete training and after-care.[1] Nevertheless, the statistics of this period challenge some of the basic assumptions about length of training and the need for full after-care.

From 1943 to 1946 the proportions avoiding reconviction fell, and in 1946 was, for the first time, under 50 per cent. But again it is not possible to know whether this was due to the difficult training conditions, or to war producing a higher proportion of more difficult boys. It should be remembered that misdemeanours of boys serving in the forces would not have counted among the reconvictions.

From the end of the war until 1955, the statistics show that the proportion reconvicted in the two years from discharge remained between 45 and 50 per cent, with about 25 to 30 per cent reconvicted more than once after three years from discharge. Since then there has been a deterioration, and of those released in 1960, 64 per cent were reconvicted once and 39 per cent twice or more after only two years from discharge. These figures compare most unfavourably with 11 per cent reconvicted twice or more after two years among boys released in 1935.

In fact, since the war the proportion of boys who have kept out of trouble has never approached that of the twenties or

---

[1] See the author's PH.D. dissertation, op. cit., for a discussion of the effect of the Services on homeless boys who enter the army on discharge.

thirties. There have been no unemployment difficulties on which to blame the lack of good results, although it is true that the institutions have been crowded with a much higher population than in pre-war years. Despite all the improvements in the system borstals are less capable of turning out reformed delinquents than in the harsh days of the Ruggles-Brise era or in the optimistic days of the late thirties. The explanation that has been most frequently offered is that youths are becoming progressively more 'difficult' to train.

The Mannheim-Wilkins prediction equation has become the standard device for assessing the difficulty of boys. The Commissioners have been making notes of the scores of all boys who have passed through the allocation centre and have reported that in 1960,

> No less than 66·4 per cent of receptions fell into the C and D categories, those with the poorest prospects of success. This compares with 56·5 per cent in 1957 and 25·5 per cent in 1946 (when the original research was undertaken) whilst the present proportion of 9·9 per cent in the A and B categories (with the best proportion of success) compares with 10·2 per cent in 1957 and 32·7 per cent in 1946. This deterioration in the quality of training material suggests that the success rate is likely to be under 40 per cent.[1]

Nearly half the boys sentenced to borstal in 1962 had six or more previous convictions. This compares very unfavourably with under 12 per cent in 1952. Mr Foster rightly asks, 'Is one of the reasons for the less satisfactory results of borstal training that too many boys are being sentenced to borstal too late?'[2]

It has also been pointed out that the 'delinquent generation effect' (with an increasing number of delinquents in the borstal age group) has added to the problems and probably affected the success rate.[3] What is more, it has been contended

---

[1] *P. C. Report*, 1960, p. 35. See also *C.A.C.A. Report*, 1961, p. 19. In the receptions for 1958, 6 per cent were in Group A, 11 per cent in Group B (3 per cent in 1946).

[2] *C.A.C.A. Report*, 1962, p. 17

[3] *C.A.C.A. Report*, 1960, pp. 17–18. See also the research note by Alan Little, 'Borstal Success and the Quality of Borstal Inmates,' *British Journal of Criminology*, Vol. 2, No. 3 (January 1962), p. 271, who rightly points out that the delinquent generation theory only tries to account for the increased

that not only are there fewer of the better boys but also that the few that remain are even faring worse than previously.[1] But this second revelation must mean that the prediction equation which was devised on the basis of data relating to pre-1950 boys is no longer related to success in the same way. The information which classified a boy as a one-in-eight chance of failure no longer does so. Other information is now needed to discriminate between the different levels of success. In view of the changes made in the institutional structure of the system, the length of training and the personalities and attitudes of the boys received,[2] it would be surprising still to find the same relationship between background information and likelihood of conviction on discharge. It could well be that social indices which were highly correlated with recidivism in 1946 have now become the property of a much larger proportion of boys. Little points out that drunkenness is now no longer such a limited phenomenon,[3] and it may be that job instability is also now more widespread. If this is so, both of these factors may not be so highly associated with recidivism as they were when

---

number of delinquents, and does not state that delinquents are likely to be more serious and more likely to be recidivists. It may be, however, that the increase in the number of committals by itself is affecting the quality of training and after-care that these boys can receive. This is noted in *C.A.C.A. Report*, 1957, p. 22.

[1] See Alan Little, op. cit., p. 266ff., which shows the decrease in quality in terms of the Mannheim–Wilkins scores over the seven-year period 1950–56.

[2] The Commissioners point out that no trend was observed in the type of offence for which boys were committed nor was there a change in the distribution of intelligence and educational attainment: *P. C. Report*, 1960, p. 35. But the Director of After-Care notes that he is 'more than ever convinced that the offenders which we have been dealing with in recent years present more difficult problems than ever before. We know that they are in the main the product of homes and community groups alien to accepted attitudes towards education, work, recreation, social responsibility and religion. There is nothing new about this . . . But over and above this familiar pattern we seem now to be dealing with a generation that can best be described as having a low threshold of stress and a low tolerance of frustration . . . The result is irrational conduct often accompanied by unpremeditated offences of an almost infantile character. . . .' See *C.A.C.A. Report*, 1958, p. 13.

[3] Alan Little, op. cit., p. 272, points out that drunkenness has increased and that this places more boys in the risk groups C and D.

they were the particular behaviour of a small and difficult group. As social values change so may the strength of the variables predicting recidivism. The information which isolated boys with a 75 per cent chance of success in 1946 may now be isolating a group with only a 60 per cent chance, but only a new prediction equation can show if there is a smaller proportion of boys in the borstal population with a 75 per cent chance of success.

A prediction equation which is really an experience table must be adapted to take into account changing social conditions and a change in the 'experience'. If the Mannheim-Wilkins equation is to be used for assessing changes in types of boys over time, then a continual sequential analysis of data is needed. This equation was not devised for this purpose, its main function was as a tool for classification, and its 'life' could only be that of the 'experience' of which it was predicting results and of the relevance of the information to this experience.[1] All that recent analysis does suggest is that experience has changed, and that in general results are lower than before. It cannot be argued from the fact that boys are responding less well to institutional training than formerly that they are 'inherently more difficult', but only that they are more difficult to train under existing methods. This is the challenge for the Commissioners.

## Some Problems for the Future

(a) *Future research.* One major fault of studies which attempt to compare the effectiveness of borstal with other methods of treatment is that they define borstal training as if it were one homogeneous treatment. In fact, it is not one treatment but contains many different kinds of training situations, each of which is calculated to have a different effect. What we need

---

[1] Mannheim and Wilkins discuss this problem and suggest: 'In view of the fact that the experiences we found to be prognostic of success have, in general, been found by others over many years in many different countries, there seems to be good ground for expecting prediction based on these factors to hold for a period long enough to be administratively useful. It does not appear that much is lost because this study is based on static experience so long as the need for revision is always considered' (p. 141). There seems ample evidence for such a revision.

to know is whether counselling is more or less effective when compared with individual casework or traditional 'house-mastering' methods and, if so, for which particular types of offender.[1]

Until very recently most comparative research in this country has shown that results are similar whatever treatment is given. These results are probably mainly due to unsophisticated research methods which fail adequately to take account of real differences in the types of offenders given different treatments.[2] The work of Grant and Stuart Adams in California has shown that although the overall results of two treatments may be the same, the treatments could each have successes and failures with different types of offenders. For example, Grant set up an experiment whereby naval offenders were classified in terms of the level of their 'interpersonal maturity' and allocated either to a special intensive living unit where they received counselling or to a more conventional form of training. Grant found that taking 'mature' and 'immature' offenders together, the results in terms of reconviction were roughly the same for both treatments. However, this concealed an inter-action between the type of offender and type of treatment. Under the intensive treatment 'mature' offenders did comparatively well and 'immature' offenders comparatively badly, and vice versa for the more normal training—overall the results had balanced out to be the same.[3] Adams found a similar phenomenon.[4] Attempts such as this to develop typologies of offenders and subject them to experimental treatment situations provide the most hopeful prospect of advancing our knowledge about the effectiveness of training.

In addition to this type of research, we need to know more

[1] It is encouraging to read that research designed to investigate this issue is now under way. See *Prisons and Borstals, 1963* (formerly *P. C. Report*), p. 27.

[2] See p. 86, fn. 4 above for a short discussion of this point.

[3] J. D. and M. Q. Grant, 'A Group Dynamic Approach to the Treatment of Non-Conformists in the Navy,' *Annals* (March 1959). See also, M. Q. Grant, 'Interaction between Kinds of Treatment and Kinds of Delinquent' in *Inquiries Concerning Kinds of Treatment for Kinds of Delinquents*, California Board of Corrections Monograph No. 2 (1961).

[4] S. Adams, 'Interaction between Individual Interview Therapy and Treatment Amenability of Older Youth Authority Wards,' California Board of Corrections Monograph No. 2 (1961)

about how the training process actually works. Gordon Rose has asked: 'What is meant by "making an effort" and "taking his training seriously" . . . what is the relation of anti-authority behaviour in the institution to anti-authority behaviour outside?'[1] The problem of what is actually meant by 'training' and what in practice it consists of should be, as Mr Foster rightly asserts, the subject of 'intensive and objective investigation'.[2] There is a great danger that training is simply presumed to exist—with some boys taking advantage of it and others not. We cannot afford to assume this and concentrate entirely on follow-up studies of reconviction rates. More should be known about how boys perceive training and how the organization of the regime affects them. In the United States, Polsky has shown how a progressive therapeutically orientated regime was in fact dominated by the inmate social structure. He was able to suggest that one of the major reasons for this was the separation of the therapeutic staff from the cottage community where the major relationships of the boys were formed. Apart from Alan Little's pioneering study in an open borstal almost no progress has yet been made along these lines. When new methods of treatment are introduced it is imperative that an evaluation should be made of their impact on the offender.

It will be particularly necessary to reconsider the role of research in future developments. In the United States experiments have been conceived as part of a research programme and sophisticated models employed so that treatment can be assessed in a scientific manner. In this country, what have been called 'experiments' are really 'innovations' or new developments and have not been formulated as research models. Researchers have not played a dynamic role in suggesting and evaluating new treatments but have had to content themselves with *ex-post-facto* assessments of training methods. Faced with its present difficulties, borstal must be prepared for new ideas, dynamic experiments and objective evaluation.

(*b*) *Some basic problems.* Although, on the surface, the borstal system has made vast progress in the last thirty years, there is little evidence to show that it has come any nearer to the

[1] G. Rose, 'Status and Grouping in a Borstal Institution,' *British Journal of Delinquency*, Vol. 9, No. 4 (April 1959), p. 273
[2] *C.A.C.A. Report*, 1961, p. 20

solution of its major problem—the training and reformation of the 'hard-core' of its inmates. It is to this large segment of the borstal population that attention should be directed, particularly as it appears to be growing in size. Because of their likelihood of absconding or contaminating 'better' boys, the criminally sophisticated and aggressive anti-social personalities have by and large been allocated '*en bloc*' to some of the closed borstals. Here, they are themselves contaminated by strong inmate traditions and a culture more like that of a prison than a training school. In the past these types of offender—who are clearly not responsive to traditional methods—have never been the recipients of progressive innovations. In the context of the large institutions, such as Portland, in which they are housed it is understandably difficult to completely alter the regime, custody and control being an essential element. The existence of large institutions, even of 150 boys, is in itself perhaps one of the major barriers to progress. It would seem worth while to experiment with small groups of offenders, living either in houses or in small semi-secure camps where they can receive intensive treatment.[1] In such small groups anti-authority inmate traditions will perhaps be easier to control and the staff can have more direct influence over the boys. The experience of the special home, 'Northways', for institutionalized homeless boys has already indicated the value of developing methods particularly appropriate to the problems of distinct groups of offenders. Specialized methods of dealing with egocentric aggressive offenders, incipient psychopaths, the 'mature professional', and other difficult types could similarly be experimented with, without any increased danger to the public, and with some hope of success.

There appear to be two main factors blocking such experimentation with treatment methods: first, the cost and the difficulties involved in getting suitably qualified staff; and second, the basic commitment of borstal to *institutional* training. True, small camps have been established at various times, but no innovations such as hostels in the community, intensive small therapeutic units or entirely educational groups have been tried. Now that Miller has demonstrated the favourable

---

[1] The term 'treatment' is here used in its generic sense, to cover any kind of reformative measure.

response of the socially-inadequate and over-institutionalized boy to the regime of 'Northways', it would seem appropriate to allocate these boys straight to such a home rather than insisting that they first complete normal borstal training. But it is perhaps felt that this would nullify the intention of the courts in imposing 'custodial training'. It is in this phrase that a major barrier to experiments with non-institutional methods lies. The belief in the value of long-term reformatory training in institutions is deeply embedded in English penal philosophy. If an offender has not responded to the less severe sanctions available to the court, it is concluded that he must both suffer and need long-term training. The fact that custodial training is intended to be a more *severe* sanction than detention centres or probation makes it difficult to experiment with methods which perhaps do not look 'severe'. It has always been for this reason that a minimum period of training—now of six months—has been imposed to stop early discharge.

The only way this difficulty could be overcome is through the abolition of the distinction between short-term and long-term custodial training. The offender could then be committed for 'training' with a maximum sentence of two years (and perhaps a lower maximum for more trivial offenders), and the choice of treatment left to penal administrators. Such a situation has already been established in part by the amalgamation of borstal and prison sentences. It would simply need to be extended to include the detention centres. Under such a system it would be possible for the penal administrators to develop a wide variety of training methods. The court would still have a basic choice between committal for training and treatment in the community.[1] The choice of training would depend on an assessment of treatment needs at special classifying centres. In this way offenders could be sent to the most appropriate type of training facility. But before such a system could be made acceptable it would be necessary for there to be expertly staffed classifying centres, a *real* choice between different treatments, and a continuous experimentation with, and evaluation of, methods. Too often classifying systems look progressive on paper but in fact conceal poor facilities for

[1] This has already been suggested by Nigel Walker in 'The Sentence of the Court', *The Listener*, 28 June 1962.

diagnosis and observation and a similarity between institutions that consequently severely limits the choice of the allocating board. Such a difficulty can only be overcome by a great increase in the expenditure normally made on classifying centres. In the long run, however, intensive short-term methods could prove much cheaper than lengthy institutionalization.

It would seem that a choice has to be made between persevering with the present system of custodial training, or replacing the whole edifice with a complex and flexible range of training and treatment facilities. The latter choice implies a complete re-thinking of the principles on which borstal training has been developed over the last fifty years.

# APPENDIX A

## Opening and Closing of Institutions 1908-1962

| CLOSED BORSTALS | Date first opened | Type of buildings | Dates closed | Re-opened |
|---|---|---|---|---|
| Rochester | 1902 | Converted convict prison | 1940–42 reduced in size | |
| Feltham | 1911 | Old walled reformatory | 1914–17 and 1941–45 became a reception centre, prison, and borstal for sixty only | In full use again in 1945 |
| Portland | 1921 | Converted convict prison | An extra house added in 1928 was closed in 1935 | |
| Camp Hill | 1931 | A preventive detention prison. Cellular | 1940–46 and 1949 onwards | |
| Sherwood | 1932 | Old single-block prison, converted | 1940–41 became licence-revokee centre. Closed 1949 onwards | |
| Dartmoor | 1946 | A borstal in one block of the prison | Closed from 1947 onwards | |
| Hull | 1950 | Old prison, part-converted, new wing 1959 | Closed 1961 | |
| Buckley Hall | 1955 | A converted institution, semi-secure | Reclassified 1961 as a detention centre | |

| CLOSED BORSTALS | Date first opened | Type of buildings | Dates closed | Re-opened |
|---|---|---|---|---|
| Dover | 1957 | Formerly a medium-security prison for corrective detainees | | |
| Northallerton | 1958 | Formerly a central prison for preventive detainees | Reclassified 1962 as a young prisoners' centre | |
| Everthorpe | 1958 | A new, large maximum-security prison taken over immediately as a borstal | | |
| Huntercombe | 1961 | This former open borstal was converted into a medium-security borstal by a fence | | |
| Hindley | 1962 | A new maximum security prison, opened in 1961. Taken over from use as a young prisoners' centre | | |
| Swinfen Hall | 1963 | A newly-built secure borstal | | |
| Wellingborough | 1964 | A newly-built secure borstal | | |

| OPEN BORSTALS | Date first opened | Type of buildings | Dates closed | Re-opened |
|---|---|---|---|---|
| Lowdham Grange | Purchased 1930 First party in 1931 Still not complete in 1938 | Administrative and separate house blocks built by inmate labour | 1940–41 | In full use again in 1941 |
| North Sea Camp | 1934 | Hutted camp on salt marshes | Sept. 1963. Converted in part to open senior detention centre | |
| Hollesley Bay Colony | 1938 | An administrative block and houses spread out on a large estate—extra accommodation built 1959 | | |
| Usk and Prescoed Camp | 1939 | Based on an old prison and linked to a new hutted camp | Nov. 1939– June 1940 | In full use again in 1940 |
| Gaynes Hall | 1946 | Country house and house blocks in the grounds, remnants of a wartime camp— extra accommodation built in 1959 | | |
| Huntercombe | 1946 | Country house with wartime camp in the grounds. 1960 —in process of adaptation to medium-security borstal. Completed 1961 | | |

| OPEN BORSTALS | Date first opened | Type of buildings | Dates closed | Re-opened |
|---|---|---|---|---|
| Hewell Grange | 1946 | Country house with wartime camp | | |
| Gringley and Hatfield | 1946 1949 | Gringley was a wartime farming estate; Hatfield an army camp. A joint institution | | |
| Pollington | 1950 | An army camp | 1955–57 | Re-opened as a special institution 1957 |
| Morton Hall | 1958 | Formerly R.A.F. establishment. Immediately occupied and converted over two years by staff and boys | | |
| Wetherby | 1958 | Formerly Royal Navy training establishment. Immediately occupied and converted over two years by staff and boys | | |
| Finnamore Wood Camp | 1960 | A hutted open satellite camp for Feltham. Adapted and repaired by borstal work parties | | |
| Guy's Marsh | 1962 | A hutted camp. Formerly a satellite for Portland during building operations in 1961 | | |

| SPECIAL INSTITUTIONS | *Dates in use* |
|---|---|
| *Reception Centres* | |
| Wandsworth | 1923–31. Came into full operation in 1926. |
| Wormwood Scrubs | 1931–40. 1946 onwards. Closed during the war. |
| Feltham | 1941–45. Most of Wormwood Scrubs young prisoners' side was transferred here during the war. |
| Latchmere House | First independent reception centre opened 1946. |
| *Recall Centres* | |
| Canterbury | 1911–23. |
| Wormwood Scrubs | 1923–31. |
| Wandsworth | 1931–40. |
| Sherwood | 1940–41, as a temporary measure only. |
| Chelmsford | 1941–48. |
| Portsmouth | 1948 onwards. The first recall centre not part of a prison in use for ordinary prisoners. |
| Reading | 1960 onwards, began to take some recalls as well as boys needing correction. All trained under the same regime. |
| *Correctional Centres* | |
| Wormwood Scrubs | 1923–31. Combined activities with being recall centre. |
| Wandsworth | 1931–40 and 1946–51. |
| Reading | 1951 onwards. First correctional centre not part of a prison having other functions. |

# APPENDIX B

## Dates of Some Important Innovations in the System

1922　New Chairman of Prison Commission Sir Maurice Waller; and Alexander Paterson appointed as Commissioner.

1923　Camps started. Success of camp for Rochester boys.
Full strength of housemasters first employed.
Boys allowed home on parole for special reasons.
New shops available for industrial training. An industrial expert is appointed.
First experiment in plain clothes for officers during week-ends at Feltham.

1924　Experiment in sending boys to a technical school in evenings copied from Italy.
Officers began to wear plain clothes continually.

1930　The first open institution purchased.

1931　Boys go to work in the open on the new institution. Experiment in value of constructive work for the inmates, and in shorter training.

1933　Christmas leave for high-grade boys at Feltham.

1934　Gradually spread—was the basis of the home leave experiment.
The start of the pioneering principle at North Sea Camp. North Sea Camp opened without any prison officers, only housemasters.

1936　Age limit increased from 21 to 23: boys to be trained in one institution at Sherwood and treated more like men—allowed to wear trousers, etc.
Use made of experiments in vocational guidance carried out by Institute of Industrial Psychology.

1938　Experiment in smaller groups at the widespread Hollesley Bay Colony.

1939　Mass discharge of all boys who had served six months. Breakdown of traditions.

1946   The controversy over Dartmoor. Closed within a year.
       Vocational training scheme starts. Six-month courses for
          the Ministry of Labour Certificate, taking the place
          of the old trade training.
1947   Increase in the educational facilities given by Local
          Authorities.
1948   Age limit again reduced to 21.
       Home leave for five days generally introduced for all at
          some time during training.
1950   Penal borstal opened at Hull for most difficult cases.
1954   Mannheim-Wilkins Prediction Study.
1957   Pollington Borstal used for boys with best chances of
          success.
       The prediction technique is used to aid allocation.
       The beginning of group counselling methods at Polling-
          ton.
1961   Sentence reduced to maximum of two years.
       After-care made standard period of two years following
          discharge.
       Borstal and long-term imprisonment joined into the
          single system of 'custodial training'.

# BIBLIOGRAPHY

### References to Developments in the Borstal System

ALPER, B. (1951). 'The Borstal system of training for young offenders.' Tappan, P. W. (ed.): *Contemporary Correction*. New York: McGraw Hill.

BARMAN, S. (1934). *The English Borstal System*. London: King.

BENNY, M. (1937). *Low Company*. London: Peter Davies.

BENSON, SIR GEORGE (1959). 'Prediction methods and young prisoners.' *Brit. J. Delinq*. 5, 191.

BIRD, M. (1961). 'Group counselling at Pollington.' *Prison Service J*. 1, No. 2, 33.

BISHOP, N. (1960). 'Group work at Pollington Borstal.' *Howard J*. 10, No. 3, 185.

B.M.A. (1951). *The adolescent delinquent boy:* A Report of the joint committee on psychiatry and the law appointed by the British Medical Association and the Magistrates' Association.

BURKHART, W. R. (1956). *A study of the Borstal after-care system*. Unpublished M.A. thesis: University of London.

CAPE, C. T. (1941). 'Administrative and other experiences of a Borstal governor.' *Public Administration*. 19, 61.

CONRAD, J. P. (1960). 'The assistant governor in the English prison.' *Brit. J. Delinq*. 10, 245.

EDWARD, L. (1939). *Borstal Lives*. London: Gollancz.

ELKIN, W. A. (1957). *The English Penal System*. London: Penguin.

ELKIN, W. A. and KITTERMASTER, D. B. (1950). *Borstal: A Critical Survey*. London: The Howard League.

FENTON, N. (1958). *An Introduction to Group Counselling in State Correctional Service*. New York: The American Correctional Association.

FENTON, N. (1961). *Group Counselling: A Preface to its use in Correctional and Welfare Agencies.* California: Institute for the Study of Crime and Delinquency.

FOSTER, F. C. (1952). 'Borstal after-care in England and Wales.' *International Review of Criminal Policy.* No. 2, 27.

FOX, L. W. (1934). *The Modern English Prison.* London: Geo. Routledge.

—— (1947). 'Borstal since the war.' *The Magistrate.* 7, 80.

—— (1952). *The English Prison and Borstal Systems.* London: Routledge and Kegan Paul.

FRY, M. (1940). 'The Borstal system.' Radzinowicz, L. and Turner, J. W. C. (eds.): *Penal Reform in England.* London: Macmillan.

—— (1950). 'The effects of the Criminal Justice Act on the Borstal system.' *J. Criminal Science.* 2, 60.

GIBBENS, T. C. N. assisted by MARRIAGE, A. and WALKER, A. (1963). *Psychiatric Studies of Borstal Lads.* Institute of Psychiatry. Maudsley Monographs 11. Oxford: University Press.

GORDON, J. W. (1932). *Borstalians.* London: Hopkinson.

GOULD, A. (1958). 'Time and training.' *Howard J.* 10, No. 1, 50.

GRUNHUT, M. (1948). *Penal Reform.* Oxford: Clarendon Press.

—— (1955). 'Juvenile delinquents under punitive detention.' *Brit. J. Delinq.* 5, 191.

—— (1960). 'After effects of punitive detention.' *Brit. J. Delinq.* 10, 178.

HAWKINS, G. *Alec Paterson: An Appreciation.* Private circulation.

HEALY, W. and ALPER, B. (1941). *Criminal Youth and the Borstal System.* New York: The Commonwealth Fund.

HENRIQUES, B. (1937). 'Young delinquents.' *The Magistrate.* 4, 1213.

—— (1947). 'Crime and punishment.' *Social Service.* 21, No. 2, 62.

HOBHOUSE, S. and BROCKWAY, F. (1922). *English Prisons Today.* London: Longmans Green.

HOME OFFICE (1945, 1950, 1957, 1960). *Prisons and Borstals.* H.M.S.O.

HOOD, R. (1963). *The Borstal System: An Historical and Empirical Study of some of its Aspects.* Unpublished PH.D. thesis: University of Cambridge.

IREMONGER, T. L. (1962). *Disturbers of the Peace.* London: Johnson.

I.S.T.D. (1960). *Penal practice in a changing society: a critical examination of the White Paper policy.* London.

JONES, H. (1963). *Crime and the Penal System.* London: U.T.P.

KENYON, H. (1952). 'The concept of shared responsibility in Borstal training.' *Howard J.* 8, No. 3, 189.

KING, J. F. S. (1958). *The Probation Service.* London: Butterworth.

LEITCH, A. (1944). 'A survey of reformatory influence in Borstal training—A socio-psychological study.' *Brit. J. Med. Psychol.* 21, 77.

LE MESURIER, L. (1931). *Boys in Trouble.* London: John Murray.

—— (1935). *A Handbook of Probation and Social Work of the Courts.* London: National Assoc. of Probation Officers.

LESLIE, SHANE (1938). *Sir Evelyn Ruggles-Brise: A Memoir of the Founder of Borstal.* London: John Murray.

LITTLE, A. N. (1961). *Borstal: a study of inmates' attitudes to the staff and the system.* Unpublished PH.D. thesis: University of London.

—— (1961). 'The Borstal boys.' *The Twentieth Century.* Winter, 35.

—— (1962). 'Borstal success and the quality of Borstal inmates.' *Brit. J. Criminol.* 2, 271.

—— (1963). 'Penal theory, penal reform and Borstal practice.' *Brit. J. Criminol.* 3, 257.

LLEWELLIN, W. W. (1933). 'Lowdham Grange—a Borstal experiment.' *Howard J.* 3, No. 4, 36.

—— (1936). 'The North Sea Camp—a fresh Borstal experiment.' *Howard J.* 3, No. 2, 252.

MANNHEIM, H. (1940). *Social Aspects of Crime in England between the Wars*. London: Allen and Unwin.

MANNHEIM, H. and SPENCER, J. C. (1949). *Problems of Classification in the English Penal and Reformatory Systems*. London: I.S.T.D.

MANNHEIM, H. and WILKINS, L. T. (1955). *Prediction Methods in Relation to Borstal Training*. H.M.S.O.

MAXWELL, SIR A. (1937). *Treatment of Crime*. Barnet House Papers No. 21.

MAXWELL, R. (1956). *Borstal and Better*. London: Hollis and Carter.

MILLER, D. (1964). *Growth to Freedom*. London: Tavistock.

MORRIS, PAULINE (1960). *Prison After-Care: Charity or Public Responsibility?* Fabian Research Series, 218.

MORRISON, A. C. L. (1930). 'Impressions of Borstal.' *Justice of the Peace*. 95, 351.

MORRISON, R. L. (1957). 'Borstal allocation.' *Brit. J. Delinq.* 8, 95.

—— (1961). 'Group counselling in penal institutions.' *Howard J.* 10, No. 4, 279.

MORRISON, W. D. (1896). *Juvenile Offenders*. London: T. Fisher Unwin.

MOSELEY, S. A. (1926). *The Truth about Borstal*. London: Cecil Palmer.

MULLINS, C. (1936). 'The treatment of young offenders.' *The Magistrate*. 4, 991.

NORWOOD-EAST, W. (1942). *The Adolescent Criminal*. London: Churchill.

OGDEN, D. G. (1954). 'A Borstal typological survey.' *Brit. J. Delinq.*

PAKENHAM/THOMPSON COMMITTEE (1961). *Problems of the Ex-Prisoner*. London: National Council of Social Service.

PATERSON, A. (1911). *Across the Bridges*. London: Arnold.

PETERSON, A. W. (1960). 'Modern developments in the prison system.' *Howard J.* 10, No. 3, 167.

PRISON COMMISSION (1925). *The principles of the Borstal system.* London: Unpublished for general circulation. .

—— (1962). 'Group counselling: an instruction by the Prison Commissioners.' *Howard J.* 11, No. 1, 37.

RADZINOWICZ, L. and TURNER, J. C. (eds.) (1945). *The Modern Approach to Criminal Law.* London: Macmillan.

RECKLESS, W. C. and SHERVINGTON, P. P. (1963). 'Gauging the impact of the institution on the delinquent youth.' *Brit. J. Criminol.* 4, 7.

ROBERTON, A. (1961). 'Casework in Borstal.' *Prison Service J.* 1, No. 2, 15.

RODGER, A. (1932). 'Vocational guidance in Borstal.' *Howard J.* 3, No. 2, 51.

—— (1937). *A Borstal Experiment in Vocational Guidance.* Industrial Health Research Board Pamphlet, No. 78, H.M.S.O.

ROSE, A. G. (1954). *Five Hundred Borstal Boys.* Oxford: Basil Blackwell.

—— (1956). 'The sociological analysis of Borstal training.' *Brit. J. Delinq.* 6, 202.

—— (1956). 'Sociometric analysis and observation in a Borstal institution.' *Brit. J. Delinq.* 6, 285.

—— (1959). 'Status and grouping in a Borstal institution.' *Brit. J. Delinq.* 11, 258.

RUCK, S. K. (ed.) (1951). *Paterson on Prisons.* London: Muller.

RUGGLES-BRISE, SIR E. (1921). *The English Prison System.* London: Macmillan.

RUSSELL, C. E. B. and RIGBY, L. M. (1905). *The Making of the Criminal.* London: Macmillan.

SCOTT, H. (1947). 'Developments in after-care.' *Probation.* 5, No. 11, 147.

SILLITOE, A. (1959). *The Loneliness of the Long-Distance Runner.* London: W. H. Allen.

TEETERS, N. (1944). *World Penal Systems.* Philadelphia: Pennsylvania Prison Society.

TEMPLEWOOD, LORD (1947–48). 'The outlook for penal reform.' *Howard J.* 7, No. 3, 166.

WALLER, M. L. (1921). 'New points in the Borstal system.' *The Magistrate.* 1, 8.

WARDROP, K. R. H. (1957). 'Treatment of the adolescent offender.' *Brit. J. Delinq.* 8, 106.

WEEKS, H. A. (1958). *Youthful Offenders at Highfields.* Ann Arbor: University of Michigan Press.

WILLS, D. (1941). *The Hawkspur Experiment.* London: Allen and Unwin.

WILKINS, L. T. (1958). 'A small comparative study of the results of probation.' *Brit. J. Delinq.* 8, 201.

—— *Classification and contamination*: Unpublished memorandum.

—— (1960). *Delinquent Generations.* A Home Office Research Unit Report. London: H.M.S.O.

## Official Reports

*Report from the Departmental Committee on Prisons,* 1895, C. 7702.

*Report of the Prison Officers' Pay Committee,* 1923 (Cmd. 1959).

*Report of the Departmental Committee on the Treatment of Young Offenders,* 1927 (Cmd. 2831).

*Report of the Departmental Committee on Persistent Offenders,* 1932 (Cmd. 4090).

*Report of the Departmental Committees on the Employment of Prisoners, Part I: Employment of Prisoners,* 1933 (Cmd. 4462).

*Report of the Departmental Committee on the Employment of Prisoners, Part II: Employment on Discharge,* 1935 (Cmd. 4897).

*Report of the Departmental Committee on the Social Services in Courts of Summary Jurisdiction,* 1936 (Cmd. 5122).

*Report of the Committee to Review Punishments in Prisons, Borstal Institutions, Approved Schools and Remand Homes, Part II, Borstal Institutions,* 1950–51 (Cmd. 8256).

*Seventh Report of the Select Committee on Estimates: Session 1951–52.*

*Report of the Committee on Discharged Prisoners' Aid Societies,* 1952–53. Home Office.

*The After-Care and Supervision of Discharged Offenders:* A Report of the Advisory Council on the Treatment of Offenders, 1958. Home Office.

*Penal Practice in a Changing Society—Aspects of Future Developments* (England and Wales), 1959 (Cmd. 645).

*The Treatment of Young Offenders:* A Report of the Advisory Council on the Treatment of Offenders, 1959. Home Office.

*Disturbances in the Carlton House Approved School on 29th and 30th August 1959:* A Report of the Enquiry by Mr Victor Durand, Q.C., 1960 (Cmd. 937).

*Report of the Committee on Children and Young Persons,* 1960 (Cmd. 1191).

*Work and Vocational Training in Borstal* (England and Wales). A Report of the Advisory Council on the Employment of Prisoners, 1962. Home Office.

*The Organization of After-Care.* A report of the Advisory Council on the Treatment of Offenders, 1963. Home Office.

# INDEX

absconders: *see* escapes

Adams, S., 87 *n*, 216 *n*

Advisory Council on Treatment of Offenders, 148, 149–51, 189

after-care, 59, 61, 136; administration, 183–4; assessment of, 197–202; beginnings of, 162–4; casework and supervision, 192–7; concept of, 190–7; effects of unemployment on, 168–9, 176–8; expansion of, 173–6; legislation for, 164–7, 188, 189; probation officers and, 175–6, 184–7; problem cases, 178-80; reorganization of, 187–90; role of, 190–7; under A. Paterson, 172, 173 ff; under Sir A. Ruggles-Brise, 167–73; voluntary committees, 175, 187; Voluntary Associates, 173–6, 184–7; *see also* licence, release on and supervision

age of admissions to borstals, 1, 7–9, 18–19, 20, 41; alterations to, 49, 71, 89; Home Secretary's powers on, 21

Allchin, Dr W. H., 88 *n*

allocation centres: *see* classifying centres, reception centres

Alper, B., on voluntary and official services, 129

Alper, B. S., 118 *n*: *see also* Healy, W. and Alper, B. S.

appeals against sentences, 61: *see also* Court of Criminal Appeal

approved schools, comparison with borstals, 90

Astbury, B. E., 128 *n*

attendance centres, 61, 72–3

Avory, Mr Justice, views of, on borstal training, 51, 53

Bagthorpe Prison, 48

Baker, Dr, and research on prisoners' height and weight, 8

Barman, S., 32 *n*, 55 *n*, 58 *n*, 94 *n*, 122 *n*, 123, 126 *n*, 128 *n*, 132 *n*

Bazeley, E. T., 130 *n*

Beauchamp, Earl, 29 *n*

Bedford Prison, first borstal experiments at, 1 *n*, 14

Benny, M., 139 *n*, 178 *n*

Benson, Sir George, on borstal system, 82, 84, 85–6, 88 *n*

Bird, M., 144 *n*

Bishop, N., 143 *n*

Borstal (Rochester), 1 fn; establishment of juvenile-adult reformatory, 14–15; allocation to, 113–14; Governor's views on, 30, 53–4, 111; high failure rate at 76; outline of new treatment at, 15; shortage of work for boys at, 124

Borstal Association

and after-care, 136, 163 ff; attacks on, 34–5, 172–3; complaints about prison atmosphere, 99–100, 102; criticism of Sir E. Ruggles-Brise, 171–2; early years, 163–4; on escapes, 69; on success of training, 50–1; on trade-learning, 28, 97–8; praise for, 170; recognition of, 165; views on staff, 109, 120 *n*, 121 *n*

*Borstalian, The* (later *The Phoenix*), 107 *n*, 111, 122 *n*

British Medical Association, report, 150 *n*

Brockway, A. Fenner, 168, 179 *n*; criticism of borstals, 35, 37, 42, 105

Buckingham (suicide of), 34

Burkhardt, W. R., 162 *n*

Burt, Sir C., 106 *n*

Butler, R. A.

on borstal discipline, 83; on Criminal Justice Act (1961), 75–6